MyMaths
for Key Stage 3

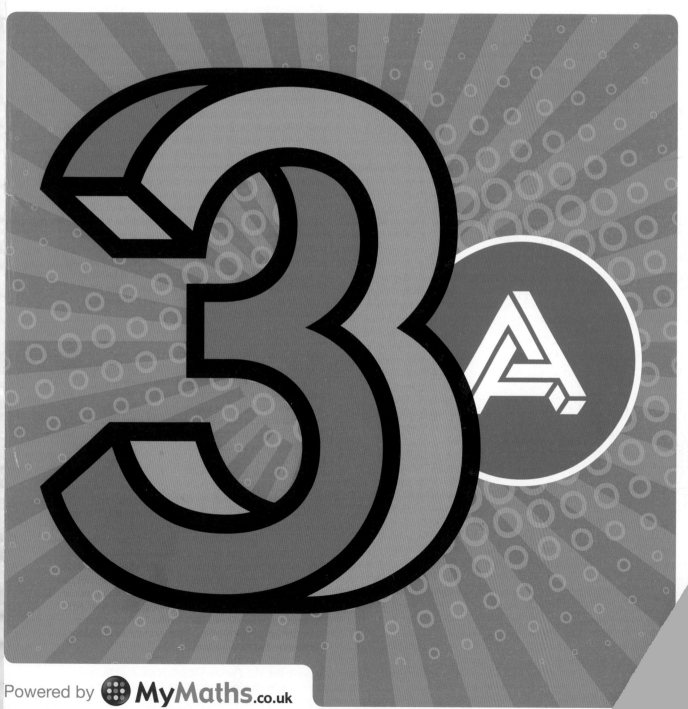

3A

Powered by **My**Maths.co.uk

FSC
www.fsc.org

MIX
Paper from responsible sources
FSC® C007785

Acknowledgements

Although we have made every effort to trace and contact copyright holders before publication this has not been possible in all cases. If notified, the publisher will rectify any errors or omissions at the earliest opportunity.

p5: SALi-uk/iStockphoto; **p7:** (t) Luis Santos/Dreamstime, (a) Olga Danylenko/Shutterstock, (b) Design56/Dreamstime, (c) Sociologas/iStockphoto, (e) cris180/iStockphoto, (f) Luis Santos/Shutterstock, (g) Ian 2010/Shutterstock, (h) Coprid/Shutterstock, (i) Newlight/Dreamstime, (j) Ariene/iStockphoto; **p14:** Getty Images; **p15:** PCN Photography/Alamy; **p22:** (t) Michal Steckiw/Dreamstime, (m) susandaniels/iStockphoto, (b) Xacto/iStockphoto; **p25:** RGB Ventures LLC dba SuperStock/Alamy; **p43:** Christopher Clavius (1537–1612) Aged 69, published by Jean Le Clerc, c.1606-07 (engraving), French School, (17th century)/Fitzwilliam Museum, University of Cambridge, UK/The Bridgeman Art Library; **p61:** (b) Pablo Paul/Alamy; **p65:** (t) BortN66/Shutterstock; **p68:** Jeff Thrower/Shutterstock; **p69:** (t) Yuri/Istockphoto; **p81:** dieKleinert/Alamy; **p124:** David W. Leindecker/Shutterstock.com; **p125:** (t) Claude Huot/Shutterstock, **p125:** (bl) Anthony Pierce/Alamy, (br) Dianamower/Dreamstime; **p127:** Dimedrol68/Shutterstock; **p135:** schantalao/Shutterstock.com; **p141:** Public domain; **p142:** Viktor1/Shutterstock, **p148:** Oleksiy Maksymenko Photography/Alamy; **p163:** saiko3p/Shutterstock; **p168:** Dimedrol68/Shutterstock; **p207:** Alexey Repka/Shutterstock; **p217:** Stephen Clarke/Shutterstock; **p242:** Joshua Haviv/Dreamstime; **p243:** Maica/iStockphoto; **p261:** Johan Swanepoel/Shutterstock; **p277:** (r) Oleksiy Maksymenko Photography/Alamy; **p279:** (l) lsantilli/Shutterstock, (m) Nkrivko/Shutterstock; **p286:** Jacob Hamblin/Shutterstock, (br) Gjermund/Shutterstock; **p294:** Aperture51/Shutterstock

Case Studies:

Online Creative Media/iStockphoto; OUP.Corel; Dean Turner/iStockphoto; Scol/Dreamstime; Stefan Klein/iStockphoto; Mary Evans/iStockphoto; Mikhail Kokhanchikov/iStockphoto; Kmitu/iStockphoto; Juri Samsonov/Dreamstime; Terraxplorer/iStockphoto; Timothy Large/iStockphoto; Martin Applegate/iStockphoto; Lisa F Young/Dreamstime; Blackred/iStockphoto; Robert Mizerek/Dreamstime; Jf123/Dreamstime; Andy Brown/Dreamstime; Heather Down/iStockphoto; Hulton Archive/iStockphoto; James Davidson/Dreamstime; Brianna May/iStockphoto; Stefanie Leuker/Dreamstime; Viktor Pravdica/Dreamstime; Karam Miri/iStockphoto; Giorgio Fochesato/iStockphoto; Greenwales/Alamy; Mehmet Salih Guler/iStockphoto; Mediagfx/Dreamstime; Dusan Zidar/Dreamstime; Achim Prill/iStockphoto; Lucian Coman/iStockphoto; Sierpniowka/Dreamstime; Felinda/iStockphoto; Robyn Mackenzie/Dreamstime; Elena Elisseeva/Dreamstime; TT/iStockphoto; Fernando Soares/Dreamstime; Jan Rihak/iStockphoto; Gerald Hng Wai Chuin/Dreamstime; Hanquan Chen/iStockphoto; Yakobchuk/Dreamstime; Valentin Garcia/Dreamstime; fotolinchen/iStockphoto; Dmitry Kovyazin/Dreamstime; Rixie/Dreamstime; Feng Yu/Dreamstime; Valentin Garcia/Dreamstime; John Archer/iStockphoto; Christophe Test/Dreamstime.

Artwork by; Phil Hackett , Erwin Haya, Paul Hostetler, Dusan Pavlic, Giulia Rivolta, Katri Valkamo & QBS.

Contents

About this book

MyMaths for Key Stage 3 is an exciting new series designed for schools following the new National Curriculum for mathematics. This book has been written to help you to grow your mathematical knowledge and skills during Key Stage 3.

Each topic starts with an Introduction that shows why it is relevant to real life and includes a short *Check in* exercise to see if you are ready to start the topic.

Inside each chapter, you will find lots of worked examples and questions for you to try along with interesting facts. There's basic practice to build your confidence, as well as problem solving. You might also notice the **4-digit codes** at the bottom of the page, which you can type into the search bar on the *MyMaths* site to take you straight to the relevant *MyMaths* lesson for more help in understanding and extra practice.

At the end of each chapter you will find *MySummary*, which tests what you've learned and suggests what you could try next to improve your skills even further. The *What next?* box details further resources available in the supporting online products.

Maths is a vitally important subject, not just for you while you are at school but also for when you grow up. We hope that this book will lead to a greater enjoyment of the subject and that it will help you to realise how useful maths is to your everyday life.

1 Whole numbers and decimals

Introduction

On the 3rd January 2004 the Mars Exploration Rover landed on the Martian surface within 200 m of its target. Navigators used radio signals sent by three antennae spread around the Earth's surface, to control the flight of the spacecraft. An error in their distance calculations of even 5 cm on Earth would have led to an error on Mars of over 400 m.

In a journey of 300 million miles the navigators and scientists needed to work to incredibly high levels of accuracy.

What's the point?

Scientists, engineers and nurses need to know how accurate their measurements must be, otherwise there could be disastrous consequences. An understanding of rounding is vital in all walks of life.

Objectives

By the end of this chapter, you will have learned how to …

- Multiply and divide by 10, 100, 0.1 and 0.01.
- Round positive whole numbers to the nearest 10, 100 or 1000.
- Round decimals to the nearest whole number or one decimal place.
- Use the BIDMAS rules to do a calculation in the correct order.
- Find factors, multiples and test numbers for divisibility.
- Identify prime numbers and write a number as the product of its prime factors.
- Find lowest common multiples (LCM) and highest common factors (HCF).
- Order decimals.

Check in

1 Copy and complete these problems by inserting the correct operation (+, −, × or ÷).

   a   16 ☐ 4 = 4   **b**   6 ☐ 4 = 24   **c**   13 ☐ 13 = 26

   d   18 ☐ 2 = 9   **e**   9 ☐ 3 = 27   **f**   18 ☐ 18 = 0

2 A number **squared** is a number multiplied by itself.

   Nine squared is written 9^2... which is $9 \times 9 = 81$.

   What are these squared numbers worth?

   a 3^2 **b** 5^2 **c** 7^2 **d** 10^2 **e** 8^2

3 Work out these multiplications in your head, as quickly as you can.

   a 9×3 **b** 8×9 **c** 8×7 **d** 7×6

4 Work out these divisions in your head.

   a $48 \div 6$ **b** $45 \div 5$ **c** $24 \div 3$ **d** $63 \div 9$

Starter problem

Pets come in all shapes and sizes from gerbils to Irish wolfhounds, but about how much does it really cost to keep a pet?

1a Powers of 10

You **multiply** by 10 quickly by moving the digits *one* place to the *left*.
You multiply by 100 quickly by moving the digits *two* places to the *left*.

Example

Find

a 6.5×10

b 3.4×100

a $6.5 \times 10 = 65$

b $3.4 \times 100 = 340$

	× **10**		
T	U	.	$\frac{1}{10}$
	6	.	5
6	5		

		× **100**		
H	T	U	.	$\frac{1}{10}$
		3	.	4
3	4	0		

Multiplying by 10 makes a number 10 times bigger.

You **divide** by 10 quickly by moving the digits *one* place to the *right*.
You divide by 100 quickly by moving the digits *two* places to the *right*.

Example

Find

a $26 \div 10$

b $25 \div 100$

a $26 \div 10 = 2.6$

b $25 \div 100 = 0.25$

	÷ **10**		
T	U	.	$\frac{1}{10}$
2	6	.	
	2	.	6

	÷ **100**			
T	U	.	$\frac{1}{10}$	$\frac{1}{100}$
2	5			
	0	.	2	5

Dividing by 100 makes a number 100 times smaller.

Look at the calculation 3×0.1
It means 'what is 3 lots of 0.1?'
$3 \times 0.1 = 0.3$, which is the same as $3 \div 10$

⬤ Multiplying by 0.1 is the same as *dividing* by 10.

Look at the calculation $3 \div 0.1$
It means 'how many times does 0.1 divide into 3?'
$3 \div 0.1 = 30$ which is the same as 3×10

⬤ Dividing by 0.1 is the same as *multiplying* by 10.

Multiplying by 0.1 makes a number 10 times smaller. Dividing by 0.1 makes a number 10 times bigger.

Exercise 1a

1 Multiply each number in this grid by 10.

4	9	18	37
64	80	256	457
101	6.5	4.8	11.2
0.5	0.65	0.07	0.063
1.05	0.009	20.3	70.07

2 Divide each number in this grid by 10.

40	70	120	250
620	410	45	32
51	125	207	648
7	4.8	1.4	0.62
0.3	0.403	0.07	20.05

3 Multiply each number in this grid by 100.

5	8	23	14
24	62	6.7	1.9
23.4	3.71	6.48	9.06
24.56	7.617	13.582	12.003
2112	0.67	100.1	30.08

4 Divide each number in this grid by 100.

400	600	800	2600
1800	8700	550	470
615	904	2850	6057
62	57	23.9	20.01
0.3	0.46	7.01	70.08

5 Copy each calculation and choose the correct answer from the box.

a $7 \times 0.1 = $ | 7, 70 or 0.7

b $6 \div 0.1 = $ | 60, 0.6 or 6

c $9 \times 0.1 = $ | 0.9, 90 or 9.1

d $4 \times 0.1 = $ | 4, 0.4 or 40

e $12 \div 0.1 = $ | 12, 120 or 1.2

f $16 \times 0.1 = $ | 160, 1.6 or 16

6 Copy each calculation and choose the correct answer from the box.

a $5 \div 0.01 = $ | 0.05, 50 or 500

b $5 \times 0.01 = $ | 0.05, 50 or 500

c $8 \div 0.01 = $ | 800, 8 or 0.8

d $7 \times 0.01 = $ | 700, 0.07 or 7

e $25 \times 0.01 = $ | 2.5, 0.25 or 2500

f $19 \div 0.01 = $ | 0.19, 1900 or 1.9

7 Copy and complete these calculations with either 0.1 or 0.01 .

a $8 \times \square = 0.8$ **b** $8 \times \square = 0.08$

c $6 \div \square = 600$ **d** $5 \div \square = 50$

e $9 \times \square = 0.9$ **f** $7 \div \square = 700$

g $12 \times \square = 1.2$ **h** $15 \div \square = 150$

i $18 \div \square = 1800$ **j** $24 \times \square = 2.4$

k $26 \times \square = 0.26$ **l** $40 \div \square = 400$

Problem solving

8 Alice is trying to save for a mobile phone. She wants to save £259 in 10 weeks. How much does she need to save each week?

9 Year 9 would like to hold a fund-raising event for charity. There are 100 students in year 9. If every student collects £4.27, how much money would year 9 raise?

Charity cake sale

MyMaths.co.uk   🔍 1027, 1392   **SEARCH**

1b Rounding

Rounding makes working with numbers easier.

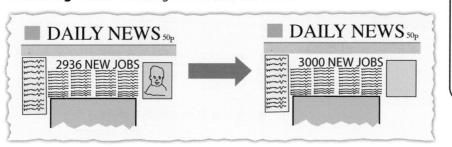

When you round a number check that your answer is a reasonable approximation to the number.

When rounding, make sure you are aware of the value of the digits in each **column**.

Thousands	Hundreds	Tens	Units	.	Tenths	Hundredths

⬤ Always **round up** from the **midpoint**.

You can use a number line when rounding.

Example

a Round 25 to the nearest 10.　　　　**b** Round 614 to the nearest 100.
c Round 7500 to the nearest 1000.

a

20 21 22 23 24 25 26 27 28 29 30
　　　　　　　　　　▲

25 rounded to the nearest 10 is 30.

25 is the **midpoint** of 20 and 30.

b

600 610 620 630 640 650 660 670 680 690 700
　　　　▲

614 rounded to the nearest 100 is 600.

614 is nearer to 600 than to 700.

c

7000 7100 7200 7300 7400 7500 7600 7700 7800 7900 8000
　　　　　　　　　▲

7500 rounded to the nearest 1000 is 8000.

7500 is the midpoint of 7000 and 8000.

Example

a Round 5.8 to the nearest whole number.
b Round 3.762 to one decimal place (1dp)

a

5.0 5.1 5.2 5.3 5.4 5.5 5.6 5.7 5.8 5.9 6.0
　　　　　　　　　　▲

5.8 rounded to the nearest whole number is 6.

5.8 is nearer to 6 than to 5.

b

3.7 3.71 3.72 3.73 3.74 3.75 3.76 3.77 3.78 3.79 3.8
　　　　　　　　　▲

3.762 rounded to one decimal place is 3.8.

3.762 is nearer to 3.8 than 3.7.

Exercise 1b

1 Round each of these numbers to the nearest 10.

a	25	**b**	31	**c**	83
d	36	**e**	98	**f**	101
g	215	**h**	305	**i**	1693
j	1555	**k**	17	**l**	202

2 Round each of these numbers to the nearest 100.

a	181	**b**	431	**c**	23
d	50	**e**	251	**f**	443
g	652	**h**	3518	**i**	1215
j	2879	**k**	250	**l**	249

3 Here are the populations of some towns.

Bideford	14599	Keswick	4984
Brecon	7901	Ludlow	10500
Ely	15102	Redruth	12352
Filey	6560	Shanklin	8055
Heysham	4397	Tetbury	5250

Round each of the figures to the nearest 1000.

Then write the towns in order of their population size, smallest to largest.

4 Round each of these numbers to the nearest whole number.

a	2.8	**b**	0.3	**c**	14.2
d	3.5	**e**	1.4	**f**	21.8
g	28.4	**h**	40.2	**i**	99.6
j	49.5	**k**	0.57	**l**	9.9

5 Round each of these numbers to one decimal place.

a	0.27	**b**	0.15	**c**	4.25
d	8.74	**e**	8.06	**f**	2.41
g	0.222	**h**	1.45	**i**	0.59
j	0.955	**k**	9.99	**l**	0.099

Did you know?

Reading in Berkshire is the most populated town in the UK with a population of 220000.

Problem solving

6 Sarah is a shopkeeper. She decides to make things easier by rounding the prices in her shop to the nearest 10p.
Round the price of each product to the nearest 10p.

a Toffee £2.39 **b** Tennis balls £5.54 **c** Mug £3.15 **d** Game £11.75 **e** Biscuits 55p

7 A customer buys one of each product in Sarah's shop. Does the customer spend more or less now that the prices have been rounded?

f Oil £3.95 **g** Comb 97p **h** Mints 54p **i** Map £4.99 **j** Tea bags £1.03

There are rules to tell you which order to do the calculations in.

To remember the rules you can use the term **BIDMAS**.

Calculations are *not* worked out by going from left to right.

Example

Work out $4^2 + (3 \times 2) \div 2 - 10$

$4^2 + (3 \times 2) \div 2 - 10 = \square$

$\downarrow$

3×2

$\downarrow$

$4^2 + \quad 6 \quad \div 2 - 10 = \square$

$\downarrow$

4×4

$\downarrow$

$16 + \quad 6 \quad \div 2 - 10 = \square$

$\downarrow$

$6 \div 2$

$\downarrow$

$16 + \quad \quad 3 \quad - 10 = \square$

$\downarrow$

$16 + 3$

$\downarrow$

$19 \quad \quad \quad \quad - 10 = 9$

$4^2 + \quad (3 \times 2) \div 2 - 10 = 9$

B Do calculations in **brackets** first.

I Next, multiply out the **indices**.

D **M** Next complete any division or multiplication.

A **S** Finally, complete any addition or subtraction.

Try this example on your calculator. It will use BIDMAS automatically.

Example

Work out $3^2 + (6 + 2) \div 4 - 5$

$3^2 + (6 + 2) \div 4 - 5 = \square$

$\downarrow$

Brackets

$3^2 + \quad 8 \quad \div 4 - 5 = \square$

$\downarrow$

Indices

$9 + \quad 8 \quad \div 4 - 5 = \square$

$\downarrow$

Multiplication and division

$9 + \quad \quad 2 \quad - 5 = \square$

$\downarrow \quad \quad \quad \downarrow$

Addition and subtraction

$11 \quad \quad \quad - 5 = 6$

$3^2 + (6 + 2) \div 4 - 5 = 6$

Exercise 1c

1 Here is a calculation: $10 - 2 \times 3$.

Sam says

$10-6$

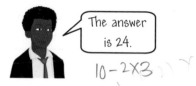

The answer is 24.

$10-2\times3$

Jack says

The answer is 4.

Who is correct? Explain your answer.

Jack

2 Work out these using the correct order of operations.

a $5 - 2 \times 3$ **b** $10 \div 2 + 3$

c $5 + 3 \times 4$ **d** $6 \times 2 - 5$

e $6 + 10 \div 5$ **f** $11 \times 2 - 7$

g $18 - 16 \div 2$ **h** $24 \div 12 + 5$

i $4 + (5 \times 2)$ **j** 2×4^2

k $3^2 \times (2 + 8)$ **l** $(4 \times 4) \div 2$

m $5^2 - (4 \times 5) + 10$ **n** $5 + 3^2 - (9 - 4)$
          9

o $6 \times (10 - 7)^2 + 12$ **p** $50 - (10 \div 2) \times 3^2$
       66 5

q $2^2 + 3^2 \times (7 - 5)$ **r** $3 \times 5^2 - 100 \div 4$
    22 50

3 Use a calculator to work out these.

a $(9 + 16) \times 21$

b $257 - (142 - 63)$

c $18 \times (46 - 24)$

d $192 \div (8 + 4)$

e $(7 + 21) + (87 - 13)$

f $(2 \times 6) \times (91 - 68)$

4 Work out these.

a $7 + (6 \div 3) - 4 + 3^2$

b $4^2 - 5 + (4 \times 3) - 10$

c $3^2 + (7 - 2) + (8 - 3)$

d $14 - 2^2 + (15 - 7) + 3^2$

e $(3 \times 6) - 3^2 + 16 - (9 \div 3)$

f $(4 + 2 \times 3)^2 \div 5 + 1$

5 Lauren says that these three calculations will have the same answer.

a $100 \div 10 \div 5$

b $(100 \div 10) \div 5$

c $100 \div (10 \div 5)$

Lauren is wrong. Work out which one is different and explain why it gives a different answer.

Problem solving

6 Write these calculations in the correct order to get the answer given.

a $\boxed{+4}$ $\boxed{8}$ $\boxed{\times 2}$ = 20

b $\boxed{3}$ $\boxed{+}$ $\boxed{\times}$ $\boxed{5}$ $\boxed{2^2}$ = 35

c $\boxed{4}$ $\boxed{3^2}$ $\boxed{\times}$ $\boxed{+}$ $\boxed{2}$ = 17

d $\boxed{2^2}$ $\boxed{\div}$ $\boxed{5}$ $\boxed{10}$ $\boxed{+}$ = 6

e $\boxed{+3}$ $\boxed{-1}$ $\boxed{\times 2}$ $\boxed{8}$ = 13

f $\boxed{-4}$ $\boxed{+2}$ $\boxed{4^2}$ $\boxed{\div 2}$ = 6

7 Use the operations $\div$, $\times$, $+$, $-$ to make the calculations below correct:

a $8 \ \square \ 2 \ \square \ 5 = 9$

b $8 \ \square \ 2 \ \square \ 5 = 18$

c $8 \ \square \ 2 \ \square \ 5 = 11$

d $8 \ \square \ 2 \ \square \ 5 = -2$

e $4 \ \square \ 4 \ \square \ 4 = -12$

f $4 \ \square \ 4 \ \square \ 4 = 4$

1d Multiples, factors, divisibility and prime numbers

You should know your times tables.
The 5 times table is: 5   10   15   20   25   30 ...

> ● A **multiple** of a number is a number in its times table.

20 is a multiple of 4, 5 and 20 because:

20 appears in the 4 times table   4   8   12   16 (20)...
           the 5 times table   5   10   15 (20)   25 ...
    and the 20 times table (20)   40   60   80   100 ...

> ● A **factor** is a number that divides exactly into another number.

4, 5 and 20 are some of the factors of 20.

> ● To find all of the factors of a number, write them down in factor pairs.

There are some simple divisibility tests you can use.

Divisibility tests	
2	number ends in 0, 2, 4, 6 or 8
3	sum of digits is a multiple of 3
4	half the number is even
5	number ends in 0 or 5
10	number ends in 0

20 ends in 0 so 2, 5 and 10 are factors. Half of 20 is 10 which is even, so 4 is a factor.

The factors of 20 are 1, 2, 4, 5, 10 and 20.
The factor pairs are 1 and 20, 2 and 10, and 4 and 5.

> ● A **prime number** has only two factors, 1 and itself.

Find all the factors of these numbers and say if they are prime.

a 12   **b** 13   **c** 1

a $12 = 1 \times 12$
     $12 = 2 \times 6$
     $12 = 3 \times 4$
The factors of 12 are
1, 2, 3, 4, 6, and 12
12 is not a prime number.

b $13 = 1 \times 13$
The factors of 13 are
1 and 13.
13 is a prime number.

c   1 is not a prime number.

Exercise 1d

1 List the first six multiples of
   a   3   **b**   7   **c**   10

2 List all the factors of
   a   10   **b**   16   **c**   35
   d   36   **e**   48   **f**   100

3 Is 38 a multiple of 8?

4 Is 4 a factor of 30?

5 Test these numbers to see if they are divisible by 3.
   a   15   **b**   23   **c**   31
   d   42   **e**   57   **f**   265

6 Which of these numbers are divisible by 5 but not by 10?
   a   1005   **b**   2010   **c**   2005
   d   100   **e**   4035   **f**   1 000 005

7 a Show that Peter's statement is not true.

250 is divisible by 10 and by 3.

Problem solving

10 a What is the smallest number which is divisible by
    i   2, 3 and 5
    ii   3, 4 and 5
    iii 2, 5 and 7?
  b **i**   Can you line up 500 soldiers in rows of 3? Explain your answer.
      ii   How many more soldiers would you need to be able to make rows of 3?

7 b Which of Alice's statements are true?

A Any number which is divisible by 10 is divisible by 5.

B Any number which is divisible by 5 is divisible by 10.

C If you can divide a number by 6, you can divide the number by 2.

8 Find the factors of these numbers and say whether or not they are prime.
   a   18   **b**   19   **c**   27
   d   1005   **e**   92   **f**   51
   g   31   **h**   42   **i**   41

9 Here is a list of numbers.
   6   7   8   15   17   35
   From this list, write down
   a   the multiples of 7
   b   the factors of 48
   c   the prime numbers.

Did you know?

TOP BANK   Date *January 2014*

Pay World's Largest Prime Number

Amount Really, truly, seriously big   £ $2^{57,885,161} - 1$

Leonard Euler

Cheque No.   Branch Sort Code   Account No.
"095395"   "095395"   "0123456789"

Around 300 BC, a Greek mathematician called Euclid proved that there are an infinite number of prime numbers. Many mathematicians search for large prime numbers. In 2013, the largest prime number found had a staggering 17 425 170 digits! There are substantial prizes offered for breaking the record on the largest known prime number.

You can always write any number as a **product of its prime factors**.

A factor tree can help you do this.

Example

Write 12 as a product of its prime factors.

12 written as a product of its prime factors is 2 × 2 × 3.

or 12 = 2² × 3.

When you find a prime number, circle it.

These are the factors of 12 and 18	Here are some multiples of 12 and 18
12: ①, ②, ③, 4, ⑥, 12	12: 12, 24, ㉖, 48, 60, ⑫...
18: ①, ②, ③, ⑥, 9, 18	18: 18, ㉖, 54, ⑫, 90, 108...

1, 2, 3 and 6 are common factors but 6 is the **highest common factor** (HCF).

36, 72,... are common multiples but 36 is the **lowest common multiple** (LCM).

> ⬤ You can use the product of prime factors and a **Venn diagram** to find the LCM and HCF of two numbers.

Example

Find the HCF and LCM of 84 and 120.

p.298 >

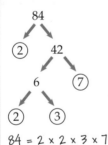

84 = 2 × 2 × 3 × 7

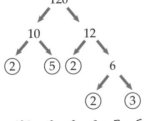

120 = 2 × 2 × 2 × 3 × 5

This is the Venn diagram for the prime factors.

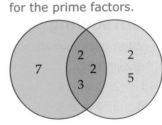

The HCF of 84 and 120 = 2 × 2 × 3 = 12

The HCF is the product of the shared prime factors.

The LCM of 84 and 120 = 2 × 2 × 3 × 7 × 2 × 5 = 840

The LCM is the product of the shared *and* not shared prime factors.

5

Exercise 1e

1 Write these numbers as products of their prime factors.

   a 24   **b** 45   **c** 36

   d 80   **e** 50   **f** 60

   g 100   **h** 72   **i** 250

2 A class are asked to find the highest common factor of 75 and 250.

Zach says   Lauren says

> $75 = 3 \times 5 \times 5$ and $250 = 2 \times 5 \times 5 \times 5$. So the HCF of 75 and 250 is $5 \times 5 = 25$.

> 75 and 250 are both divisible by 5. The HCF of 75 and 250 is 5.

Who is correct? Show your workings to explain your answer.

3 A class are asked to find the lowest common multiple of 12 and 18.

Sam says   Jack says

> $12 \times 18 = 216$ so 216 is the lowest common multiple of 12 and 18.

> $12 = 2 \times 2 \times 3$ and $18 = 2 \times 3 \times 3$. So the lowest common multiple of 12 and 18 is $2 \times 2 \times 3 \times 3 = 36$.

Who is correct? Show your workings to explain your answer.

4 Use a Venn diagram to find the highest common factor of

   a 36 and 48   **b** 144 and 252

   c 168 and 280   **d** 135 and 360

5 Use a Venn diagram to find the lowest common multiple of

   a 36 and 45   **b** 70 and 84

Problem solving

6 Jon, Jim and Jan are three security guards. They have to contact the control centre at regular times.

Jon has to call in every 30 minutes.
Jim has to call in every 40 minutes.
Jan calls in every 50 minutes.

If they all start at the same time, how long is it before they all call in at the same time?

7 Pick two numbers, say 18 and 48, and use a Venn diagram to find their HCF and LCM. Calculate the product of your two numbers and the product of the HCF and LCM, what do you notice? Can you explain why this is always true?

1f Ordering decimals

The red line is 3 cm long.

This means that it is
3 whole cm and no $\frac{1}{10}$'s cm.

T	U	•	$\frac{1}{10}$
	3	•	0

This line is 2.7 cm long.
It is shorter than the 3 cm line.

This means that it is
2 whole cm and $\frac{7}{10}$ cm

T	U	•	$\frac{1}{10}$
	2	•	7

⬤ To order numbers, start by comparing the largest place value of
each number.

Even though 2.7 shows 7 in the $\frac{1}{10}$'s column, it shows only 2 in the
units column, so 2.7 is smaller than 3 or 3.0.

You can write | 3.0 > 2.7 or 2.7 < 3.0. |

⬤ You can use the symbol < to mean 'less than' and > to mean
'greater than'.

I jumped
3.42 metres in
the long jump this
morning.

I jumped 3.6
metres. 3.6 is
greater than 3.42
so I jumped farther
than you.

▲ The world record
for the women's
long jump is 7.52 m
held by Galina
Chistyakova.

Example

Write these numbers in order from largest to smallest:
3.139, 2.397, 2.593, 2.511

Compare the largest place value first.	3.139 is the largest.
Then look at the next place value.	2.397 is the smallest as 3 < 5.
Then look at the next place value.	2.593 > 2.511 as 9 > 1.

So the order is 3.139, 2.593, 2.511, 2.397

Number Whole numbers and decimals

Exercise 1f

1 Write down the positions of each of these arrows on this number line using decimals. Arrow F is at 3.2.

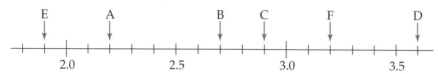

2 Write these numbers as decimals.

  a 1 unit and $\frac{3}{10}$

  b 6 units and $\frac{8}{10}$

  c 7 units and $\frac{1}{10}$

  d 0 units and $\frac{9}{10}$

  e 1 ten, 3 units and $\frac{6}{10}$

  f 2 tens, 5 units and $\frac{5}{10}$

3 Use this place value table to re-write these numbers in order, smallest first.

10.0, 0.9, 5.2, 9.0, 6.1, 12.3, 8.3

T	U	•	$\frac{1}{10}$
1	0	•	0
	0	•	9
	5	•	2
	9	•	0
	6	•	1
1	2	•	3
	8	•	3

4 Use the correct sign ($<$ or $>$) to order these pairs of decimal numbers.

a	4.0	0.4	b	0.8	2.1
c	0.7	1.0	d	10.01	0.12
e	1.03	0.71	f	2.32	0.95
g	1.5	2	h	0.8	1
i	12	1.2	j	6.32	0.85
k	0.7	9	l	9.8	10

5 Estimate the decimal value for both arrows on each number line.

  a
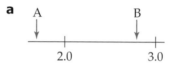

  b
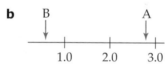

  c

Estimate your answers to 1 decimal place.

Problem solving

6 In the London 2012 Olympics, the men's 100m final results were given in seconds as:

9.75, 9.63, 11.99, 9.94, 9.98, 9.79, 9.8, 9.88

Put these times in order starting with the fastest.

7 a Find a decimal that is between 0.9 and 1.

  b Find another decimal this is between your first decimal and 1.

  c How many decimals are there between 0.9 and 1?

Check out

You should now be able to ...

Test it ➡
Questions

✓	Multiply and divide by powers of 10.	6	1
✓	Round whole numbers and decimals.	5	2
✓	Work out calculations using BIDMAS.	5	3
✓	Identify multiples, factors and prime numbers.	5	4–8
✓	Use product of prime factors to find HCF and LCM.	5	9, 10
✓	Order decimals.	5	11

Language	Meaning	Example
Rounding	Writing a number with fewer non-zero digits. It makes numbers easier to work with.	$123 = 120$ to the nearest 10 $6.75 = 6.8$ to one decimal place
BIDMAS	BIDMAS helps you to remember the order of operations: brackets, indices, division, multiplication, addition and subtraction.	$(4 \times 3 - 2)^2 + 3 = 103$ $4 \times 3 - 2^2 + 3 = 11$
Factor	A number which divides exactly into another number.	1, 3, 9 and 27 are all factors of 27. $27 = 1 \times 27 = 3 \times 9$
Highest common factor (HCF)	The highest number that is a factor of two or more numbers.	The HCF of 24 and 36 is 12.
Lowest common multiple (LCM)	The smallest number that is a multiple of two or more numbers.	The LCM of 24 and 36 is 72.
Multiple	A multiple of a number is a number in its times table.	12 and 18 are multiples of 6. $12 = 2 \times 6$, $18 = 3 \times 6$
Prime	A prime number has two factors.	2, 3, 5, 7, 11 ... are prime. 1 is *not* a prime number

1 Calculate

a $78 \div 10$ b $325 \div 100$

c 9×0.1 d 6×0.01

e $0.7 \div 0.01$ f 170×0.01

g $35 \div 0.1$ h 0.92×0.1

2 Round 6096.5

a to the nearest whole number

b to the nearest 10

c to the nearest 100

d to the nearest 1000

3 Calculate these using the correct order of operations.

a $23 + 5 \times 2$

b $24 - 8 \div 4$

c $(25 + 7) \times 3$

d $65 - 3 \times (4 + 1)$

e $2 \times 4^2 + 3 \div 3$

f $\dfrac{(2 + 1)^2}{15 - 4 \times 6}$

4 Which of the following numbers are factors of 8?

1 2 3 8 12 16 24

5 Which of the following numbers are multiples of 8?

1 2 3 8 12 16 24

6 Use divisibility tests to answer these questions and explain your answer.

a Is 3 a factor of 564?

b Is 610 a multiple of 4?

c Is 103 a prime number?

d Is 6745 divisible by 5?

7 Write each of these numbers as a product of its prime factors.

a 42 b 175

8 Which of the following numbers are prime numbers?

1 3 6 7 9

9 Find the highest common factor of each pair of numbers.

a 18 and 45 b 96 and 180

10 Find the lowest common multiple of each pair of numbers.

a 11 and 8 b 28 and 70

11 Put these decimals in order from smallest to largest.

a 3.5 3.2 3.0 4

b 0.1 0.01 0.12 0.21

c 9.8 9.08 8.99 9.91

d 0.8 0.78 0.09 0.81

What next?

Score		
	0 – 4	Your knowledge of this topic is still developing. To improve look at Formative test: 3A-1; MyMaths: 1003, 1004, 1027, 1032, 1034, 1035, 1044, 1072, 1167 and 1392
	5 – 9	You are gaining a secure knowledge of this topic. To improve look at InvisiPen: 111, 112, 114, 124, 171, 172 and 173
	10 – 11	You have mastered this topic. Well done, you are ready to progress!

1 MyPractice

1a

1 Find the answer to each of these multiplication problems.

   a 3.2×100 **b** 4.63×10 **c** 0.72×1000

   d 0.092×10 **e** 37.6×100 **f** 4.9×1000

   g 0.3×10 **h** 0.476×100 **i** 32.7×1000

2 Find the answer to each of these division problems.

   a $21 \div 10$ **b** $3.7 \div 10$ **c** $6.21 \div 10$

   d $37 \div 100$ **e** $2.9 \div 100$ **f** $4.7 \div 1000$

   g $6.92 \div 10$ **h** $63.7 \div 100$ **i** $47.9 \div 1000$

1b

3 Round each of these numbers to the nearest whole number.

   a 2.8   **b** 7.4   **c** 11.9

   d 15.5   **e** 29.4   **f** 0.3

4 Round each number to the nearest 10.

   a 23   **b** 35   **c** 46

   d 98   **e** 104   **f** 225

5 Round each number to the nearest 100.

   a 55   **b** 236   **c** 250

   d 43   **e** 661   **f** 919

1c

6 Calculate these, remembering the BIDMAS rule.

   a $3 \times 3 + 4 =$ **b** $12 - 8 \div 2 =$

   c $3 + 3 \times 4 =$ **d** $3 \times 4 + 9 \div 3 =$

   e $25 - 5 \times 5 + 2 =$ **f** $5 + 3^2 \times 2 =$

   g $(4 + 9) - 6 + 3^2 =$ **h** $4^2 + (6 - 2) \times 5 =$

   i $8 + (8 - 3) + (6 + 2) \times 2 =$ **j** $20 + 2^2 + (12 - 7) - 3^2 =$

1d

7 List the first six multiples of 7.

8 Jane says that 6 is a factor of 84.

Anita says that Jane is wrong, because 7 is a factor of 84.

Who is correct?

Explain your answer.

9 **a** Test these numbers to see if they are divisible by 3.

     i 21   **ii** 28   **iii** 32

     iv 84   **v** 96   **vi** 1011

  b Which of the numbers in part **a** are divisible by 2?

10 Use divisibility tests to say whether or not these numbers are prime.

    a 2   **b** 18   **c** 29   **d** 81   **e** 87

    f 58   **g** 51   **h** 41   **i** 43   **j** 20970

11 Copy and complete these diagrams and then write each number as a product of its prime factors.

a

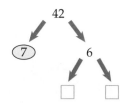

b

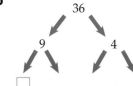

c

d

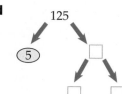

12 a Copy and complete these diagrams.

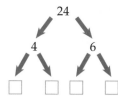

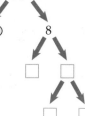

  b Find the HCF of 24 and 56.

13 Put these numbers in order, starting with the smallest.

1.32, 13.2, 0.13, 0.2, 2.1, 0.5, 3, 0.001.

MyMaths.co.uk

2 Measures and area

Introduction

The fastest man in the world is Usain Bolt. In 2009 he ran 100 metres in 9.58 seconds. His average speed for the race was 10.44 m/s but his top speed during the race was 12.27 m/s. However, Usain would be chasing the tails of creatures such as greyhounds, antelopes, cheetahs and even the domesticated cat, which all can run faster.

What's the point?

Being able to measure distances and times accurately means that you can work out speed, which is highly useful in our increasingly fast-moving world!

Objectives

By the end of this chapter, you will have learned how to …
- Convert one metric unit to another.
- Know rough metric equivalents of some imperial units.
- Calculate the area of a rectangle.
- Deduce and use the formula for the area of a triangle.
- Calculate the area of a parallelogram.
- Use π (pi) to calculate the circumference of a circle.

Check in

1 Sort these units into **metric** and **imperial** measures.

pint gram millimetre ounce foot kilometre inch mile litre pound centimetre kilogram millilitre yard

Metric	Imperial

2 Which is greater?

   a 1 mile or 1 kilometre   **b** 1 pound or 1 kilogram

   c 1 foot or 1 metre   **d** 1 inch or 1 centimetre   **e** 1 pint or 1 litre

3 What is the area of each shape in square centimetres (cm²)?

a
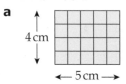
4 cm
← 5 cm →

b
3 cm
← 6 cm →

c
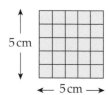
5 cm
← 5 cm →

Starter problem

A surveyor has 60 m of fencing. He wants to mark out the largest area he can for the construction of a house.

Investigate.

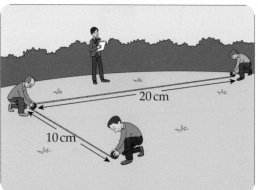

20 cm

10 cm

21

2a Metric measures

These are the basic units of **metric** measurement.

● **Length:** millimetres (mm), centimetres (cm), metres (m), kilometres (km)

10 millimetres = 1 centimetre	
100 centimetres = 1 metre	
1000 metres = 1 kilometre	

● **Mass:** grams (g), kilograms (kg), tonnes (t)

1000 grams = 1 kilogram	
1000 kilograms = 1 tonne	

● **Capacity:** millilitres (ml), centilitres (cl), litres (l)

10 millilitres = 1 centilitre	
1000 millilitres = 1 litre	
100 centilitres = 1 litre	

Example

a How many centilitres are there in half a litre?

b How many metres are there in 10 kilometres?

a There are 100 centilitres in one litre.

There are 50 centilitres in half a litre.

b 1 km = 1000 metres

10 km is 10 × 1000 = 10 000 metres.

Example

Jake is 1.68 m tall.
What is his height in millimetres?

I am 1.68 metres tall.

Do the calculation in two steps.
1 m = 100 cm
1.68 m is 1.68 × 100 = 168 centimetres.
1 cm = 10 mm
168 cm is 168 × 10 = 1680 millimetres.

Exercise 2a

1 **a** How many centimetres are there in 6.5 metres?

  b How many centilitres are there in 1.5 litres?

  c How many millimetres are there in 4.5 centimetres?

  d How many millimetres are there in 2.3 metres?

  e How many millilitres are there in 19 centilitres?

  f How many kilograms is 2400 grams?

  g How many tonnes is 4500 kilograms?

  h 42 millilitres are poured from a 1-litre bottle.
    How much is left?

  i 1 kilogram of flour is shared equally into 10 bags.
    How many grams of flour are there in each bag?

2 Carla measures her garden, in metres.
  Convert each measurement into centimetres.

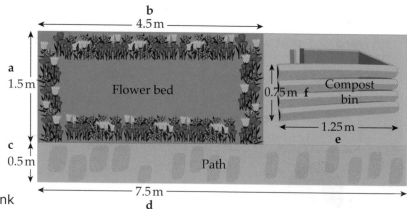

3 Choose the most sensible estimate for

  a the mass of an apple
    10 g   100 g   1 kg

  b the capacity of a can of drink
    33 ml   33 cl   33 litres

  c the distance from Madrid to Lisbon.
    600 cm   600 m   600 km

Problem solving

4 A 10 kg sack of flour is divided into packs with a mass of 500 g.
  How many packs can be filled from the sack?

5 One lap of the school playing field is 650 metres.
  Ahmed runs six laps.
  How many more metres does he have to run to complete 4 kilometres?

6 Ameera is preparing a party for 35 people.
  A bottle of cordial has the instructions 'mix one part cordial to five parts water'.
  Ameera plans on providing enough for three drinks each.
  Her cups hold 150 ml each.
  How many bottles of cordial will she need?

How many of these do I need to buy?

2b Imperial measures

When people first started measuring things they used **non-standard** measures.

▲ The Romans used the length of a human foot as a unit of measure.

▲ King Henry I decided that the distance from the tip of his nose to the tip of his fingers was 1 yard.

▲ Edward II decided that the length of three barleycorns laid end-to-end was 1 inch.

In 1824 British imperial units of measurement were made **standard** so that 1 **yard** or 1 **pint** were the same everywhere in the land.

You will need to recognise imperial units and know how to convert between imperial and metric units.

Length	Weight	Capacity
inches, feet, yards, miles	ounces, pounds, stones, tons	pints, quarts, gallons
12 inches = 1 foot 3 feet = 1 yard 1760 yards = 1 mile	16 ounces = 1 pound 14 pounds = 1 stone 160 stones = 1 ton	2 pints = 1 quart 8 pints = 1 gallon

Example

James weighs 151 pounds. How much does he weigh in stones and pounds?

There are 14 pounds in 1 stone, so divide 151 by 14.

```
    10  r 11
14)151
    140     10 × 14
    ‾‾‾
     11
```

Answer: 10 stones and 11 pounds.

Example

Mia runs in a 5 mile off-road race. How many kilometres is this?

1 mile ≈ 1.6 km

5 miles is 5 × 1.6 = 8 km

Answer: Mia runs about 8 kilometres.

Length
1 inch ≈ 2.5 cm
1 mile ≈ 1.6 km

Mass
1 ounce ≈ 30 grams
1 pound ≈ 500 g
more accurately,
1 kg ≈ 2.2 pounds

Capacity
1 litre ≈ $1\frac{3}{4}$ pints
1 gallon ≈ 4.5 litres

Exercise 2b

1 a How many feet are there in 5 yards?

b How many inches are there in 6 feet?

c How many ounces are there in 3 pounds?

d How many pints are there in 6 gallons?

e How many pounds are there in 5 stones?

f How many inches are there in 1 yard?

2 Callum has a box of 6-inch square tiles. He has to stick them in a row 3 feet long. How many tiles will he use?

3 A barrel holds 5 gallons of vinegar.

How many one-pint bottles can be filled from the barrel?

4 What is the total mass, in pounds, of Edith's shopping?

12 ounces   15 ounces   2 pounds

8 ounces   13 ounces

5 Which is greater?

a 10 inches or 15 centimetres

b 5 pounds or 3 kilograms

c 110 centimetres or 4 feet

d 100 grams or 3 ounces

e 8 pints or 6 litres

f 3 stones or 12 kilograms

g 6 kilometres or 3 miles

h 14 litres or 4 gallons

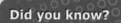

Problem solving

6 Granny reads her shopping list to Nikki over the phone. Convert the measurements into metric measurements.

4 pounds of potatoes ...
5 pints of milk ...
$3\frac{1}{2}$ yards of string ...
a packet of 6-inch nails ...
and 10 ounces of toffee.

That's about ? kilograms.
That's about ? litres.
That's about ? metres.
That's about ? centimetres.
That is about ? grams.

Did you know?

In 1999 NASA lost a $125 million spacecraft when it crashed into Mars. The reason? One team of engineers did all their calculations in metric units and another team used imperial units!

2c Area

A 2D shape is a 'flat' shape.

> ● 2D shapes have **area**.
> ▶ Area is the amount of surface the shape covers.
> ▶ Area is measured in square units using ^{2}.

p.260 >

> ● You find the area of a rectangle by multiplying its **length** by its **width**.
> Area = $l \times w$

Units for area are cm^2 (square centimetres), m^2, mm^2 or km^2.

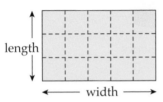

length

width

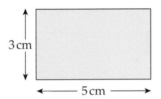

3 cm

5 cm

You can find the area of the rectangle by counting the squares. There are 15 centimetre squares. The area is $15\,cm^2$.

You can find the area of the rectangle more quickly using the formula.
Area $= l \times w$
$= 5\,cm \times 3\,cm = 15\,cm^2$

Example

Find the area of the rectangle.

3.7 cm

6.3 cm

Area = $l \times w$
$= 6.3 \times 3.7$ Use a calculator.
$= 23.31\,cm^2$
The area of the rectangle is $23.31\,cm^2$.

Example

Find the area of the rectangle.

46 cm

1.3 m

You must make sure the units are the same before finding the area.

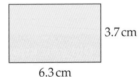

You can convert 1.3 m to centimetres or 46 cm to metres.

Area = $l \times w$
$= 1.3 \times 0.46$
$= 0.598\,m^2$

Alternatively, in centimetres
Area = 130×46
$= 5980\,cm^2$

The area of the rectangle is $0.598\,m^2$ or $5980\,cm^2$.

Exercise 2c

1 Calculate the area of each of these rectangles.

a

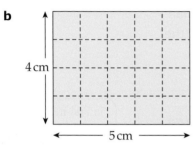

3 cm

7 cm

b

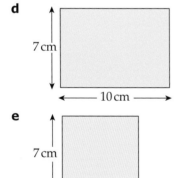

4 cm

5 cm

c

5 cm

7 cm

Area has square units.
You write 6 square
centimetres as 6 cm².

d

7 cm

10 cm

e

7 cm

7 cm

2 Calculate the area of each of these. Take care to use the correct unit.

a A photograph is 11 cm long and 6 cm wide.

b A sheet of gold leaf is 5 cm long and 9 cm wide.

c A wall is 5 m long and 3 m wide.

d A tennis court is 10 m by 23 m.

3 Find the area of each of these rectangles.

a

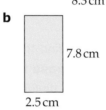

2.9 cm

8.3 cm

b

7.8 cm

2.5 cm

4 Find the area of each of these rectangles.

a

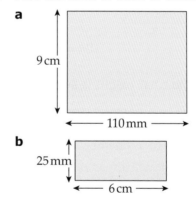

9 cm

110 mm

b

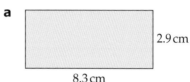

25 mm

6 cm

Problem solving

5 How many of the smaller rectangles fit into the square?

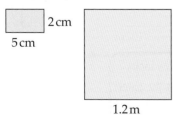

2 cm

5 cm

Not drawn to scale

1.2 m

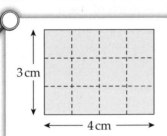 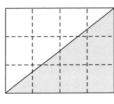 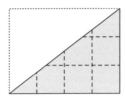

3 cm

4 cm

Use this method to investigate the area of other triangles.

The area of this rectangle is 12 cm².
Area = *l* × w
= 3 cm × 4 cm
= 12 cm²

Divide the rectangle with a diagonal line. The blue area is half of 12 cm² = 6 cm².

The area of the triangle is half the area of the rectangle.

● The area of a triangle is half the area of the rectangle drawn around it.

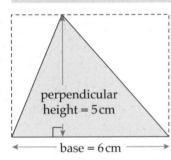

perpendicular height = 5 cm

base = 6 cm

You find the area of a triangle by multiplying the **base** by the **perpendicular** height and then dividing this result by 2.

Area = $\frac{1}{2} \times b \times h$
= $\frac{1}{2} \times 6\,cm \times 5\,cm = \frac{1}{2} \times 30\,cm^2$
= 15 cm²

The area of the triangle is 15 cm².

To find half of an amount you divide it by 2.

● The perpendicular height is at right angles (90°) to the base.

● The **formula** for finding the area of a triangle is
Area = $\frac{1}{2} \times$ base × height
▶ This is often written as $A = \frac{1}{2}bh$

Example

Find the area of this triangle.

The base is 10 cm and the perpendicular height is 6 cm.

Area = $\frac{1}{2} \times b \times h$
= $\frac{1}{2} \times 10\,cm \times 6\,cm$
= $\frac{1}{2} \times 60\,cm^2$
= 30 cm²

The area of the triangle is 30 cm².

6 cm

10 cm

This triangle looks 'awkward' but the same formula still applies.

Exercise 2d

1 For each diagram
   i find the area of the rectangle
   ii find the area of the blue triangle.

a

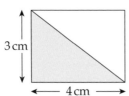
3 cm
4 cm

b

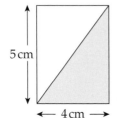
5 cm
4 cm

c

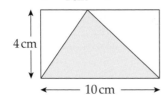
4 cm
10 cm

d

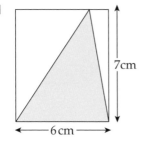
7 cm
6 cm

2 Calculate the area of each of these triangles.

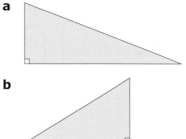

a 2 cm, 5 cm

b 3 cm, 6 cm

c 6 cm, 5 cm

d 6 mm, 4 mm

e 6 cm, 6 cm

f 9 m, 10 m

3 Carefully measure each of these triangles. Use your measurements to calculate their areas.

a

b

Problem solving

4 Ryan's boat has two triangular sails.
   What is the total area of the sails, in square metres?

3 m 4 m 3 m 1.5 m

2e Area of a parallelogram

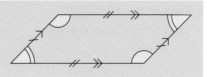

- A **parallelogram** is a quadrilateral.
  ▶ Opposite sides are equal in length.
  ▶ Opposite sides are parallel to each other.
  ▶ Opposite angles are equal.

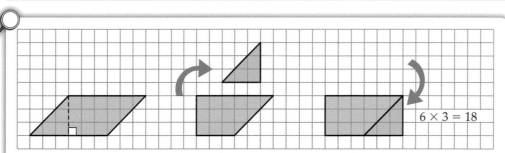

| Make a perpendicular cut to give a triangle at one end. | Slide the triangle to the other end. | Now you have a rectangle. The area of the rectangle is 6 cm × 3 cm = 18 cm². |

Use this method to find the area of other parallelograms.

- You find the area of a parallelogram by multiplying the base by the **perpendicular height**.

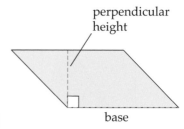

You can write a formula for the area of a parallelogram.

The formula uses A for area, b for base and h for perpendicular height.

Area = base × height
A = bh

**Example**

Find the area of the parallelogram.

a
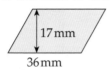
17 mm
36 mm

b
2.3 cm   3.2 cm
4.1 cm

a   A = b × h
Area = 36 × 17
= 612 mm²
The area of the parallelogram is 612 mm².

b   A = b × h
Area = 4.1 × 2.3
= 9.43 cm²
The area of the parallelogram is 9.43 cm².

Be careful! You must use the perpendicular height, 2.3 cm, not the slant height, 3.2 cm

Exercise 2e

1 Find the area of each of these parallelograms.

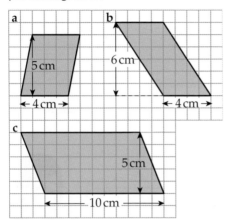

2 Calculate the area of each parallelogram using the formula Area = $b \times h$.

a

5 cm

11 cm

b

6 m

5 m

c
$2\frac{1}{2}$ cm
6 cm

3 Find the area of these parallelograms.

a

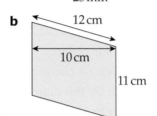
16 mm
20 mm
25 mm

b

12 cm
10 cm
11 cm

4 Find the area of these shapes.

a

9 cm
5 cm
8 cm

b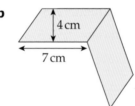

4 cm
7 cm

These two parallelograms are congruent.

Problem solving

5 Jenny designed a logo.
Find the area of the shaded region.

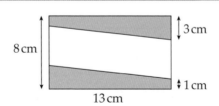
8 cm
3 cm
1 cm
13 cm

6 Amir draws a parallelogram with area 36 cm² and perimeter 28 cm.

a Which parallelogram cannot be Amir's shape?

i

4.5 cm
6 cm
8 cm

ii

4 cm
5 cm
9 cm

iii

6 cm
6 cm
9 cm

b Draw another possibility for Amir's parallelogram.

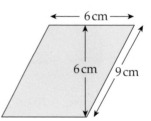

MyMaths.co.uk   🔍 1108   SEARCH

circumference
diameter

● The **circumference** of a circle is the distance all around its edge.

● The **diameter** of a circle is the distance across the circle through the centre.

Find some different circular objects.
Measure the diameter and the circumference using a piece of string.
Divide the circumference by the diameter.
What is the link between the circumference and diameter?

The circumference of a circle is just over three times longer than its diameter. More accurately, the circumference of a circle is 'pi' times the diameter.

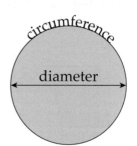

Pi is written using the Greek letter π.

● The formula for finding the circumference of a circle is
circumference = π × diameter

A whiteboard pen has diameter 1.5 cm. What is its circumference?

For an **estimate** you can use π ≈ 3.

To calculate more accurately, you use more decimal places.

Circumference = π × diameter		
Estimate $C = 3 \times 1.5$	Using π = 3.1	$C = 3.1 \times 1.5$
$= 4.5$ cm		$= 4.65$ cm
		$= 4.7$ cm (1 decimal place)

Example

i Estimate the circumference of each circle using π ≈ 3.

ii Estimate the circumference of each circle using π ≈ 3.1.

a

Diameter = 10 cm

b

Diameter = 80 mm

a circumference = π × diameter
  i $C ≈ 3 \times 10$ cm
    $= 30$ cm
  ii $C = 3.1 \times 10$ cm
    $= 31$ cm

b circumference = π × diameter
  i $C ≈ 3 \times 80$ mm
    $= 240$ mm
  ii $C = 3.1 \times 80$ mm
    $= 248$ mm

Exercise 2f

1   Estimate the circumference of each of
    these circles.
    Use π ≈ 3.

a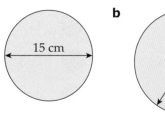
15 cm

b
25 cm

c
7 cm

d
32 mm

2   Using π ≈ 3.1, find the circumference of
    these circles.

a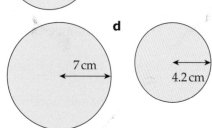
3 cm

b
9 mm

c
7 cm

d
4.2 cm

Problem solving

3   The Round Table of Arthur in the Great Hall in Winchester has a diameter of 5.5 m.

   a   Calculate its circumference using π ≈ 3.1.
           Round your answer to 1 decimal place.

   b   Each of Arthur's knights needed 1 m of elbow room at the table.
           How many of Arthur's twenty-four knights could
           sit together at the table at one time?

4   The circumference of this peg is 14.9 cm.
    The diameter of the hole is 4.7 cm.
    Will the peg fit exactly into the hole, fall through the
    hole or not go into the hole at all?
    Show your working.

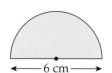
4.7 cm

14.9 cm

5   **a**   The diameter of this log is 38 cm.
            What distance does it travel in one full revolution?
            Use π ≈ 3.1.

   b   What distance does the log travel in ten revolutions?

6   What is the total length
    of the edges of these shapes?
    use π ≈ 3.1

   a
   ←— 6 cm —→

   b
   ←— 4 cm —→

2 MySummary

Check out
You should now be able to ...

Test it
Questions

✓ Convert one metric unit to another.	⑤	1
✓ Convert some metric units to imperial units and vice versa.	⑤	2, 3
✓ Find the area of a rectangle by using the formula.	⑤	4
✓ Find the area of a triangle by using the formula.	⑥	5
✓ Find the area of a parallelogram by using the formula.	⑥	6
✓ Find the circumference of a circle by using the formula.	⑥	7, 8

Language	Meaning	Example
Metric units	Metres (m) measure length, grams (g) measure mass and litres (l) measure capacity.	1000 ml = 1 litre 100 cm = 1 m 1000 g = 1 kg
Imperial	Some of the imperial units are inches, feet, miles, ounces, pounds, stones, pints and gallons.	5 miles ≈ 8 kilometres 1 kilogram ≈ 2.2 pounds 1 gallon ≈ 4.5 litres
Area	Area is the amount of surface that a shape covers.	Area of rectangle = length × width
Circumference and diameter	The circumference of a circle is the distance around its edge. The diameter of a circle is the distance across the circle through the centre.	circumference / Diameter (circle diagram)

1 a How many millimetres are there in 25 cm?
   b How many centilitres are there in 2.5 litres?
   c How many metres are there in 12 km?
   d How many grams are there in 4.3 kg?

2 a How many inches are there in 2 feet?
   b How many ounces are there in 5 pounds?

3 Which is bigger
   a 10 kg or 20 pounds
   b 10 km or 7 miles?

4 Calculate the area of this rectangle and state the units of your answer.

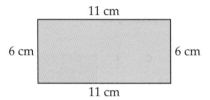

5 Calculate the area of these triangles. State the units of your answers.
   a

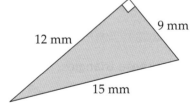

5 b

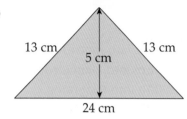

6 Calculate the area of these parallelograms.
   a

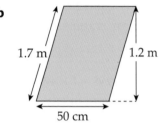

   b

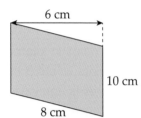

7 Calculate the circumference of the circle.

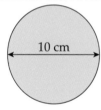

8 A wheel has a diameter of 24 cm. What is its circumference?

What next?

Score	0 – 3	Your knowledge of this topic is still developing. To improve look at Formative test: 3A-2; MyMaths: 1061, 1084, 1088, 1091, 1108, 1129
	4 – 6	You are gaining a secure knowledge of this topic. To improve look at InvisiPen: 313, 314, 315, 332, 333 and 351
	7 – 8	You have mastered this topic. Well done, you are ready to progress!

2a

1   Convert these.

   a   300 cm into metres
   b   40 mm into centimetres
   c   2000 m into kilometres
   d   4000 ml into litres
   e   8000 g into kilograms
   f   8 km into metres
   g   6 cm into millimetres
   h   4 kg into grams
   i   2 litres into millilitres
   j   5 m into centimetres

2b

2   Approximately ...

   a   how far is 5 miles in kilometres?
   b   how many pints would 3 litres be equivalent to?
   c   30 centimetres is equivalent to how many inches?
   d   how many ounces are there in 90 grams?
   e   1 metre is equivalent to how many feet?
   f   7 kilograms is the same as how many pounds?

2c

3   Use the formula $A = l \times w$ to calculate the areas of these rectangles.
   (Give your answers in cm².)

   a
   7 cm
   4 cm

   b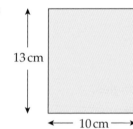
   13 cm
   10 cm

   c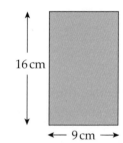
   16 cm
   9 cm

2d

4   Use the formula $A = \frac{1}{2} \times b \times h$ to calculate the areas of these triangles.

   a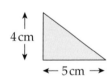
   4 cm
   5 cm

   b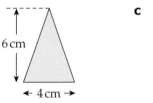
   6 cm
   4 cm

   c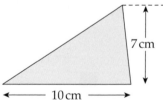
   7 cm
   10 cm

   d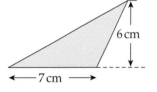
   6 cm
   7 cm

   e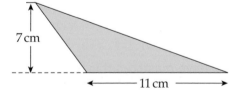
   7 cm
   11 cm

5 Use the formula $A = b \times h$ to calculate the areas of these parallelograms.

a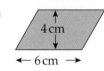
4 cm
← 6 cm →

b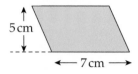
5 cm
← 7 cm →

c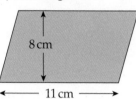
8 cm
← 11 cm →

d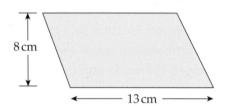
8 cm
← 13 cm →

e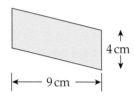
4 cm
← 9 cm →

6 Find the area of these shapes.

a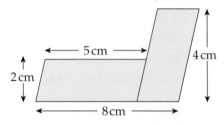
5 cm
4 cm
2 cm
8 cm

b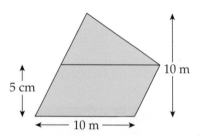
10 m
5 cm
10 m

7 Estimate the circumference of each of these circles.
Use $\pi \approx 3.1$.

a
8 cm

b
9.3 cm

c
15 mm

d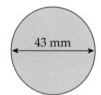
43 mm

8 Estimate the circumference of each of these circles.
Use $\pi \approx 3.1$.

a
6 cm

b
3.8 cm

c
21 mm

d
57 mm

9 The diameter of a wheel is 48 cm.
  a Find the circumference of the wheel.
  b How many full revolutions does the wheel need to turn to travel 1 km?

10 The circumference of a circle is 52.7 mm.
Find the diameter of the circle.

MyMaths.co.uk

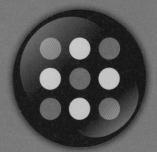

3 Expressions and formulae

Introduction

The most famous scientists have used mathematical formulae to describe their ideas. When an apple famously dropped on his head, Sir Isaac Newton used the formula

$$F = \frac{Gm_1m_2}{r^2}$$

to describe what he called gravity.

When Albert Einstein said that you could convert between mass and energy he changed the world and used the formula

$$E = mc^2$$

to show how it could be calculated.

What's the point?

A formula shows how one quantity is linked to another. Using formulae helps us to understand how our world is connected.

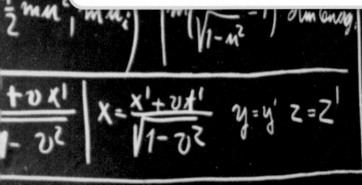

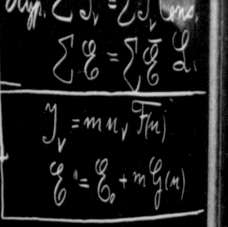

Objectives

By the end of this chapter, you will have learned how to …

- ⦿ Simplify expressions by collecting like terms.
- ⦿ Expand brackets.
- ⦿ Substitute values into expressions with brackets.
- ⦿ Substitute into formulae.
- ⦿ Rearrange basic formulae.
- ⦿ Form expressions.

Check in

1 Work out

a $1 + 4 + 7 + 6 + 3$ b $5 + 3 - 4$ c $4 + 3 + 2 - 5 + 2 - 1$

d $3 - 6 + 2 + 4 - 2$ e $4 - 7 + 2$ f $5 - 3 - 4 + 1 - 2$

2 Work out

a 3×6 b 7×4 c 5×9 d 12×7

e 6×8 f 9×7 g 3×7 h 8×4

3 Work out

a -3×4 b 2×-5 c -5×9 d -4×-6

e 6×-8 f -9×-2 g -5×5 h -7×-4

4 Find the perimeter of each shape.

a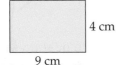

b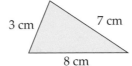

c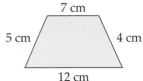

Starter problem

This L-shape is drawn on a 10×10 grid numbered from 1 to 100.

It has 5 numbers inside it.

We can call it L_{35} because the largest number inside it is 35.

The total of the numbers inside L_{35} is 138.

Pretend you are a famous scientist and see if you can find a connection between the L number and the total of the numbers inside the L shape.

You should try to write your connection as a formula.

1	2	3	4	5	6	7	8	9	10
11	12	13	14	15	16	17	18	19	20
21	22	23	24	25	26	27	28	29	30
31	32	33	34	35	36	37	38	39	40
41	42	43	44	45	46	47	48	49	50
51	52	53	54	55	56	57	58	59	60
61	62	63	64	65	66	67	68	69	70
71	72	73	74	75	76	77	78	79	80
81	82	83	84	85	86	87	88	89	90
91	92	93	94	95	96	97	98	99	100

3a Simplifying expressions

Here are five cards.

You can group or **collect** the cards together into **like** colours. The red cards together and the black cards together.

There are two red and three black or 2 red + 3 black.

You can collect symbols or **terms** in the same way.

p.192 > $a + b + b + b + a = 2a + 3b$ $x + x + 2x - x + 3y + y = 3x + 4y$

> Like terms have the same letter or symbol.

⬤ You can only collect like terms together.

Be careful with negative numbers. $5m + n - 3m - 4n = 2m - 3n$

$$1n - 4n = \text{-}3n$$

⬤ In algebra you often make the × sign invisible.

$2 \times 3x = 2 \times 3 \times x = 6 \times x = 6x$

When there is more than one unknown value, the **expression** could look like this.

$3x \times 2y = 3 \times x \times 2 \times y = 6 \times x \times y = 6xy$

⬤ You can write divisions as fractions or with a ÷ sign.

$$\frac{12a}{4} = 3a \quad \text{or} \quad 12a \div 4 = 3a$$

Example

Simplify these expressions.

a $3e + 5e - 7e$ b $4t - 5u + 5t + 6u$ c $5 \times t$ d $5g \times 3k$ e $\frac{24d}{6}$

a $3e + 5e - 7e = e$ b $4t - 5u + 5t + 6u = 9t + u$ c $5 \times t = 5t$

d $5g \times 3k = 15gk$ e $\frac{24d}{6} = 4d$

Example

Write an expression for the perimeter of this triangle. Simplify the answer as much as possible.

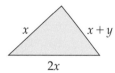

The perimeter $= x + x + y + 2x$
$= 4x + y$

Exercise 3a

1 Simplify these expressions by collecting the terms.
   a $h + h + h + h$
   b $j + j + j + j + j + j$
   c $m + m + m + 2m$
   d $t + t + t + t - t$
   e $f - f + f$
   f $n + 3n + 2n - n$

2 Each expression has unlike terms. Simplify them by collecting like terms together.
   a $w + 2w + 3v + v$
   b $2m + 5n + 5n + 8m$
   c $6y + 5x + x + 4x$
   d $7t + 5q + 2q + 3t$
   e $3e - e + g + 6g$
   f $6h - 7h + 5j + 4j$

3 Complete the puzzles by adding the expressions in the direction of the arrows.

   a
   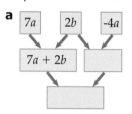

   b
   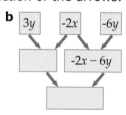

4 Write an expression for the perimeter of each of these shapes.
   Simplify your expressions.

   a
   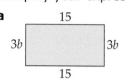

   b
   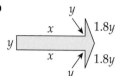

   c
   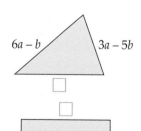

5 Simplify these expressions by multiplying and dividing.

   > Use the invisible × sign.

   a $5 \times 2a$ b $6 \times 5m$
   c $3s \times 5$ d $2 \times 4 \times 5f$
   e $6a \times 4b$ f $5r \times 5s$
   g $10m \times 3n$ h $8t \times 7v$
   i $15h \div 5$ j $60y \div 5$
   k $\dfrac{12x}{6}$ l $\dfrac{18t}{3t}$
   m $12 \times 6k$ n $\dfrac{18v}{20}$
   o $\dfrac{100f}{20f}$ p $5u \times 20v$
   q $\dfrac{36x}{9x}$ r $2b \times 6a$

Problem solving

6 a The perimeter of this triangle is $8a + 4b$.
     Find the length of the third side.
   b A shape has a perimeter of $6x - 12y + 18$.
     Sketch and label the sides of a possible shape.

7 a The area of this rectangle is $12a$.
     Find the length of the missing side.
   b A rectangle has area $24xy$.
     Sketch and label the sides of a possible shape.
   c The area of the triangle is $30uv$.
     Find the length of the missing side.

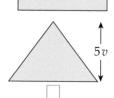

3b Using brackets

When Michelle works out the bills for her customers she uses **symbols** to stand for the cost of each item on the menu.

For fish and chips she writes $f + c$.
The bill is £4.50 + £1.20 = £5.70.

The bill for 2 portions of fish and
2 portions of chips is

$f + f + c + c$.

Michelle writes $2 \times (f + c)$ or $2(f + c)$.

To work out the total of the bill, Michelle
substitutes the price of each item.
$$2(f + c) = 2 \times (£4.50 + £1.20)$$
$$= 2 \times £5.70$$
$$= £11.40$$

MENU
Chips	...... £1.20
Fish	...... £4.50
Sausage	...... £0.80
Bread	...... £0.50
Tea	...... £1.00
Cola	...... £1.10

Example

a   Use symbols to write expressions for the cost of these orders. Use brackets.
  i   '4 teas (t) and 4 colas (k) please.'
  ii   '2 portions of chips (c) and 3 sausages (s) please.'
b   Substitute the prices of the items to find the cost of the orders.

a   i $t + t + t + t + k + k + k + k$ ii $c + c + s + s + s = 2c + 3s$
      $= 4t + 4k$
      $= 4(t + k)$
b   i $4(t + k) = 4 \times (£1.00 + £1.10)$ ii $2c + 3s$
        $= 4 \times £2.10$ $= 2 \times (£1.20) + 3 \times £0.80$
        $= £8.40$ $= £2.40 + £2.40$
                    $= £4.80$

● To expand the brackets means to multiply everything in the
  brackets by the term outside the brackets.

Example

Expand these brackets.
a $4(x + y)$ b $3(2x - 3y)$

a $4(x + y) = 4x + 4y$ b $3(2x - 3y) = 6x - 9y$

Multiplying out brackets and expanding brackets both mean the same thing.

Exercise 3b

1 Use the symbols on the menu to write expressions for the cost of these orders. Use brackets.

Menu

Chips .... *c* £1.20
Fish .... *f* £4.50
Sausage ..... *s* £0.80
Bread .... *b* £0.50
Tea .... *t* £1.00
Cola .... *k* £1.10

a 2 portions of chips and 2 portions of bread

b 3 colas and 3 teas

c 2 sausages, 2 portions of bread and 2 teas

d 3 portions of fish and 4 portions of chips

e 4 portions of bread and 3 portions of chips

2 Substitute the prices of the items to find the cost of the orders in question **1**. The first one is completed for you.

a $2(c + b) = 2 \times (£1.20 + £0.50)$
$= 2 \times £1.70$
$= £3.40$

3 Expand the brackets in these expressions.

a	$3(x + y)$	**b**	$6(a - b)$
c	$10(w - v)$	**d**	$3(x + y + z)$
e	$4(2x + 3y)$	**f**	$5(3p - 2q)$
g	$7(2m - 5n)$	**h**	$8(2t - 3s + r)$
i	$9(10u + 4v)$	**j**	$6(j + 5k)$
k	$2(3 + 2f)$	**l**	$5(4 + 7t)$
m	$4(2r + 8)$	**n**	$4(3r + 6s)$
o	$7(5h + 6i)$	**p**	$3(13q - 5h)$

4 You can write this expression for the perimeter of a rectangle.

$2(x + y)$

a Multiply out the brackets.

b If $x = 17.5\,$cm and $y = 8.5\,$cm, what is the perimeter of the rectangle, in centimetres?

Did you know?

Christopher Clavius suggested the use of brackets in 1608. He thought it would be useful to use brackets to group terms.

Problem solving

5 A regular shape has perimeter of $6(x + y)$ cm.

a Sketch the shape.

b Label the sides with their measurements.

c If the perimeter of the shape is 60 cm, suggest some pairs of values for x and y.

A regular shape has all its sides equal and all its angles equal.

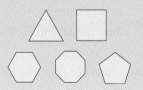

6 The perimeter of this rectangle is $6y + 6x$. What is its width?

$3y + x$

?

3c Formulae

> 📀 A formula is a rule, written as an equation, which you use to find values.

Formulae is the plural of formula.

Your average speed on a bike can be calculated by dividing the distance by the time for which you travel.

As a formula this is written

speed = distance ÷ time

or $s = d ÷ t$

or $s = \dfrac{d}{t}$

You can **substitute** the values of d and t into the formula.

Example

Jo cycles 60 km and it takes 3 hours.
What is Jo's average speed?

Use the formula, $s = \dfrac{d}{t} = \dfrac{60}{3}$

$s = 20$

Jo travels at 20 km per hour.

You can rearrange the formula to find the distance or the time.
This triangle helps.

To work out s

cover s and you see
d over t.

$s = \dfrac{d}{t}$

To calculate t

cover t and you see
d over s.

$t = \dfrac{d}{s}$

To find d

cover d and you see
s times t.

$d = s \times t$

Example

a Start with the formula for area of a rectangle $A = l \times w$.
Rearrange the formula to find the width.

b Use your formula to find the width if the area = 25 cm² and the length = 10 cm.

a $A = l \times w$

$w = \dfrac{A}{l}$

b $w = \dfrac{A}{l} = \dfrac{25}{10}$

$w = 2.5$ cm

Exercise 3c

1 The formula for the area of a rectangle is
$A = l \times w$.
(l = length and
w = width)

a Use the formula to calculate the area of each of these rectangles.

   i $l = 20\,cm$, $w = 3\,cm$

   ii $l = 3\,cm$, $w = 18\,cm$

   iii $l = 14.5\,cm$, $w = 6\,cm$

   iv $l = 25\,cm$, $w = 12\,cm$

b Rearrange the formula $A = l \times w$ so that you can calculate the width, w, of a rectangle.

   $w =$ ......

c Use the rearranged formula to calculate the width of each of these rectangles.

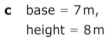

   i Area = $40\,cm^2$, length = $10\,cm$

   ii Area = $40\,cm^2$, length = $15\,cm$

   iii $A = 81\,cm^2$, $l = 9\,cm$

   iv $A = 51\,cm^2$, $l = 17\,cm$

2 To find the area of a triangle you multiply the base by the perpendicular height and divide the result by 2.

As a formula this is
$A = \dfrac{1}{2} \times b \times h$.

Use the formula to calculate the area of each of these triangles.

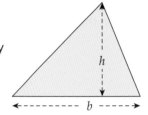

Make sure you use the correct units for your answers.

a base = $5\,cm$, height = $10\,cm$

b base = $7\,cm$, height = $6\,cm$

c base = $7\,m$, height = $8\,m$

d $b = 8\,cm$, $h = 15\,cm$

e $b = 7\,cm$, $h = 25\,cm$

f $b = 21\,cm$, $h = 11\,cm$

g $b = 0.5\,m$, $h = 0.5\,m$

h $b = 50\,cm$, $h = 1\,m$

i $b = 30\,cm$, $h = 0.3\,m$

Problem solving

3 a Rearrange the formula for the area of a triangle so that you can calculate the height of a triangle.

   b Use the formula to calculate the height of a triangle with an area of $90\,cm^2$ and a base of $3\,cm$.

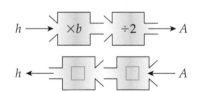

4 The voltage V in an electrical circuit with current I and resistance R, is given by the formula: $V = IR$.

   a Rearrange the formula so that you can calculate the current, I in the circuit.

   b Use your formula to find I when $V = 60$ and $R = 12$.

5 Here is a formula connecting speed and acceleration.

$$v = u + at$$

   a Find v if $u = 1$, $a = 3$ and $t = 4$.

   b Find u if $v = 10$, $a = 2$ and $t = 4$.

   c Find t if $v = 12$, $u = 3$ and $t = 3$.

Inside the bag there are *n* marbles.

Outside the bag there are 5 marbles.

+

> *n* + 5 is an expression.

Altogether there are *n* + 5 marbles.

n stands for the number of marbles in the bag.

> ● An expression is made up of terms.
> ● An expression has no equals sign.

This bag contained *m* marbles but 3 marbles rolled out.

There are *m* − 3 marbles left in the bag.

There are *t* pins in each box.

p.192 >

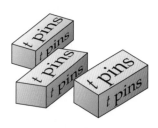

> In algebra you don't write the times sign, so it should be 3*t* not 3 × *t*.

There are 3 boxes here, so there are 3 × *t* = 3*t* pins altogether.

Example

There are *t* pins in a box.

How many pins are there in

a 10 boxes

b 2 full boxes and 15 loose pins?

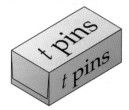

- - - - - - - - - - - -

a 10*t*   In 10 boxes there are 10 × *t* or 10*t* pins.

b 2*t* + 15   In 2 full boxes there are 2 × t or 2*t* pins.
                    Adding 15 loose pins makes 2*t* + 15 pins.

Exercise 3d

1   Write an expression to say how many
    marbles there are in each picture.
    Use the symbol *n* for the unknown
    number of marbles in each bag.

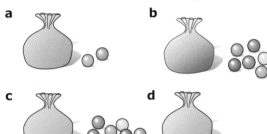

a
b

c
d

2   There were *m* marbles in each bag, but
    some marbles have rolled out.
    How many marbles are left in each bag?

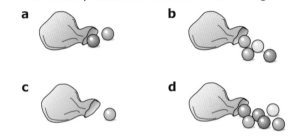

a
b

c
d

3   There are *c* chocolates in a box.
    How many chocolates
    are there in:

a   3 boxes
b   6 full boxes and
    2 extra chocolates
c   1 box after 4 have been eaten?
d   If *c* stands for 12 chocolates, how
    many is *c* + 6?

4   Write the shortest
    expression you can for
    the perimeters of these
    shapes.
    One shape has three
    different lengths and
    uses unlike symbols.

> **Remember:**
> perimeter is the
> distance around
> the edge of a
> shape.

a
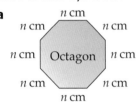

b

c
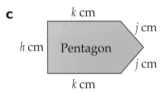

d   If *n* is 5 cm, what is the perimeter
    of the octagon?
e   If *x* is 9 cm, what is the perimeter
    of the square?
f   If *h* = 5 cm, *j* = 3 cm and *k* = 8 cm,
    what is the perimeter of the pentagon?
g   A regular hexagon has sides of length
    z cm.
    i   Write an expression for the
        perimeter of the hexagon.
    ii Find the perimeter if *z* = 3.5 cm.

Problem solving

5   Jan and Dean are sharing their earphones.
    Each of their wires is *y* cm long.
    Make an expression using *y* cm for the
    furthest distance apart that Jan and Dean
    can be.

Check out

You should now be able to ...

✓ Simplify expressions by collecting like terms.	5	1, 2
✓ Expand brackets.	5	3
✓ Substitute values into expressions with brackets and formulae.	5	4
✓ Rearrange basic formulae.	5	5
✓ Form expressions.	5	6

Language	Meaning	Example
Expression	An expression is made up of terms but has no equals sign.	$2x - 6y + 3z$
Simplify	Simplify means to write an expression as simply as possible.	$3x + 5x - x = 7x$ $3a \times 4b = 12ab$
Expand	Expanding brackets means to multiply out the brackets.	$3(2x - 5y) = 6x - 15y$
Formulae	Formulae is plural of formula. A formula is a rule linking two or more variables.	The formula for finding the circumference of a circle is $C = \pi d$
Substitution	Substitution is when you replace the letter in an expression or formula with a number.	$P = 2l + 5w$ Find P when $l = 5\,\text{cm}$ and $w = 4\,\text{cm}$. $P = 2 \times 5 + 5 \times 4 = 30\,\text{cm}$

1 Simplify these expressions by collecting like terms together.
   a $b + 2b + b$
   b $5n + 9m - n + 3m$
   c $11g - 14h + 2h - 10g$
   d $6j + 3 - 2i - 8i + 5j + 2$

2 Simplify these expressions by multiplying and dividing.
   a $2a \times 12$ b $3c \times 4d$
   c $24h \div 8$ d $\dfrac{30v}{15v}$
   e $2 \times 7 \times 3x$ f $\dfrac{9y}{3 \times y}$
   g $5p \times 2 \times 3q$ h $6 \times 4s \div 3s$

3 Expand the brackets.
   a $12(a + b)$ b $4(3v - 4)$
   c $2(3x + 1)$ d $5(2s - 4t)$
   e $3(7 - 4s)$ f $4(p + 2q - 3r)$
   g $6(3 + \tfrac{1}{2}t)$ h $\tfrac{1}{2}(8m + 4n)$

4 The formula for the area of a parallelogram is
   $A = b \times h$
   where b is the length of the base and h is the perpendicular height.
   a Find the area of a parallelogram with $b = 9\,$cm and $h = 11\,$cm.
   b Find the base of a parallelogram with Area = 27 cm² and height = 9 cm.

5 Tim has t apples and Phil has p apples.
   a Write an expression for the number of apples they have all together.
   b Tim eats one of his apples. How many apples does he have now?
   c Katie has twice as many apples as Phil. Write an expression for the number of apples that Katie has.

6 Find a formula for the perimeter, P, of each shape.
   Simplify your answers.
   a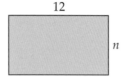
   b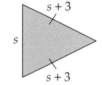
   c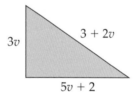
   d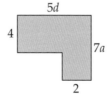

What next?

Score		
0 – 2		Your knowledge of this topic is still developing. To improve look at Formative test: 3A-3; MyMaths: 1158, 1178, 1179, 1187 and 1247
3 – 5		You are gaining a secure knowledge of this topic. To improve look at InvisiPen: 211, 212, 213, 214, 251, 252, 254 and 255
6		You have mastered this topic. Well done, you are ready to progress!

3 MyPractice

1 Simplify these expressions.

   a $x + x + x + x$ **b** $2p + 3p$

   c $6y - 3y$ **d** $9a + 2a - 4a$

   e $15d - 10d + 2d - 3d$ **f** $20g - 2g - 10g + 4g$

2 Simplify these expressions by collecting like terms together.

   a $m + 5m + 3n - n$ **b** $12r + r - 9s + 3r$

   c $8x - 6y - x - 4y$ **d** $12e - 15e + 5f + 3e$

   e $8t - 3t + 6u - 6u - 5t$ **f** $20p + 13q + 7q - p$

3 Simplify these expressions.

   a $4t \times 8$ **b** $5m \times 6$

   c $2a \times b$ **d** $4x \times 6y$

   e $\dfrac{36j}{9}$ **f** $\dfrac{40n}{8}$

   g $\dfrac{15f}{f}$ **h** $\dfrac{20z}{4z}$

   i $2 \times 3 \times 4p$ **j** $8s \times 7t$

   k $\dfrac{4 \times 6p}{8q}$ **l** $\dfrac{2a \times 8b}{4a}$

4 Multiply out the brackets in these expressions.

   a $6(n + k)$ **b** $3(f + g)$

   c $-2(p + r)$ **d** $15(x + 2y)$

   e $9(2d - 4y)$ **f** $4(5p - 8q)$

   g $5(5f - 4g)$ **h** $12(5t - 4r + 2)$

   i $20(5b + 4c)$ **j** $15(3m + 6n - 4)$

5 Use brackets to write an expression for the perimeter of this rectangle.

   $5x$
   $8y$ □

6 **i** Use brackets to write an expression for the area of each rectangle.

   ii Multiply out the brackets in your expression for the area.

   a $x + 6$ **b** $2a + 3b$
       3 □   4 □

   c $t - 4$ **d** $2q - 3r + 5$
       2 □   3 □

7 The formula for the area of a trapezium is

Area $= \frac{1}{2} \times (a + b) \times h$.

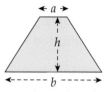

Use the formula to calculate the area of each of these trapeziums. All measurements are in centimetres.

a $a = 6, b = 5, h = 10$

b $a = 8, b = 6, h = 7$

c $a = 15, b = 5, h = 9$

d $a = 11, b = 8, h = 10$

Make sure you use the correct units for your answers.

8 The formula for converting temperatures from Centigrade to Fahrenheit is $C = \frac{5}{9}(F - 32)$

a Find the temperature in °C when F = 95°

b Find the temperature in °F when C = -40°

9 Write the perimeter of each shape as an expression.
Write your answers in their simplest form.

a

y

x ☐

Rectangle

b

a a

b b

Kite

c

y y

x x

x

Pentagon

10 There are *s* sweets in a bag.
How many sweets are there in

a 2 bags?

b 5 full bags and 4 extra sweets?

c 1 bag after 3 have been eaten?

11 a A catering company uses this rule to work out the number of sandwiches to make for lunch meetings at an office.
For each group, the number of sandwiches is two per person plus four.
Write this rule as an algebraic formula.
(Let *s* stand for sandwiches and *p* stand for people.)

b How many sandwiches need to be made for 12 people?

c How many sandwiches need to be made for 9 people?

d If 36 sandwiches are made, how many people are expected at the meeting?

MyMaths.co.uk

Bikes are ingeniously simple structures which are very efficient at getting us around quickly and cheaply. This case study shows how bikes have developed over the years into the sophisticated machines they are today.

Task 1

The pedals of a penny-farthing bicycle were fixed directly to the front wheel so the wheel turned once for every turn of the pedals. The larger the wheel, the further the bike travelled for each turn.

This penny-farthing has a wheel diameter of 1.5 m.

a How far would the bike travel for one turn of the pedals?
Remember: $C = πd$

b How many turns of the pedals would be needed to travel 1 km?

Task 2

If you remember riding a tricycle like this, you will know that you had to pedal quite quickly even at low speeds!

a With a 30 cm diameter front wheel, how many turns of the pedals would be needed to travel 500 m?

b Why does a child have to pedal quickly on this type of tricycle?

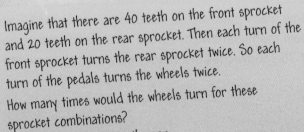

Task 3

As bikes developed, their wheels became smaller and a crank and chain drive was used. The larger front sprocket means that the wheel turns several times for each turn of the pedals.

Imagine that there are 40 teeth on the front sprocket and 20 teeth on the rear sprocket. Then each turn of the front sprocket turns the rear sprocket twice. So each turn of the pedals turns the wheels twice.

How many times would the wheels turn for these sprocket combinations?

a 36 teeth front, 12 teeth rear
b 42 teeth front, 28 teeth rear

Task 4

Most bikes now have several gears which select different numbers of teeth on the front and rear sprockets.

This allows you to alter the number of turns of the wheels for each turn of the pedals.

$\pi = 3.1$

a A 7-speed touring bike has wheel diameter 70 cm.
  Find the distance travelled for each turn of the wheel, giving your answer to 1 d.p.

b Copy and complete this table, which shows different gear selections for the bike.
  Give your answers to 1 d.p. where appropriate.

number of teeth front sprocket	number of teeth rear sprocket	number of turns of the wheel per turn of the pedals	distance travelled per turn of the pedals (m)
		4	8.7
48	12		
48	14		
			6.5
48	16		
48	18	$2\frac{2}{3}$	
48	20		
48	24		
48	28		

c With these gear selections, what is the fewest number of turns of the pedal that would be needed to travel 1 km?

Task 5

When riding comfortably, a cyclist makes between 40 and 90 turns of the pedals per minute.

Look again at the table in task 4.

What range of speeds will a cyclist travel at in each gear? Give your answers in kilometers per hour.

a Describe the amount of overlap between the speed ranges in different gears.

b Why would this be a good thing?

c What would the speed ranges be in miles per hour?
  1 km ≈ $\frac{5}{8}$ mile

d What would the speed ranges be if the cyclist were using their 32 teeth front sprocket?

Extension

If you have a bike, estimate how quickly you turn the pedals and work out the speed ranges for your gears.

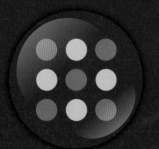

4 Fractions, decimals and percentages

Introduction

Fractals are at the cutting edge of modern mathematics, but are based on the simple idea of fractions. A fractal is a picture that, as you zoom in to any part of it, looks like the original picture! If the picture is infinitely detailed, then you should be able to zoom in forever and you will end up with what you started with.

What's the point?

Fractals are vitally important in biology and medicine for understanding the organs of the human body at microscopic level; they are also useful for describing complex and irregular real world objects such as clouds, coastlines and trees. They are frequently used in computer games to generate 'real-life' environments.

Objectives

By the end of this chapter, you will have learned how to …
- Add and subtract fractions.
- Find the fraction of a quantity.
- Multiply and divide integers by fractions.
- Convert fractions to decimals.
- Compare fractions and decimals.
- Find the percentage of a quantity.
- Find a percentage increase or decrease.
- Write one number as a percentage of another.
- Calculate percentage changes.

Check in

1 This bar has been divided into ten equal sections.

Copy the diagram and complete the labelling of the bar.

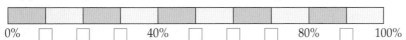

0% ☐ ☐ ☐ 40% ☐ ☐ ☐ 80% ☐ 100%

2 What is $\frac{1}{2}$ of these amounts?

   a £10   **b** 16 kg   **c** 24 cm   **d** 50 mm

3 Find the fraction of the shaded part for each diagram.

   a   **b**   **c**

   d   **e**   **f**

Starter problem

Andy buys a new car for £12 000.

He borrows the money from a bank.

The bank charges a fee of 10% per year in interest.

Andy pays back £1000 per year.

Investigate what happens.

The flag of Eire has three equal sections. Each section is $\frac{1}{3}$ of the whole flag.

The flag of Mauritius has four equal sections. Each section is $\frac{1}{4}$ of the whole flag.

The flag of Samoa is divided into four equal sections.
Each section is $\frac{1}{4}$ of the whole flag.
The **proportion** of the flag which is red is $\frac{1}{4} + \frac{1}{4} + \frac{1}{4} = \frac{3}{4}$.

The **denominator** tells you that the flag has four equal parts.

$\frac{3}{4}$

The **numerator** focuses on three of the four parts.

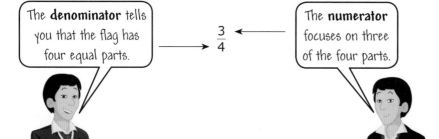

⬤ In a fraction, the denominator is how many parts are in the whole and the numerator is how many parts you have.

⬤ You can add or subtract fractions only when the denominators are the same.
  ▶ You do this by adding or subtracting the numerators only.

Example

a Which of these flags is divided into halves $\left(\frac{1}{2}s\right)$?

Greenland

Qatar

Nigeria

b What fraction of the Nigerian flag is green?
c Add these fractions together. $\frac{1}{8} + \frac{1}{8} + \frac{3}{8}$

---

a Greenland
The red area is equal to the white area.

b The fraction of the flag which is green is $\frac{1}{3} + \frac{1}{3} = \frac{2}{3}$.

c $\frac{1}{8} + \frac{1}{8} + \frac{3}{8} = \frac{1 + 1 + 3}{8} = \frac{5}{8}$

Exercise 4a

1 a Which of these flags are divided into quarters $(\frac{1}{4}s)$?

Jordan   NATO   Sweden

Mauritius   Scotland

b Even without careful measuring, you can see that the flag of Scotland is not divided into quarters. Explain why.

c What fraction of the Mauritian flag is red and yellow?

d What fraction of the Mauritian flag is *not* green?

2 Here is a flag made from equal-sized triangles.

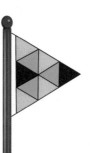

a What proportion of the flag is
  i orange
  ii green
  iii black?

b What fraction of the flag is either green or black?

3 Lizzie and Charlie order a take-away pizza. The pizza is cut into eight equal pieces.

a What fraction is each piece?

Lizzie eats $\frac{5}{8}$ of the pizza.

Charlie eats $\frac{2}{8}$ of the pizza.

b What fraction do they eat altogether?

c What fraction of the pizza is left over?

4 Add these fractions.

a $\frac{2}{5} + \frac{2}{5}$ **b** $\frac{1}{4} + \frac{2}{4}$ **c** $\frac{1}{7} + \frac{3}{7} + \frac{1}{7}$

d $\frac{1}{9} + \frac{1}{9} + \frac{4}{9}$ **e** $\frac{5}{6} + \frac{1}{6}$ **f** $\frac{4}{8} + \frac{3}{8} + \frac{1}{8}$

5 Are these statements true or false?

a $\frac{5}{5}$ is the same as 1.

b $\frac{3}{2}$ is less than 1.

c $\frac{10}{10}$ take away $\frac{1}{10}$ is $\frac{9}{10}$.

d $1 - \frac{2}{5} = \frac{3}{5}$

6 Subtract these fractions.

a $\frac{4}{5} - \frac{2}{5}$ **b** $\frac{7}{8} - \frac{5}{8}$ **c** $\frac{9}{10} - \frac{3}{10}$

d $\frac{19}{20} - \frac{9}{20}$ **e** $\frac{6}{7} - \frac{3}{7}$ **f** $\frac{7}{9} - \frac{2}{9} - \frac{2}{9}$

Problem solving

7 Use $+$ and $-$ signs in this string of fractions to make the total equal to one tenth.

$$\frac{3}{10} \quad \frac{7}{10} \quad \frac{4}{10} \quad \frac{5}{10} = \frac{1}{10}$$

8 Copy and complete the pyramids. To find a fraction add the two bricks below it.

a

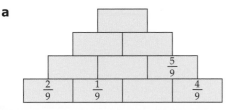

b

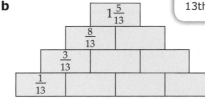

MyMaths.co.uk   🔍 1017   **SEARCH**

Steve and Dave share a bar of chocolate.

The bar has ten equal pieces.

Each piece is $\frac{1}{10}$ of the whole bar.

Steve eats $\frac{1}{2}$ of the bar and Dave eats $\frac{1}{5}$ of the bar.

● You can only add fractions which have the same **denominators**.

When Steve eats $\frac{1}{2}$ of the bar, it is the same as eating $\frac{5}{10}$ of the bar.

When Dave eats $\frac{1}{5}$ of the bar, it is the same as eating $\frac{2}{10}$ of the bar.

To work out how much they ate altogether you need to add the fractions.

Now that both fractions have the same denominator, you can add them together.

$$\frac{5}{10} + \frac{2}{10} = \frac{7}{10}$$

The fraction of the bar that remains uneaten is

$$1 - \frac{7}{10}.$$

So $\frac{10}{10} - \frac{7}{10} = \frac{3}{10}$

I whole bar is $\frac{10}{10}$.

● When adding fractions with different denominators, use equivalent fractions to change the fractions so the denominators are the same.

Example

A bar of flapjack has six sections.

June eats $\frac{1}{3}$ of the bar and Megan eats $\frac{1}{2}$ of it.

a How much of the bar do they eat altogether?

b As a fraction of the whole bar, how much more flapjack does Megan eat than June?

a June eats $\frac{1}{3}$.

$\frac{1}{6}$	$\frac{1}{6}$	$\frac{1}{6}$
$\frac{1}{6}$	$\frac{1}{6}$	$\frac{1}{6}$

$\frac{1}{3} = \frac{2}{6}$

Megan eats $\frac{1}{2}$.

$\frac{1}{6}$	$\frac{1}{6}$	$\frac{1}{6}$
$\frac{1}{6}$	$\frac{1}{6}$	$\frac{1}{6}$

$\frac{1}{2} = \frac{3}{6}$

Altogether they eat $\frac{2}{6} + \frac{3}{6} = \frac{5}{6}$

b The difference is $\frac{1}{2} - \frac{1}{3} = \frac{3}{6} - \frac{2}{6}$

$= \frac{1}{6}$

Exercise 4b

1   Mike and Chris share a box of chocolates.
    There are 20 chocolates in the box.

> Each chocolate is $\frac{1}{20}$ of the box.

Chris eats $\frac{2}{5}$ of the box and Mike eats $\frac{1}{10}$.
   a   Use the picture to calculate the total
       fraction of the box that they eat.
   b   What fraction of the box of
       chocolates is left?

2   Bella cooks a pizza and slices it into eight
    equal pieces.

Bella eats $\frac{3}{8}$ of the pizza and her mum
eats $\frac{1}{4}$ of it.
   a   Who eats more of the pizza?
   b   Change $\frac{1}{4}$ into $\frac{1}{8}$s: $\frac{1}{4} = \frac{\square}{8}$
   c   What fraction of the pizza did they
       eat altogether?

3   Another pizza is cut into eight equal
    pieces, like the one in question **2**.
    James eats $\frac{1}{4}$ of the pizza and Ross
    eats $\frac{1}{2}$ of it.
   a   What fraction of the pizza do they eat
       altogether?
   b   Ross eats more of the pizza than James.
       As a fraction of the whole pizza,
       how much more pizza does Ross eat
       than James?

4   The diagram shows a rectangle divided
    into $\frac{1}{12}$s.

$\frac{1}{12}$	$\frac{1}{12}$	$\frac{1}{12}$	$\frac{1}{12}$
$\frac{1}{12}$	$\frac{1}{12}$	$\frac{1}{12}$	$\frac{1}{12}$
$\frac{1}{12}$	$\frac{1}{12}$	$\frac{1}{12}$	$\frac{1}{12}$

Use the diagram to help you add or
subtract these fractions.

   a $\dfrac{1}{2} + \dfrac{3}{12}$ b $\dfrac{1}{2} - \dfrac{1}{12}$ c $\dfrac{11}{12} - \dfrac{1}{2}$

   d $\dfrac{5}{12} + \dfrac{1}{4}$ e $\dfrac{1}{3} + \dfrac{1}{12}$ f $\dfrac{1}{3} - \dfrac{1}{12}$

   g $\dfrac{1}{3} + \dfrac{1}{4}$ h $\dfrac{3}{4} + \dfrac{1}{12}$ i $\dfrac{2}{3} - \dfrac{1}{12}$

   j $\dfrac{1}{2} - \dfrac{1}{3}$ k $\dfrac{1}{2} + \dfrac{1}{4} + \dfrac{1}{6}$

Problem solving

5   In a survey of Year 9 students, $\frac{1}{4}$ preferred Indian curry
    and $\frac{1}{5}$ preferred Thai curry.
    The rest of the students did not vote for curry at all.
   a   What fraction of students voted for curry?
   b   What fraction did not vote for curry?

4c Fraction of a quantity

To find one third $\left(\frac{1}{3}\right)$ of these 9 bananas, you **divide** the number of bananas by 3.

$\frac{1}{3}$ of 9 = 3   9 ⟶ ÷3 ⟶ 3

⬤ To calculate a fraction of a number, you divide the number by the **denominator** of the fraction and then multiply this by the **numerator**.

To calculate $\frac{2}{3}$ of 9, first find $\frac{1}{3}$ of 9 by dividing by 3, then find $\frac{2}{3}$ by multiplying by 2.

 9 ⟶ ÷3 ⟶ ×2 ⟶ 6   so $\frac{2}{3}$ of 9 = 6

Example

a Which of these function machines do you use to calculate $\frac{1}{5}$ of a quantity?

A ⟶ ×5 ⟶   B ⟶ +5 ⟶

C ⟶ ÷5 ⟶   D ⟶ -5 ⟶

b Calculate $\frac{1}{10}$ of £60.

c Calculate $\frac{1}{2}$ of 5 kg.

d What is $\frac{3}{4}$ of 20 cm?

a To calculate $\frac{1}{5}$ of a number you divide by 5.

⟶ ÷5 ⟶

b $\frac{1}{10}$ of £60 = £60 ÷ 10 = £6

c $\frac{1}{2}$ of 5 kg = 5 kg ÷ 2 = $2\frac{1}{2}$ kg or 2.5 kg

d **Either**
First find $\frac{1}{4}$.
20 cm ÷ 4 = 5 cm
Then multiply the result by 3.
5 cm × 3 = 15 cm

or

Use a function machine.

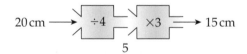
20 cm ⟶ ÷4 ⟶ ×3 ⟶ 15 cm

Exercise 4c

1 Calculate these.

a $\frac{1}{5}$ of £50   **b** $\frac{1}{3}$ of £12

c $\frac{1}{6}$ of 24 mm   **d** $\frac{1}{10}$ of 80 cm

e $\frac{1}{2}$ of 50 kg   **f** $\frac{1}{7}$ of €35

g $\frac{1}{9}$ of $36   **h** $\frac{1}{4}$ of 120 g

i $\frac{1}{5}$ of 45 tonnes   **j** $\frac{1}{6}$ of 54 mm

k $\frac{1}{3}$ of 120 m   **l** $\frac{1}{10}$ of 1000 kg

2 Use two operations to calculate these.

a $\frac{2}{3}$ of £30   **b** $\frac{2}{5}$ of $15

c $\frac{3}{5}$ of 25 g   **d** $\frac{3}{10}$ of 80 cm

e $\frac{3}{4}$ of 24 g   **f** $\frac{5}{6}$ of £18

g $\frac{2}{9}$ of 36 m   **h** $\frac{2}{7}$ of €28

i $\frac{3}{5}$ of 45 volts   **j** $\frac{7}{8}$ of 32 mm

k $\frac{5}{8}$ of 40 km   **l** $\frac{9}{20}$ of 60 kg

Problem solving

3 An adult usually has 32 teeth.
People sometimes lose some of their teeth.
Pat has only $\frac{5}{8}$ of her teeth left.
How many teeth has she lost?

4 A bus can carry 72 passengers.
The bus is $\frac{3}{4}$ full.

    a How many passengers is it carrying?
    b How many more people can it carry?

5 In the 2012 London Olympic Games
Team GB won a total of 65 medals.
29 were Gold.
17 were Silver.
19 were Bronze.
What fraction of the medals were gold?

6 Which is greater in value: $\frac{3}{7}$ of £1001 or 50% of £858?

Did you know?

Some people use fractions in their jobs – chefs must make different quantities of food all the time. They have to reduce or increase all the ingredients at the same time by the same fraction.

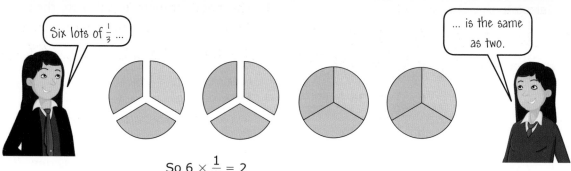

Six lots of $\frac{1}{3}$ ...

... is the same as two.

So $6 \times \dfrac{1}{3} = 2$

This is the same as $6 \div 3 = 2$.

● $\frac{1}{3}$ is the same as dividing by 3.

Example

a Work out $30 \times \frac{1}{2}$.

b A bar of chocolate weighs $\frac{1}{2}$ kg.
How much do eight bars weigh?

a $30 \times \frac{1}{2} = 30 \div 2 = 15$

b You need to multiply $\frac{1}{2}$ by 8.

$8 \times \frac{1}{2} = 8 \div 2 = 4$ kg

Three is the same as ...

... six lots of $\frac{1}{2}$.

So $3 \div \frac{1}{2} = 6$.

Which is the same as $3 \times \frac{2}{1} = 6$.

● When you divide by a fraction, you 'flip' the fraction and multiply.

So dividing by $\frac{1}{2}$ is the same as multiplying by $\frac{2}{1}$ or 2.

The diagram shows that $3 \div \frac{1}{2} = 6$ and $3 \times \frac{2}{1} = \frac{6}{1} = 6$ ✔

Example

Work out **a** $10 \div \frac{1}{3}$.

b $12 \div \frac{1}{4}$

a $10 \div \frac{1}{3} = 10 \times \frac{3}{1} = 30$

b $12 \div \frac{1}{4} = 12 \times \frac{4}{1} = 48$

Exercise 4d

1 Here are eight $\frac{1}{4}$ kg weights.

   a What is the total mass of the weights?

   b You add one more weight.
     What is the total mass now?

2 Work these out.

   a $\frac{1}{3} \times 30$ **b** $\frac{1}{4} \times 16$ **c** $\frac{1}{2} \times 20$

   d $\frac{1}{6} \times 30$ **e** $\frac{1}{6} \times 48$ **f** $\frac{1}{5} \times 60$

   g $\frac{1}{2} \times 120$ **h** $\frac{1}{8} \times 40$ **i** $35 \times \frac{1}{7}$

   j $45 \times \frac{1}{9}$ **k** $\frac{1}{8} \times 72$ **l** $100 \times \frac{1}{10}$

   m $72 \times \frac{1}{12}$ **n** $42 \times \frac{1}{7}$ **o** $121 \times \frac{1}{11}$

3 The length of a tile is $\frac{1}{5}$ m.
Twenty tiles are laid edge to edge in a line.

How long is the line of tiles?

4 A roll of adhesive tape is 10 m long.

1m	2m	3m	4m	5m	6m	7m	8m	9m	10m

How many half-metre strips can be cut
from the 10 m piece of tape?

5 Divide these whole numbers by fractions.

   a $30 \div \frac{1}{2}$ **b** $25 \div \frac{1}{4}$ **c** $1 \div \frac{1}{3}$

   d $16 \div \frac{1}{2}$ **e** $5 \div \frac{1}{4}$ **f** $8 \div \frac{1}{3}$

   g $10 \div \frac{1}{5}$ **h** $20 \div \frac{1}{5}$ **i** $35 \div \frac{1}{7}$

   j $4 \div \frac{1}{9}$ **k** $4 \div \frac{1}{7}$ **l** $100 \div \frac{1}{10}$

Problem solving

6 Kerry cuts eight sandwiches into quarters.
How many quarters does she make?

7 In swimming, an 'Open Water'
race is 10 km long.
Each leg of the course
is $\frac{1}{4}$ of a kilometre long.
How many legs are there
in the race?

8 A marathon is a running event which is a staggering
distance of 26 miles and 385 yards.
An athlete ran exactly two fifths of a marathon
before being injured.
How far did the athlete run?
You may find it useful to use 1 mile = 1760 yards

‹ p.24

MyMaths.co.uk   🔍 1046   **SEARCH**

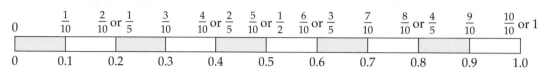

🔘 You can use this scale to **convert** some fractions into decimals.

| 0 | $\frac{1}{10}$ | $\frac{2}{10}$ or $\frac{1}{5}$ | $\frac{3}{10}$ | $\frac{4}{10}$ or $\frac{2}{5}$ | $\frac{5}{10}$ or $\frac{1}{2}$ | $\frac{6}{10}$ or $\frac{3}{5}$ | $\frac{7}{10}$ | $\frac{8}{10}$ or $\frac{4}{5}$ | $\frac{9}{10}$ | $\frac{10}{10}$ or 1 |

| 0 | 0.1 | 0.2 | 0.3 | 0.4 | 0.5 | 0.6 | 0.7 | 0.8 | 0.9 | 1.0 |

You can see that $0.3 = \frac{3}{10}$ and that $\frac{2}{5}$ is less than 0.5.

The fraction $\frac{1}{8}$ is not easy to place on the scale.

🔘 To convert a fraction to a decimal divide the numerator by the denominator.

$\frac{1}{8}$ means 1 ÷ 8. You can use your calculator to do the **division**.

1÷8
0.125

$\frac{1}{3}$ means 1 ÷ 3. The answer is called a **recurring decimal**.

1÷3
0.333333333333

When you have a very long answer you should **round** it to a smaller number of places.

So, $\frac{1}{3} \approx 0.33$ rounded to 2 dp.

Example

a Convert these fractions into decimals.

   i $\frac{1}{4}$ **ii** $\frac{2}{9}$

b Use your answer to part **a** to explain which is larger, $\frac{1}{4}$ or $\frac{2}{9}$.

- -

a **i** $\frac{1}{4}$ means 1 ÷ 4.   **ii** $\frac{2}{9}$ means 2 ÷ 9.

     0.25   0.2222222

$\frac{1}{4} = 0.25$. $\frac{2}{9} = 0.22$ (2dp)

b $0.25 > 0.22$ so $\frac{1}{4}$ is larger than $\frac{2}{9}$.

> The answer is a recurring decimal so round to 2 decimal places.

Exercise 4e

0	$\frac{1}{10}$	$\frac{2}{10}$ or $\frac{1}{5}$	$\frac{3}{10}$	$\frac{4}{10}$ or $\frac{2}{5}$	$\frac{5}{10}$ or $\frac{1}{2}$	$\frac{6}{10}$ or $\frac{3}{5}$	$\frac{7}{10}$	$\frac{8}{10}$ or $\frac{4}{5}$	$\frac{9}{10}$	$\frac{10}{10}$ or 1
0	0.1	0.2	0.3	0.4	0.5	0.6	0.7	0.8	0.9	1.0

1 Use the fraction-to-decimal scale to convert these fractions into decimals.

a $\frac{1}{10}$ b $\frac{1}{2}$ c $\frac{7}{10}$

d $\frac{1}{5}$ e $\frac{9}{10}$ f $\frac{3}{5}$

g $\frac{8}{10}$ h $\frac{7}{10}$ i $\frac{4}{5}$

2 Use the scale to say which is the larger number in each of these pairs.
Use a < or > sign.
If you think that the two numbers are equal use the = sign.

a $\frac{1}{2}$ or $\frac{4}{10}$ b $\frac{3}{5}$ or 0.6 c $\frac{1}{5}$ or $\frac{3}{10}$

d 0.4 or $\frac{2}{5}$ e 0.8 or $\frac{7}{10}$ f 0.1 or $\frac{10}{10}$

g $\frac{5}{10}$ or $\frac{1}{2}$ h $\frac{3}{5}$ or 0.7 i $\frac{1}{5}$ or 0.2

3 Use a calculator to convert these fractions into decimals.
Round the number when the answer is a recurring decimal.

a $\frac{1}{20}$ b $\frac{3}{4}$ c $\frac{5}{8}$

d $\frac{2}{7}$ e $\frac{5}{6}$ f $\frac{1}{9}$

g $\frac{2}{11}$ h $\frac{7}{20}$ i $\frac{3}{8}$

4 a Convert these fractions to decimals.

i $\frac{3}{8}$ and $\frac{2}{5}$

ii $\frac{5}{6}$ and $\frac{4}{5}$

iii $\frac{2}{3}$ and $\frac{3}{4}$

b Use your answers to part **a** to say which is the larger number in each of the pairs.
Use a < or > sign.

5 Rearrange these fractions in order from the smallest to the biggest.
You will find it easier to convert them into decimals first.

$\frac{2}{5}$ $\frac{1}{4}$ $\frac{1}{2}$ $\frac{3}{10}$

Did you know?

There is evidence that Egyptians were using fractions as far back as 4000 years ago. The decimal number system we use today believed to be first used by Indian mathematicians around 2000 years ago.

Problem solving

6 James and Nessi are competing in a javelin throwing event at school.
James comes second.
His throw is $\frac{7}{8}$ of the school record.
Nessi wins the event.
His throw is $\frac{8}{9}$ of the school record.

a Use a calculator to show that Nessi has the better throw.

b In your opinion, did Nessi win by a wide margin?

- Percent means out of 100.
- Percentages are fractions of 100.
- 100% is the whole amount.

SALE 10%

20% DEPOSIT

50% EXTRA!

Some percentages are easy to work out in your head. 50% is the easiest because you just find $\frac{1}{2}$.

I think 10% is easiest to find because it's the same as one tenth and dividing by 10 is really simple.

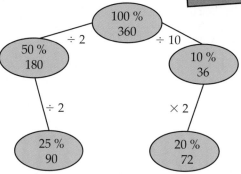

100 %
360

÷ 2

50 %
180

÷ 10

10 %
36

÷ 2

25 %
90

× 2

20 %
72

If 50% is easy to find, then so is 25% because it is $\frac{1}{2}$ of 50%.

Once you've got 10% then 20% is also easy. Just multiply by 2!

Example

a Find 10% of £60. **b** Find 70% of £60.

a 10% of £60 = £60 ÷ 10
     = £6

b 70% of £60 = £6 × 7
     = £42

- When you use a calculator to work out a percentage of a quantity, first find 1% by dividing by 100, then multiply to find the percentage you want.

On my calculator I pressed

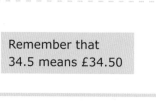

| 2 | 3 | ÷ | 1 |
| 0 | 0 | × | 1 |

| 5 | 0 | = |

34.5

Example

a Write 23% as a fraction.
b Use your answer to part **a** to calculate 23% of £150.

a 23% = $\frac{23}{100}$

b 23% of £150 = $\frac{23}{100}$ × £150

Remember that 34.5 means £34.50

23% of £150 = £34.50

Exercise 4f

1 Work out these percentages of quantities without using a calculator.

   a 10% of £50   **b** 10% of 120g

   c 10% of 200kg   **d** 10% of 75cm

   e 10% of $46   **f** 10% of 180°

2 Work out these percentages of quantities without using a calculator.

   a 20% of £50   **b** 30% of 120g

   c 40% of 50m   **d** 30% of 90 litres

   e 70% of 90cm   **f** 90% of £150

3 Write these percentages as fractions $\left(\frac{1}{100}s\right)$.

   a 45%   **b** 55%

   c 27%   **d** 90%

   e 10%   **f** 9%

   g 5%   **h** 1%

4 Calculate these percentages of quantities.

   a 25% of £80   **b** 75% of 120kg

   c 35% of £55   **d** 65% of 400cm

   e 56% of €250   **f** 9% of 500g

   g 1% of 300volts   **h** 5% of 20mm

   i 33% of 900 miles

Problem solving

5 Suzi and Austin are training for a triathlon race. Here are their personal weekly targets and their actual achievements.

		Athlete	
		Suzi	**Austin**
swimming	Target (m)	800	1100
	% achieved	73	53
cycling	Target (km)	30	25
	% achieved	55	60
running	Target (km)	9	8
	% achieved	30	45

   a Use the record to calculate

      i who swam the greater distance

      ii who cycled the greater distance

      iii who ran the greater distance.

   b In your opinion, who is more likely to succeed in the race? Explain your answer.

6 The surface area of Earth is 510065600km². Only 29% of the area is land. The other 71% is water.

   a Use your calculator to work out the areas of land and water.

   b How can you check your answers without doing the same calculations twice?

> ● You can use mental methods to calculate percentages of amounts.

> ● You can write one number as a **percentage** of another number.

Example

Kendra weighs 60 kg. Her pet dog Boxer weighs 21 kg.
What percentage of Kendra's weight is Boxer?

Write Boxer's weight as a fraction of Kendra's weight.

Fraction $= \dfrac{21}{60} = 21 \div 60$

$\qquad = 0.35$

$\qquad = 35\%$

Boxer is 35% of the weight of Kendra.

> ● You can calculate a percentage of an amount by first finding 1% and then multiplying by the percentage you want.

Example

Calculate 15% of £368.

1% of £368 = 368 ÷ 100

$\qquad = 3.68$

15% of £368 = 15 × 3.68

$\qquad = £55.20$

You can do this in one go.

15% of £368 = 368 ÷ 100 × 15

$\qquad = £55.20$

You find a percentage increase by finding the increase and then adding it to the amount you started with.

You find a percentage decrease by finding the decrease and then subtracting it from the amount you started with.

Example

a Increase £428 by 15%.

b Decrease £428 by 15%.

Find the increase or decrease by first calculating 15% of £368.

15% of £428 $= \dfrac{15}{100}$ of £428 = 428 ÷ 100 × 15 = £64.20

a Add to find the increase.

New amount = £428 + £64.20

$\qquad = £492.20$

b Subtract to find the decrease.

New amount = £428 − £64.20

$\qquad = £363.80$

Exercise 4g

Problem solving

1 a In 1977 the average family earned £3300 a year and spent 18% of their earnings on a summer holiday.
How much did the average family spend on their summer holiday?

b In 2007 the average family earned £24 500 a year and spent £3920 on their summer holiday.
What percentage of their yearly earnings is this?

2 Choose the most appropriate method to answer each of these questions.

a Alice's pocket money is £20 a week. She spends 35% of her pocket money each week on her mobile phone.
How much money does she spend on her mobile phone each week?

b Boris downloads a 140 MB file from the internet. 60% of the file downloads in 2 minutes.
How many megabytes (MB) of the file has downloaded?

c Cloud writes a 360-word story. The average length of a word is five letters. 44% of the letters are vowels.
How many vowels are there in Cloud's story?

3 a A packet of crisps normally has a weight of 150 g. The weight of the crisps is increased by 15%.
What is the new weight of the packet of crisps?

3 b A computer game normally costs £39. In a sale all the prices are reduced by 45%.
What is the new price of the computer game?

c Livchester football stadium had 53 842 seats. It was rebuilt with an increase in seating of about 19%.

How many seats are there at the new stadium? Give your answer to the nearest seat.

4 Veronica carried out a survey in which people could answer only 'yes' or 'no'. These are Veronica's results.

| Yes | 160 people | 40% |
| No | 252 people | 60% |

a Explain what is wrong with Veronica's results

b Assuming the 'Yes' vote is correct, rewrite the 'No' vote so that it is mathematically correct.

5 In December the price of a pair of trainers was £120.
In the Christmas sale the trainers were reduced in price by 15%.
A month later the price was increased by 15%.

a What is the new price of the trainers?

b Explain why the price is not the same as it was in December.

Percentages are used a lot, especially when dealing with money.
You need some efficient ways to calculate with them.

● You can calculate percentage changes using an **equivalent decimal**.

Example

Calculate
a 5% of £30 **b** 43% of £670

a 5% of £30 = $\frac{5}{100} \times 30$ **b** 43% of £670 = $\frac{43}{100} \times 670$

= 0.05 × 30 = 1.5 = 0.43 × 670 = 288.1 Use a calculator.

= £1.50 = £288.10

● You can calculate a percentage increase or decrease using a **decimal multiplier**.

Example

a Increase £50 by 15% **b** Decrease 2 kg by 25%

a You add an increase. **b** You subtract a decrease.

100% of £50 + 15% of £50 100% of 2 kg − 25% of 2 kg

= 1 × 50 + 0.15 × 50 = 1 × 2 − 0.25 × 2

= (1 + 0.15) × 50 = (1 − 0.25) × 2

= 1.15 × 50 = 0.75 × 2

= £57.50 = 1.5 kg

You could first find 15% of £50 = £7.50 and then add this to £50 to get £57.50 but 1.15 × 50 = £57.50 is faster.

● You can calculate a **repeated** percentage change using a decimal multiplier.

Example

Mandy invests £1000 in a savings account which pays 4% interest per year. How much money will she have after

a 1 year **b** 2 years **c** 10 years?

This is known as **compound** interest.

a 1.04 × 1000 = 1040

£1040

b 1000 $\xrightarrow{\times 1.04}$ 1040 $\xrightarrow{\times 1.04}$ 1081.6

This can be done in one step.

1000 × 1.04 × 1.04 = 1000 × 1.04² The index, 2, is the number of years.

= 1081.6

£1081.60

p.206 >

c 1000 × 1.04¹⁰ = 1000 × 1.48024428...

= 1480.24428...

£1480.24 Round to 2 dp for money.

On my calculator I pressed

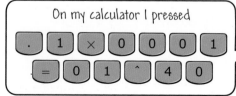

Exercise 4h

1 What equivalent decimal would you use to calculate these percentages?

   a 66%   **b** 23%

   c 77%   **d** 50%

   e 5%   **f** 7%

   g 110%   **h** 115%

2 Use an equivalent decimal to find these percentages.

   a 12% of £125   **b** 3% of 500 m

   c 57% of 34 kg   **d** 17.5% of £300

   e 34% of 4 MB   **f** 2.5% of 200 mm

3 What decimal multiplier would you use to calculate these percentage changes?

   a An increase of 25%

   b An increase of 7%

   c An increase of 130%

   d A decrease of 70%

   e A decrease of 16%

   f A decrease of 3%

4 Use a decimal multiplier to calculate these percentage changes.

   a Increase £250 by 20%

   b Increase 450 kg by 42%

   c Decrease 125 cm by 15%

   d Decrease £567 by 37%

5 Write down the decimal multiplier for each of these repeated percentage changes. Give your answers to 3 dp.

   a An increase of 40% for two years

   b An increase of 35% for 5 years

   c A decrease of 30% for 2 years

   d A decrease of 6% for 10 years

6 Use a decimal multiplier to calculate these repeated percentage changes.

   a £250 increased by 10% for 4 years.

   b £300 increased by 5% for 6 years.

   c £1000 decreased by 20% for 3 years.

   d £750 decreased by 7% for 6 years.

Problem solving

7 **a** Hollie has downloaded 45% of a 6 GB file in 5 minutes.

     i How much has she downloaded?   **ii** How much more remains?

   b The label on a 450 g packet of peanuts says they contain 0.43% salt.
     How much salt is that in grams?

   c Bettany scores 36% on her history exam. The exam is marked out of 80.
     How many marks did Bettany get?

8 **a** A regular jar of coffee weighs 175 g. Special offer jars contain 30% extra free.
     How much coffee do these jars contain?

   b At the start of the year 2000, the average price of a house in London was £161 000.
     In the next decade the average price rose by 105%. What was the average house
     price at the start of 2010?

9 **a** Suzi invests £400 in a savings account which pays 4.5% interest per year.
     How much money will Suzi have after

     i 1 year   **ii** 2 years   **iii** 5 years   **iv** 10 years?

   b A small island is being washed away by the sea. Each year it loses 6% of its area.
     Today its area is 8000 m². How big will the island be in

     i 1 year   **ii** 2 years   **iii** 5 years   **iv** 10 years?

Check out

You should now be able to ...

✓ Add and subtract fractions with the same denominator.	5	1
✓ Add and subtract fractions with different denominators.	6	2
✓ Find a fraction of a quantity.	5	3, 4
✓ Multiply and divide integers by fractions.	6	5, 6
✓ Convert fractions to decimals and compare them.	5	7, 8
✓ Find a percentage of a quantity and a percentage change.	5	9 – 12
✓ Write one number as a percentage of another.	5	13
✓ Calculate percentage changes.	7	14, 15

Language · Meaning · Example

Language	Meaning	Example
Denominator	This is the bottom number of a fraction. It tells you how many equal parts are in the whole.	The denominator for $\frac{5}{8}$ is 8. This means the whole is split into 8 equal parts.
Numerator	This is the top number of a fraction. It tells you how many parts you have.	The numerator for $\frac{5}{8}$ is 5. This means you have 5 out of the 8 parts.
Integer	An integer is zero or any positive or negative whole number.	... -3, -2, -1, 0, 1, 2, 3, 4 ...
Recurring decimal	A recurring decimal has an unlimited number of digits, which form a pattern, after the decimal point.	$\frac{2}{3} = 2 \div 3 = 0.666666....,$ the sixes do not stop.
Percentage	Percent means out of 100.	47% means $\frac{47}{100}$
Equivalent decimal	The decimal number that equals a given percentage.	The decimal equivalent of 17.5% is 0.175
Decimal multiplier	The number you multiply by to calculate a percentage change.	To increase by 25% multiply by 1.25 To decrease by 27% multiply by 0.75

1 Calculate these and simplify your answer where possible.

   a $\dfrac{3}{7} - \dfrac{1}{7}$
   b $\dfrac{2}{11} + \dfrac{4}{11} + \dfrac{5}{11}$

2 Calculate these and simplify your answer where possible.

   a $\dfrac{1}{3} + \dfrac{1}{6}$
   b $\dfrac{1}{4} - \dfrac{1}{20}$
   c $\dfrac{2}{3} + \dfrac{1}{4}$

3 Use a mental method to calculate.

   a $\dfrac{1}{5}$ of £30
   b $\dfrac{1}{8}$ of 24 students

4 Use a mental or written method to calculate.

   a $\dfrac{2}{5}$ of 40 g
   b $\dfrac{3}{7}$ of 35 cm

5 Work these out, writing your answers as whole numbers.

   a $18 \times \dfrac{1}{6}$
   b $\dfrac{1}{4} \times 60$

6 Divide these whole numbers by fractions.

   a $50 \div \dfrac{1}{3}$
   b $1 \div \dfrac{1}{5}$

7 Convert these fractions into decimals without using a calculator.

   a $\dfrac{3}{10}$
   b $\dfrac{2}{5}$
   c $\dfrac{1}{4}$

8 Use a calculator to convert these fractions into decimals. Round your answers to 2 dp.

   a $\dfrac{1}{6}$
   b $\dfrac{4}{9}$

9 Calculate these percentages of quantities using a mental method.

   a 10% of 70
   b 60% of 120

10 Calculate.

   a 75% of 280
   b 3% of 500

11 Increase £76 by 25%.

12 A toaster originally cost £18 but it reduced by 10%, what is the new price?

13 In a class of 25 students, 15 are boys. What percentage are girls?

14 Use a decimal multiplier to
   a increase £300 by 7%
   b decrease £231 by 19%.

15 You invest £740 in a savings account which page 4% interest. How much money do you have after
   a 1 year
   b 2 years
   c 10 years.

What next?

Score		
	0 – 5	Your knowledge of this topic is still developing. To improve look at Formative test: 3A-4; MyMaths: 1016, 1017, 1018, 1030, 1031, 1042, 1046, 1060 and 1075
	6 – 12	You are gaining a secure knowledge of this topic. To improve look at InvisiPen: 141, 142, 145, 151, 152, 161 and 162
	13 – 15	You have mastered this topic. Well done, you are ready to progress!

4b

1 Jan and Pauline share a box of chocolates.

There are eight chocolates in the box.

Jan eats $\frac{1}{4}$ of the chocolates and Pauline eats $\frac{3}{8}$.

a Use the picture to calculate the total fraction of the box that they eat.

> Each chocolate is $\frac{1}{8}$ of the box.

b What fraction of the chocolates is left?

2 Work these out.

a $\dfrac{1}{10} + \dfrac{1}{5}$ **b** $\dfrac{2}{5} - \dfrac{3}{10}$

c $\dfrac{4}{5} - \dfrac{2}{5}$ **d** $\dfrac{1}{2} + \dfrac{1}{10}$

> This diagram should help you.

$\frac{1}{10}$	$\frac{1}{10}$	$\frac{1}{10}$	$\frac{1}{10}$	$\frac{1}{10}$
$\frac{1}{10}$	$\frac{1}{10}$	$\frac{1}{10}$	$\frac{1}{10}$	$\frac{1}{10}$

4c

3 Calculate these.

a $\frac{1}{5}$ of £35 **b** $\frac{1}{8}$ of 40 kg

c $\frac{1}{6}$ of 30 mm **d** $\frac{1}{10}$ of 100 cm

e $\frac{1}{3}$ of 24 m **f** $\frac{1}{9}$ of €36

g $\frac{3}{10}$ of 40 cm **h** $\frac{5}{6}$ of £30

i $\frac{5}{8}$ of 24 cm **j** $\frac{7}{8}$ of 24 mm

k $\frac{3}{4}$ of 44 kg **l** $\frac{9}{16}$ of 32 kg

> Remember that to find $\frac{1}{4}$ of 20 you work out $20 \div 4$.

$$20 \longrightarrow \boxed{\div 4} \longrightarrow 5$$

> Remember that to find $\frac{3}{5}$ of 20 you work out $20 \div 5$ and then multiply the result by 3.

$$20 \longrightarrow \boxed{\div 5} \xrightarrow{4} \boxed{\times 3} \longrightarrow 12$$

4d

4 Work these out.

a $\frac{1}{9} \times 90$ **b** $\frac{1}{4} \times 24$ **c** $\frac{1}{3} \times 21$ **d** $\frac{1}{5} \times 30$

e $\frac{1}{8} \times 40$ **f** $\frac{1}{3} \times 63$ **g** $\frac{1}{4} \times 120$ **h** $\frac{1}{8} \times 72$

i $35 \times \frac{1}{5}$ **j** $45 \times \frac{1}{3}$ **k** $\frac{1}{8} \times 48$ **l** $100 \times \frac{1}{4}$

5 How many halves $\left(\frac{1}{2}\text{s}\right)$ are there in these numbers?

a 1 **b** 2 **c** 5 **d** 10 **e** 15

6 Divide these numbers by one-third $\left(\frac{1}{3}\right)$.

a 1 **b** 3 **c** 5 **d** 10 **e** 20

7 Divide these whole numbers by fractions.

a $2 \div \frac{1}{3}$ **b** $20 \div \frac{1}{5}$ **c** $5 \div \frac{1}{5}$ **d** $13 \div \frac{1}{2}$ **e** $8 \div \frac{1}{4}$ **f** $5 \div \frac{1}{4}$

4e

8 Convert these fractions into decimals. Write your answers to no more than 3 decimal places.

a $\frac{1}{10}$ b $\frac{3}{10}$ c $\frac{7}{10}$ d $\frac{1}{5}$ e $\frac{4}{5}$ f $\frac{2}{5}$

g $\frac{1}{8}$ h $\frac{1}{6}$ i $\frac{4}{11}$ j $\frac{1}{7}$ k $\frac{2}{7}$ l $\frac{3}{7}$

4f

9 Work out these percentages of quantities.

a 10% of £20 b 20% of £20 c 90% of £20

d 20% of £60 e 30% of 200 g f 70% of 50 cm

g 25% of 96 kg h 15% of 360 m i 43% of £62

10 10% of £60 is £6.

a What is 5% of £60? b What is 15% of £60?

4g

11 Choose the most appropriate method to answer these questions.

a Elliott earns £420 a week.
He spends 29% of his wage each week on his rent.
How much is his rent each week?

b A 180 g bar of high-quality cooking chocolate contains 72% cocoa solids.
What is the weight of cocoa solids in this chocolate bar?

12 a There are 32 people in Evan's class.
26 of them have black hair.
What percentage of Evan's class have black hair?

b Hugh's salary last year was £40 000. He had to pay £10 000 in tax.
Mandy's salary last year was £32 000. She had to pay £6400 in tax.
Who had to pay the higher percentage of their salary in tax?

4h

13 a A packet of biscuits normally has a weight of 250 g.
This week the packets contain 20% extra free.
What is the new weight of the packet of biscuits?

b A DVD normally costs £19.
In an 'up to 50% off' sale the price of the DVD is only reduced by 22%.
What is the sale price of the DVD?

14 Alex has invested heavily in the price of oil but the price is falling. In January he owned £50 million worth of oil but each month its value falls 2%. How much will Alex's investment be worth in

a February b March c September?

MyMaths.co.uk

These questions will test you on your knowledge of the topics in chapters 1 to 4.

They give you practice in the types of questions that you may see in your GCSE exams.

There are 90 marks in total.

1 Work these out.

    a 15×100 (1 mark)   **b** $12 \div 0.1$ (1 mark)

    c 23×0.01 (1 mark)   **d** $82 \div 0.01$ (1 mark)

2 Round these numbers to the degree of accuracy indicated.

    a 37.5 (nearest 10)   (1 mark)   **b** 1318 (nearest 100)   (1 mark)

    c 14.63 (1 dp)   (1 mark)   **d** 23 895 (nearest 1000)   (1 mark)

3 **a** Work out these **without** a calculator.

       i $3 \times 4^2 - 2$ (1 mark)   **ii** $5^2 + 7 - (3^2 + 1)$ (1 mark)

    b Work out these with a calculator.

       i $357 - (45 + 4^2) \div 4$ (2 marks)   **ii** $16 \times (5^2 - 12) \times 3$ (2 marks)

4 **a** What are the common factors of 36 and 52?   (2 marks)

    b What are the prime factors of 36 and 52?   (4 marks)

    c Find the HCF and LCM of 36 and 52.   (3 marks)

5 Which two numbers from this list are not divisible by 9?

    81   261   277   333   627   801   (2 marks)

6 Convert these measurements into the units shown in brackets.

    a 3.5 tonnes (kg)   (1 mark)   **b** 4 gallons (pints)   (1 mark)

    c 2 miles (feet)   (1 mark)   **d** 2.2 litres (cl)   (1 mark)

7 Calculate the area of these rectangles.

    a A volleyball court 18 m long by 9 m wide   (2 marks)

    b A stamp 2.1 cm by 1.8 cm   (2 marks)

    c A corn field 232 m by 200 m   (2 marks)

8 The Vanuatu flag is made from one black triangle and two identical green and red trapeziums.

Vanuatu flag

    a Find the area of the black triangle.   (3 marks)

    b Find the area of one of the trapeziums.   (3 marks)

    c What is the total area of this model flag?   (1 mark)

9 Stonehenge is a circular prehistoric monument approximately 300 feet across.

    a Calculate the circumference of this monument. Take $\pi = 3.14$ (3 marks)

b Each one of the large stones was rolled on circular logs about 12 inches in diameter. How many whole revolutions of the log would it take to move a stone 22 yards?

12 inches = 1 foot, 3 feet = 1 yard　　　　　　　　　　　　　　　　　　(5 marks)

10 Simplify these expressions by collecting like terms.

   a　$7x + 2y - x - 5y$　　　　(1 mark)　　**b**　$12u - v + 5v - u$　　　　(1 mark)

11 Multiply out these brackets.

   a　$6(3m - 2)$　　　　(1 mark)　　**b**　$3(4b + 5c)$　　　　(1 mark)

12 The sides of the triangle are $(6p - 4)$ cm, $(3p + 1)$ cm and $5p$ cm.

   a　Find the perimeter of the triangle in terms of p.　　　　(3 marks)

   b　If $p = 2$ work out the lengths of the sides of the triangle.　　　　(3 marks)

13 The formula for the power (watts) of a circuit is

$P = V \times I$　(V = voltage and I = current)

   a　Use the formula to calculate the power when $V = 240$ and $I = 3$.　　　　(1 mark)

   b　Rearrange the formula so that you can calculate the current.　　　　(2 marks)

   c　Use the rearranged formula to calculate the current when

$V = 240$ and $P = 300$.　　　　(2 marks)

14 Are these statements true or false?

If they are false then give the correct answer.

   a　$\dfrac{1}{3} + \dfrac{3}{4} = \dfrac{13}{12}$　**b**　$\dfrac{5}{8} + \dfrac{1}{4} = \dfrac{1}{2}$　**c**　$\dfrac{1}{8} + \dfrac{5}{8} - \dfrac{1}{2} = \dfrac{1}{4}$　**d**　$\dfrac{2}{9} + \dfrac{1}{3} = \dfrac{4}{9}$　(8 marks)

15 Calculate these.

   a　$\dfrac{1}{3}$ of £39　　　　(1 mark)　　**b**　$\dfrac{5}{8} \times 64$ m　　　　(1 mark)

   c　$22 \div \dfrac{1}{8}$　　　　(1 mark)　　**d**　$128 \div \dfrac{5}{16}$　　　　(2 marks)

16 a　Convert these fractions to decimals and decimals to fractions without a calculator.

     i　$\dfrac{1}{8}$　　(1 mark)　　**ii**　0.3　　(1 mark)　　**iii**　$\dfrac{4}{5}$　　(1 mark)

   b　Use a calculator to convert these fractions to decimals (to 2 dp).

     i　$\dfrac{5}{9}$　　(1 mark)　　**ii**　$\dfrac{4}{11}$　　(1 mark)　　**iii**　$\dfrac{2}{7}$　　(1 mark)

   c　Use a calculator to convert these decimals to fractions in their simplest form.

     i　0.34　　(1 mark)　　**ii**　0.08　　(1 mark)　　**iii**　0.96　　(1 mark)

17 Calculate　　**a**　56% of 2400 m　　　　(1 mark)

          b　Increase £271 by 53%　　　　(2 marks)

MyMaths.co.uk

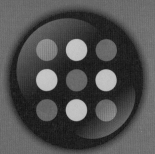

5 Angles and 2D shapes

Introduction

There are different units for measuring angles. The French tried to decimalise angles and invented a system where a right angle was equal to 100 grads. The most common measure is degrees, and there are 360 degrees in a circle. However, mathematicians prefer a unit for measuring angles called the radian, and 1 radian = 57.2958 degrees!

What's the point?

The ability to estimate, measure and describe angles is highly important to all of us, whether we are designing stage lighting, creating a pattern for a dress or lobbing a ball towards a goal.

Objectives

By the end of this chapter, you will have learned how to …

- Identify alternate and corresponding angles.
- Use side and angle properties of triangles to solve problems.
- Use the angle sum of a triangle and properties of exterior and interior angles to solve problems.
- Use the angle sum of a quadrilateral.
- Recognise, name and classify different quadrilaterals.

Check in

1 Measure these lines to the nearest millimetre (mm).

a ├────────────────┤   b ├──────────────────────────────────┤

c ├───┤   d ├─────────────────────────┤

2 Calculate the size of the lettered angles.

a

153°

b

72°

c

47°

d

262°

3 Calculate the size of the lettered angles in these triangles.

a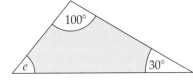

100°
30°
e

b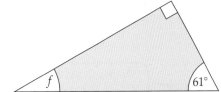

61°
f

Starter problem

You will need a 3 × 3 pinboard or a 3 × 3 dotty grid.

Make as many different quadrilaterals as you can.

● Angles on a straight line total 180°.

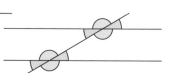

$a + b = 180°$

● When lines **intersect**, **vertically opposite** angles are equal.

Parallel lines are always the same distance apart.
Arrows are used to show the lines are parallel.

When a line intersects parallel lines there are only two different sized angles. There are some names you need to learn for these angles.

● **Corresponding** angles are the same size.

● **Alternate** angles are the same size.

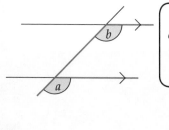

Angles *a* and *b* are corresponding angles. The lines and angles make an F shape.

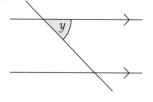

Angles *d* and *e* are alternate angles. The lines and angles make a Z shape.

Example

a Find the corresponding angle to angle *y* and colour it blue.

b Find the alternate angle to angle *y* and colour it red.

Example

Find angles *a*, *b* and *c*, giving a reason for your answers.

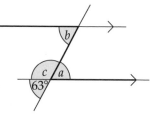

$a = 63°$
vertically opposite the angle
$b = 63°$
corresponding angle
$c = 180° - 63° = 117°$
angles on a straight line.

Exercise 5a

1 Using what you know about vertically opposite angles and angles on a straight line, find the size of the angles marked with letters.

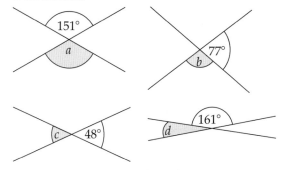

2 a Draw a line 6 cm long and label it RS.
b Draw a line parallel to the first, 3 cm below it. Label it TU.
c Draw a line parallel to the other lines, 2.5 cm below TU. Label it VW.

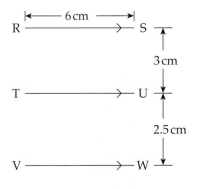

3 What is the size of these angles?
a angle r
b angle s
c angle t
d angle u

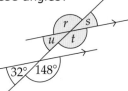

4 a Which is the corresponding angle to angle m?
b Which angle is vertically opposite angle c?
c Which is the corresponding angle to angle n?
d Which is the alternate angle to angle a?

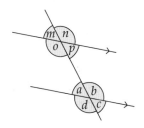

5 Find the size of the angles marked with letters.
Give a reason in each case.

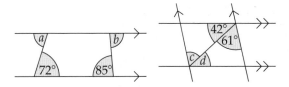

Problem solving

6 Copy and complete each statement with either alternate or corresponding.
a Angle w and angle g are ….
b Angle y and angle g are ….
c Angle f and angle x are ….
d Angle h and angle x are ….
e Angle h and angle z are ….

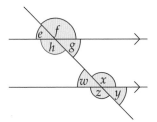

5b Angles in a triangle

You need to know the names of these triangles.

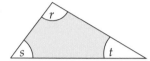

Right-angled   Isosceles   Equilateral   Scalene

Interior angles are the angles inside a shape.

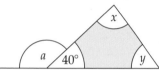

$r + s + t = 180°$

⚫ The interior angles of a triangle total 180°.

You make an exterior angle when you extend a side of a shape.

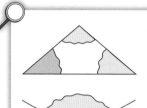

The angles on a straight line total 180°.
So $a + 40° = 180°$
$a = 140°$

The angles in a triangle total 180°.
So $x + y + 40° = 180°$
$x + y = 140°$
So $a = x + y$

⚫ The exterior angle of a triangle is equal to the sum of the two opposite interior angles.

Try tearing the corners off a triangle. Do they fit together to make a straight line?

Try to repeat this calculation using a different value than 40°. Does a still equal $x + y$?

Example

The diagram shows the exterior angles of a triangle.
Find the size of the interior angles k, l and m.

$k = 180° - 152° = 28°$
$l = 180° - 55° = 125°$
$m = 180° - 153° = 27°$

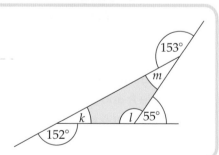

Exercise 5b

1 Find the size of the lettered angles in these triangles.

a
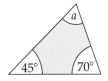

b

c
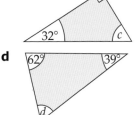

d

2 Find the third angle in each triangle. State if the triangle is right-angled, isosceles, equilateral or scalene.

a 35°, 110°   **b** 36°, 57°

c 60°, 60°   **d** 53°, 37°

e 92°, 44°   **f** 45°, 65°

g 18°, 144°   **h** 45°, 90°

3 The diagram shows the scalene triangle EFG.

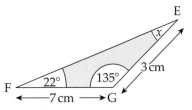

a How long is side EG?

b How many degrees is angle EGF?

c How many degrees is angle *x*?

4 The diagram shows the right-angled triangle KLM.

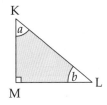

a Which is the longest side, LM, MK or KL?

b Which is the shortest side?

c How many degrees will angles *a* and *b* add up to?
Explain your answer.

Problem solving

5 a Find the size of angle *k*.

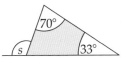

b Find the size of angle *s*.

c Find the size of angles *p* and *q*.

6 Find the size of angle *f*.

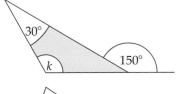

Did you know?

The Bermuda Triangle is a triangular area in the northern Atlantic between Bermuda, Florida and Puerto Rico where many boats and aircraft have allegedly gone inexplicably missing.

5c Properties of triangles

⬤ The **sum** of the angles in a triangle is 180°.

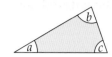

$a + b + c = 180°$

⬤ The **exterior** angle of a triangle equals the sum of the two opposite **interior** angles.

$a = x + y$

⬤ The sum of the length of the two shorter sides is greater than the length of the longest side.

Example

Which of these measurements will not make a triangle?

a 4 cm, 2 cm and 7 cm

b 4 cm, 5 cm and 7 cm

a $4 + 2 = 6 < 7$

The measurements can't make a triangle.

The sum of the length of the shorter sides is less than the length of the longest side.

b $4 + 5 = 9 > 7$

The measurements can make a triangle.

The sum of the length of the shorter sides is more than the length of the longest side.

⬤ In a triangle where two sides are equal, the angles opposite to these sides are also equal.
  ▶ The triangle is an isosceles triangle.

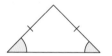

Example

Find the size of angle *w*.

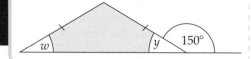

Step 1 $150° + y = 180°$ Angles on a straight line

$y = 30°$

Step 2 The triangle is isosceles.

$w = 30°$ Angles *y* and *w* are equal.

84   **Geometry and measures** Angles and 2D shapes

Exercise 5c

1 Find the size of the lettered angles in these triangles.

a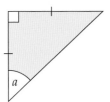

b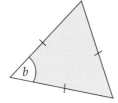

c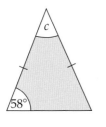

d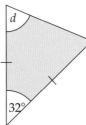

e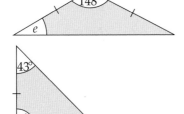

f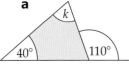

2 Find the size of the lettered angles in these triangles.

a

b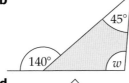

c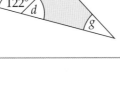

d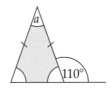

3 Which of these sets of measurements will not make a triangle?

a 6 cm, 8 cm and 5 cm

b 3 cm, 9 cm and 3 cm

c 20 cm, 30 cm and 30 cm

d 5 cm, 11 cm and 4 cm

e 16 cm, 11 cm and 28 cm

f $12\frac{1}{2}$ cm, 15 cm and $3\frac{1}{2}$ cm

4 **a** How long is side CA?

b Find the size of angle *s*.

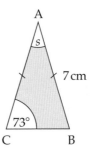

5 **a** How long is side FG?

b Find the size of angle *x*.

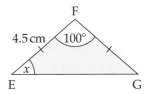

Problem solving

6 Find the size of angle *a*.

Did you know?

This is an 'impossible' triangle. On first glance it might seem fine, but try running your finger along the sides.

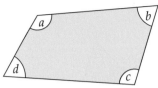

⬤ The sum of the angles in a **quadrilateral** is 360°.

$a + b + c + d = 360°$

Here is one **proof** that the sum of the angles in a quadrilateral is 360°.

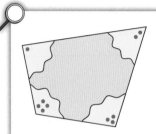

Try tearing the corners off a quadrilateral.
Do they fit together to make a full turn?

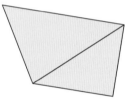

Draw a line joining opposite corners of a quadrilateral.

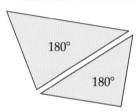

180°

180°

There are now two triangles.
The **angle sum** of a triangle is 180°.
$180° + 180° = 360°$ or $2 \times 180° = 360°$

Example

Find the size of angles p and q.

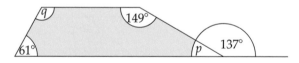

$p + 137° = 180°$ — The angles on a straight
$p = 180° - 137° = 43°$ — line total 180°.
$p = 43°$

$61° + 43° + 149° + q = 360°$ — The angle sum
$253° + q = 360°$ — of a quadrilateral
$q = 107°$ — is 360°.

Example

Find the size of angle z.

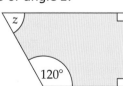

The angle sum of a quadrilateral is 360°.
$z + 120° + 90° + 90° = 360°$
$z + 300° = 360°$
$z = 60°$

Exercise 5d

1 Find the lettered angles in these quadrilaterals.

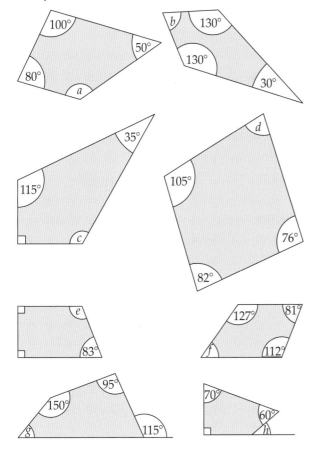

2 Use a ruler and protractor to construct this quadrilateral accurately.

Step 1

_____

6 cm

Draw a line 6 cm long.

2 **Step 2**

3 cm   120°   120°   3 cm

Draw an angle of 120° at each end of the line. Draw each side 3 cm long.

Step 3

Complete the quadrilateral by adding a fourth line.

Step 4

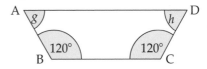

A   g   h   D
B   120°   120°   C

Label your construction as shown. Title it: 'Isosceles trapezium'.

a Measure the length of side AD.
b By measuring, decide if side BC is parallel to side AD.
c Measure angle g.
d Measure angle h.
e Add the four angles.
f What is the angle sum of your quadrilateral?
g Extend each side and measure the four external angles. What do they add up to?

Problem solving

3 Find angles a and b.

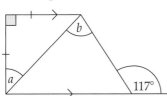

MyMaths.co.uk   Q 1141   **SEARCH**

5e Properties of quadrilaterals

⬤ A **quadrilateral** has four straight sides and four angles.

⬤ The angle sum of a quadrilateral is 360°.

You should know these quadrilaterals and their properties.

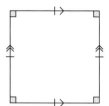

Square
4 equal angles, each 90°
4 equal sides
2 pairs of parallel sides

Rectangle
4 equal angles, each 90°
2 pairs of equal sides
2 pairs of parallel sides

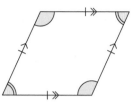

Rhombus
2 pairs of equal angles
4 equal sides
2 pairs of parallel sides

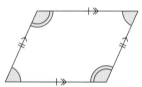

Parallelogram
2 pairs of equal angles
2 pairs of equal sides
2 pairs of parallel sides

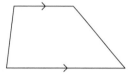

Trapezium
Usually has no equal
angles and no equal sides
Always has 1 pair of parallel sides

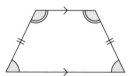

Isosceles trapezium
2 pairs of equal angles
1 pair of equal sides
1 set of parallel sides

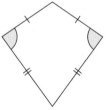

Kite
1 pair of equal angles
2 pairs of equal sides
No parallel sides

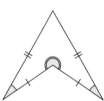

Arrowhead
1 pair of equal angles
2 pairs of equal sides
No parallel sides
1 reflex angle

Example

Find angles *a* and *b*.

$a + 61° = 180°$
$a = 180° - 61° = 119°$
$a = 119°$

Adjacent angles
total 180°.

$b = 61°$

In a parallelogram
opposite angles
are equal.

Exercise 5e

1 **a** Which quadrilaterals have only one pair of parallel lines?

b Which quadrilateral has a reflex angle?

c Which quadrilaterals have four equal angles?

d Which quadrilaterals have no parallel sides?

e Which quadrilaterals have four equal sides?

2

 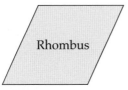

Describe one difference between a square and a rhombus.

3

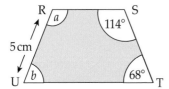

Describe one difference between a rhombus and a parallelogram.

4 This is an isosceles trapezium.

Find

a the size of angle *a*

b the size of angle *b*

c the length of ST.

5 This is a parallelogram.

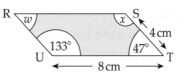

Find

a the size of angle *w*

b the size of angle *x*

c the length of RS

d the length of RU.

6 Four quadrilaterals have been cut in half.

a Match the pieces to make the four quadrilaterals.

b Name each quadrilateral.

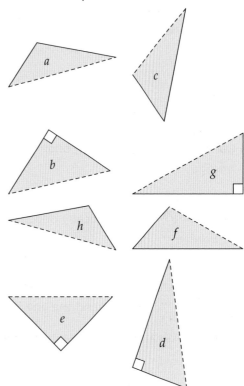

Problem solving

7 **a** How many isosceles trapeziums can you find in this diagram?

b How many parallelograms can you find?

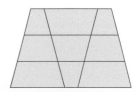

Check out

You should now be able to ...

✓ Identify alternate and corresponding angles.	6	1
✓ Use side and angle properties of triangles to solve problems.	5	2
✓ Use the angle sum of a triangle and properties of exterior and interior angles to solve problems.	5	2
✓ Use the angle sum of a quadrilateral.	6	3, 5
✓ Recognise, name and classify different quadrilaterals.	5	4, 5

Language	Meaning	Example
Parallel lines	Lines which are parallel are always the same distance apart.	
Alternate angles	Alternate angles are equal.	
Corresponding angles	Corresponding angles are equal.	
Vertically opposite	Vertically opposite angles are equal.	
Interior and exterior angles	Interior angles are angles inside a shape. Exterior angles are formed when you extend the line of a shape.	interior exterior
Quadrilateral	A quadrilateral is a shape with four straight sides.	

1 Calculate the value of the letters, give a reason for each of your answers.

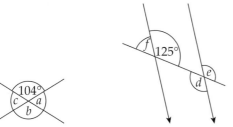

2 Calculate the value of the letters.

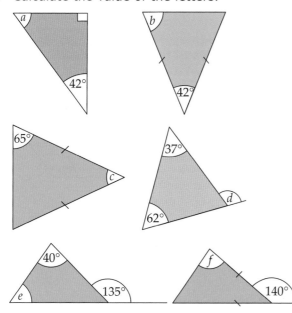

3 Calculate the value of the letters in these quadrilaterals.

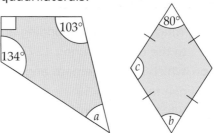

4 Which quadrilateral
  a usually has no equal angles and no equal sides but always has 1 pair of parallel sides?
  b has 4 equal angles of 90°, 2 pairs of equal sides and 2 pairs of parallel sides?

5 In this isosceles trapezium, find
  a the length of CD
  b the size of angle C
     Angles A and D are the same size
  c find the size of angle A.

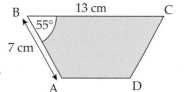

What next?

Score			
	0 – 2		Your knowledge of this topic is still developing. To improve look at Formative test: 3A-5; MyMaths: 1080, 1082, 1100, 1102, 1109 and 1141
	3, 4		You are gaining a secure knowledge of this topic. To improve look at InvisiPen: 341, 342, 343, 344 and 345
	5		You have mastered this topic. Well done, you are ready to progress!

5a

1 **a** Which is the alternate angle to the
       one measuring 127°?
   b Which is the corresponding angle
       to the one measuring 127°?
   c Which is the alternate angle to the
       one measuring 53°?
   d Which is the corresponding angle
       to the one measuring 53°?
   e What is the size of these angles?
       a angle *r*   **b** angle *s*
       c angle *t*   **d** angle *u*

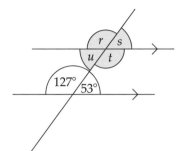

5b

2 Find the missing angle in each triangle.

   a 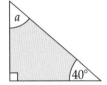   **b** 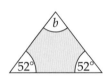   **c**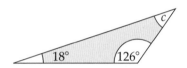

3 Using the rule
   'the exterior angle is equal to the sum of the opposite interior angles',
   calculate the sizes of angles *a*, *b* and *c*.

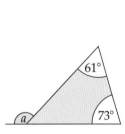   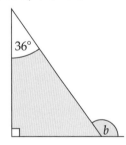   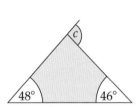

5c

4 Which of these sets of measurements will not make a triangle?
   a 4 cm, 5 cm and 8 cm
   b 6 cm, 11 cm and 7 cm
   c 12 cm, 25 cm and 20 cm
   d 3.5 cm, 1.1 cm and 1.8 cm

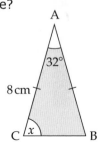

5 **a** How long is side AB?
   b Find the size of angle *x*.

6 Find the missing angle in each quadrilateral.

a

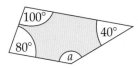

b

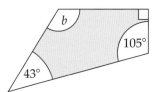

c

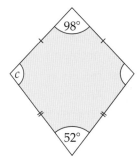

d

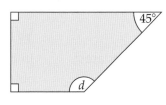

7 **a** Construct this quadrilateral using a ruler and protractor.

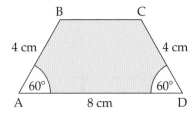

b What is the mathematical name of the quadrilateral?

c Measure side BC.

d Measure angle ABC and angle BCD.

e If sides AB and DC were extended until they meet what sort of triangle would be formed?

8 **a** Name this quadrilateral.
   b Which side is parallel to RS?
   c How long is side RU?
   d How many degrees is angle TUR?

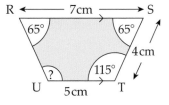

9 **a** Name this quadrilateral.
   b Which side is parallel to FG?
   c How long is side DE?
   d How many degrees is angle EFG?

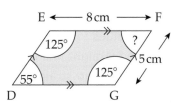

6 Graphs

Introduction

Mobile phone companies offer the latest phones with all the latest features to encourage you to spend your money with them. When you are choosing your next mobile phone it pays not only to look at the features on the phone but also to compare the price plans on offer. The price plans are often hard to compare and the best way is to represent the different set of information as graphs.

What's the point?

In business, many problems are about obtaining the best results within a given set of constraints. Answers are not often clear-cut, but the plotting of linear functions lies at the heart of the decision making process.

Objectives

By the end of this chapter, you will have learned how to ...
- Plot coordinates in all four quadrants.
- Identify and draw horizontal and vertical lines on a graph.
- Construct tables of values for graphs.
- Draw and understand straight line graphs.
- Identify the point where two straight lines intersect.
- Read and interpret real life graphs.
- Understand and draw time series graphs.

Check in

1 What is the word made by the letters at these coordinates?

(2, 8) (0, 0) (4, 3) (3, 0) (1, 2) (6, 7) (5, 5)

Write the letters in the same order as the coordinates.

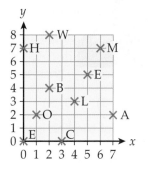

2 What numbers do the letters on this number line represent?

| f | e | d | -2 | c | 0 | 1 | a | b | 4 | 5 |

3 Use the vertical number line to answer these questions.

a What is the distance from 1 to 4?

b What is the distance from 1 to -1?

c What is the distance from -1 to -3?

d If you start at -3 and rise by 7 units, where will you be?

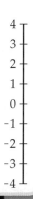

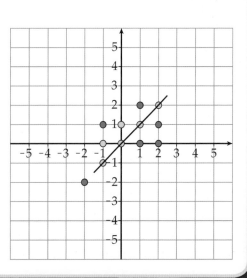

Starter problem

You need to take turns to place a counter of your colour on the grid.

To win a game of 'four-in-a-line', a player needs to have placed four of their pieces in a straight line. In this game the winning line of four is clearly marked.

What is the connection between the x- and y-coordinates of the points on the winning line? Investigate other winning lines of four possible on the grid.

6a Horizontal and vertical lines

The points on the red line share a pattern. They all have the same **y-coordinate**.

(-5, 5)   (-3, 5)   (0, 5)   (3, 5)   (6, 5)

p.164 > The equation of the line is $y = 5$ because all y-coordinates on the line equal 5.

The points on the green line also form a pattern.

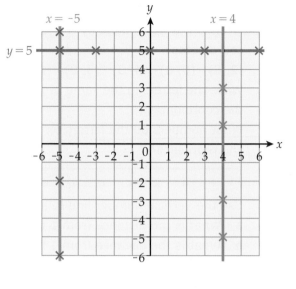

The x-coordinates are all -5.

The equation of the line is $x = -5$.

The equation of the blue line is $x = 4$.

> The equation of a vertical line is $x = $ 'a number' (these lines cross the x-axis)
> The equation of a horizontal line is $y = $ 'a number' (these lines cross the y-axis)

Example

a List any three coordinate pairs for each of the four coloured lines.

b Write down two coordinate pairs for each line, which you could see only if you extended the line.

c What are the equations of the four lines?

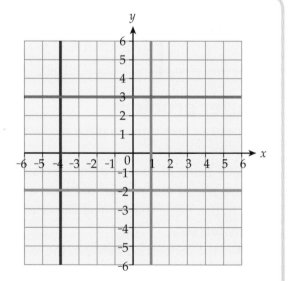

a Red: (-6, 3)   (0, 3)   (4, 3)
   Blue: (1, -3)   (1, 1)   (1, 3)
   Green: (-2, -2)   (1, -2)   (5, -2)
   Purple: (-4, 3)   (-4, -6)   (-4, 4)

b Red: (-7, 3)   (10, 3)
   Blue: (1, -9)   (1, 12)
   Green: (-9, -2)   (15, -2)
   Purple: (-4, -12)   (-4, 20)

c Red: $y = 3$
   Blue: $x = 1$
   Green: $y = -2$
   Purple: $x = -4$

Exercise 6a

1

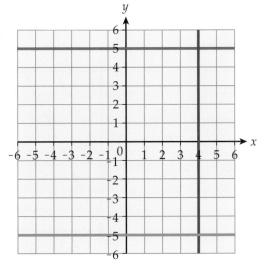

a List any three coordinate pairs for each of the three coloured lines.

b What are the equations of the three lines?

c What are the coordinates of the point at which the red and blue lines intersect?

d What are the coordinates of the point at which the green and blue lines intersect?

e If you drew the line $x = -3$, which two of the lines would it cross?

f Write down the coordinates of the points at which the two lines in part **e** would cross the line $x = -3$.

2 a Copy these axes.

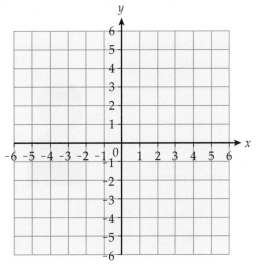

Draw the rectangle made from the four lines with these equations.
$y = 5$, $y = -3$, $x = 6$ and $x = -4$.

b List the coordinates where the lines cross.

c Find the perimeter of the rectangle.

d Find the area of the rectangle.

3 Repeat question **2** using the lines $x = -5$, $x = 5$, $y = 0$ and $y = 3$.

Problem solving

4 a Imagine the line $y = 10$.
Is it **vertical** or **horizontal**?
Give the coordinates of any point that would be on the line.

b Imagine the line $x = -20$.
Will the point (5, -20) be on the line?

c Imagine the line $y = 15$.
Give the equation of another line that will be parallel to $y = 15$.

d Imagine the line $x = 0$.
Can you think of another name for this line?

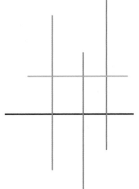

The red graph line shows the equation $y = 2x$.

The y-coordinate is always double (2 times) the x-coordinate.

To plot a graph you need coordinates.

Coordinates are taken from a table of values.

You can use a **function machine** to work out the value of the y-coordinate.

$x \longrightarrow \boxed{\times 2} \longrightarrow y$

$0 \longrightarrow 2 \times 0 = 0$
$1 \longrightarrow 2 \times 1 = 2$

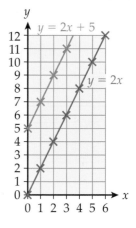

x	0	1	2	3	4	5	6
y	0	2	4	6	8	10	12

The blue graph line shows another equation,
$y = 2x + 5$.

$x \longrightarrow \boxed{\times 2} \longrightarrow \boxed{+5} \longrightarrow y$

x	0	1	2	3
$2x$	0	2	4	6
$+5$	$+5$	$+5$	$+5$	$+5$
y	5	7	9	11

First, multiply the x-coordinate by 2 and then add 5. The value of $2x + 5$ gives the y-coordinate.

⬤ Substitute the x-coordinates into the equation to find the corresponding y-coordinates.

Example

a Copy and complete this table of values for the equation $y = 3x$.

x	0	1	2	3	4	5	6
y							

b Make a table for the equation $y = 5x + 4$. Use values of x from 0 to 5.

- -

a This is the function machine for the equation $y = 3x$.

$x \longrightarrow \boxed{\times 3} \longrightarrow y$

x	0	1	2	3	4	5	6
y	0	3	6	9	12	15	18

b This is the function machine for the equation $y = 5x + 4$.

$x \longrightarrow \boxed{\times 5} \longrightarrow \boxed{+4} \longrightarrow y$

x	0	1	2	3	4	5
$5x$	0	5	10	15	20	25
$+4$	$+4$	$+4$	$+4$	$+4$	$+4$	$+4$
y	4	9	14	19	24	29

⬅ multiply the x-coordinate by 5
⬅ add 4
⬅ $5x + 4$ gives the y-coordinate

Exercise 6b

1 Copy and complete these tables of values using the function machines.

a

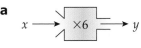

x	0	1	2	3	4	5	6
y			12				

b

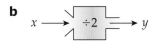

x	0	1	2	3	4	5	6
y		$\frac{1}{2}$		$1\frac{1}{2}$			

2 Copy and complete the tables of values for these equations.

a $y = 3x + 2$

x	0	1	2	3	4	5
3x						
+2	+2	+2	+2	+2	+2	+2
y						

b $y = 4x - 1$

x	0	1	2	3	4	5
4x						
-1	-1	-1	-1	-1	-1	-1
y						

3 For these equations

a $y = x + 3$ **b** $y = 3x + 4$

c $y = 5x + 2$ **d** $y = 2x + 7$

   i draw a function machine

   ii use your function machine to make tables of values.

   Use values of x from 0 to 5.

e For equation **d**, the equation $y = 2x + 7$, write a list of the x- and y-coordinates using brackets, like this. (0, 7), ...

4 Copy and complete these tables of values for these equations.

a $y = 2x - 3$

x	0	1	2	3	4	5
2x						
-3						
y						

b $y = 3x - 1$

x	0	1	2	3	4	5
3x						
-1						
y						

Problem solving

5 a Copy and complete this table of values for the equation $y = x^2 + 1$.

x	0	1	2	3	4	5	6	7	8	9	10
x^2 (= $x \times x$)	0		4								100
+1	+1	+1	+1	+1	+1	+1	+1	+1	+1	+1	+1
y	1		5								

b What do you notice about the y-coordinates?

c Copy and complete this table of values for the equation $y = x^2 + 1$.

x	-10	-9	-8	-7	-6	-5	-4	-3	-2	-1
x^2 (= $x \times x$)	100								4	
+1	+1	+1	+1	+1	+1	+1	+1	+1	+1	+1
y									5	

d What do you notice about the y-coordinates?

MyMaths.co.uk   🔍 1168   **SEARCH**

The graph shows these three equations.

$y = x$ $y = x + 3$ $y = x - 3$

These are the tables of values.

$y = x$

x	-3	-2	-1	0	1	2	3	4	5
y	-3	-2	-1	0	1	2	3	4	5

$y = x + 3$

x	-3	-2	-1	0	1	2	3	4	5
y	0	1	2	3	4	5	6	7	8

-3 + 3 = 0   -2 + 3 = 1   -1 + 3 = 2

$y = x - 3$

x	-3	-2	-1	0	1	2	3	4	5
y	-6	-5	-4	-3	-2	-1	0	1	2

-3 − 3 = -6   -2 − 3 = -5   -1 − 3 = -4

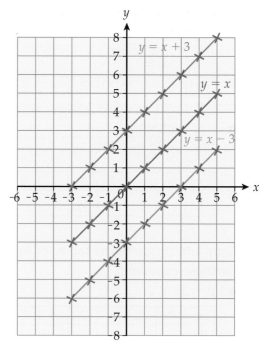

	Instructions for drawing the graph of an equation
1	Make a table of values
2	Draw and label axes
3	Plot the coordinates from the table – use small crosses
4	Draw a straight line through the crosses – use a ruler! – and label it with the equation

Example

a Make a table of values for the equation $y = 2x + 2$.

b Draw a graph of this equation for values of x between -3 and 3.

a

x	-3	-2	-1	0	1	2	3
y	-4	-2	0	2	4	6	8

2 × -3 + 2 = -4   2 × 2 + 2 = 6

2 × 0 + 2 = 2

Look at the values in the table to help you decide what values to use on the y-axis.

b

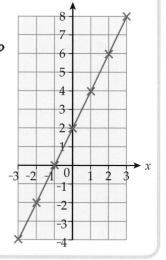

Exercise 6c

1 a Copy and complete this table of values for the equation $y = 2x + 1$.

x	0	1	2	3	4	5	6
2x	0			6		10	
+1	+1	+1	+1	+1	+1	+1	+1
y	1			7		11	

b Copy the axes.
Plot the coordinates from your table.
Join the coordinates to make a straight line.

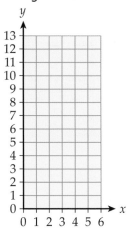

2 a Copy and complete the table of values for the equation $y = 2x$.

x	-3	-2	-1	0	1	2	3
y				0	2	4	6

b Copy the axes.
Plot the coordinates from the table.
Join the points with a straight line.

3 a Copy and complete this table of values for the equation $y = 2x - 2$.

x	-4	-3	-2	-1	0	1	2	3	4
2x		-6				2			
-2	-2	-2	-2	-2	-2	-2	-2	-2	-2
y		-8				0			

b Plot these points onto a copy of these axes and join them to make a straight line.

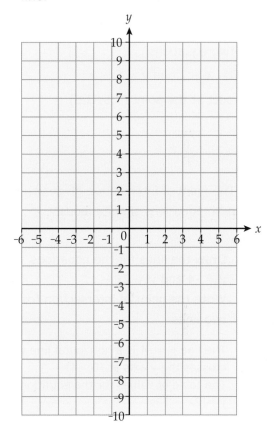

Problem solving

4 a Make a table of values for the equation $y = 3x - 4$.
Use values of x from -2 to 2.

b On the axes you drew for question **2**, plot the coordinates from your table.
Join the points with a straight line.

c What are the coordinates of the two points where this line crosses the lines you drew for questions **2** and **3**?

The graph shows these two equations.

$y = x + 2 \qquad y = 5 - x$

These are the tables of values.

$y = x + 2$

x	0	1	2	3	4	5
y	2	3	4	5	6	7

$y = 5 - x$

x	0	1	2	3	4	5
y	5	4	3	2	1	0

The two equations

$y = x + 2$ and $y = 5 - x$

intersect at the point (1.5, 3.5).

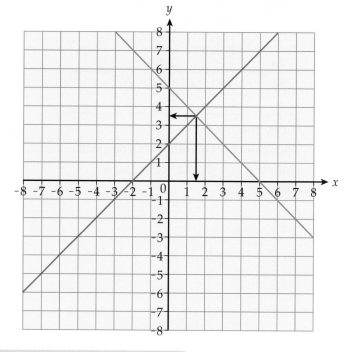

● The point of intersection gives you the solution which works for both equations simultaneously.

a Draw the lines for the equations
   $y = -4$ and $y = 2x - 1$.

b Write the point of intersection for the
   two lines.

a The line $y = -4$ is a horizontal line which
   crosses the y axis at (0, -4).
   The table of values for the equation
   $y = 2x - 1$ is

x	-2	-1	0	1	2	3
2x	-4	-2	0	2	4	6
-1	-1	-1	-1	-1	-1	-1
y	-5	-3	-1	1	3	5

Plot the graphs of $y = -4$ and
$y = 2x - 1$

b The point of intersection is where the
   two lines cross.
   (-1.5, -4)

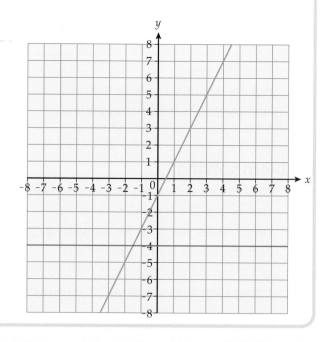

Exercise 6d

1 a Copy and complete this table of values for the equation $y = 2x$.

x	-2	-1	0	1	2	3
y		-2		2		

b Copy the axes.

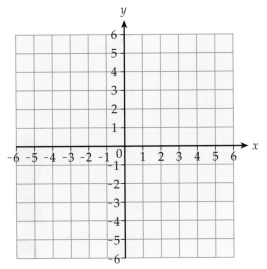

Plot the coordinates from your table. Join the coordinates to make a straight line.

c Draw the line $y = 4$ on your axes.

d Write the coordinates for the point of intersection for the lines $y = 4$ and $y = 2x$.

2 a Draw a table of values for the equation $y = 4 - x$.

b Plot the coordinates from your table on appropriate axes.
Join the coordinates to make a straight line.

c Draw the line $x = -1$ on your axes.

d Write the coordinates for the point of intersection for the lines $x = -1$ and $y = 4 - x$.

3 a Copy and complete this table of values for the equation $y = 2x + 1$.

x	-2	-1	0	1	2	3
2x	-4			2		
+1	+1	+1				
y	-3					

b Using appropriate axes plot the coordinates from your table.
Join the coordinates to make a straight line.

c Copy and complete this table of values for the equation $y = 1 - x$

x	-2	-1	0	1	2	3
y	3		1			-2

Plot your coordinates from the table on your axes.
Join the coordinates to make another straight line.

d Write the coordinates for the point of intersection for the lines $y = 2x + 1$ and $y = 1 - x$.

4 a Copy and complete this table of values for the equation $y = 5 - x$.

x	-2	-1	0	1	2	3
y	7					2

b Using appropriate axes plot the coordinates from your table. Join the coordinates to make a straight line.

c Draw a table of values for the equation $y = 2x - 1$.

d Draw the line $y = 2x - 1$ on your axes.

e Write the coordinates for the point of intersection for the lines $y = 5 - x$ and $y = 2x - 1$.

Look at these two graphs.

The **rule** for the red graph is given by this function machine.

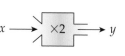

It gives coordinate pairs

(0, 0) (1, 2) (3, 6)

The blue line has coordinates (0, 5) (1, 7) (3, 11)

For the same x-coordinate the y-coordinate is increased by 5. So the blue line is five squares higher.

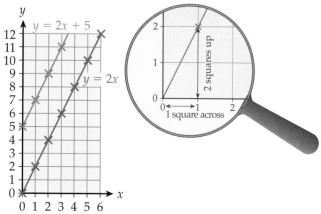

The rule for the blue line is given by this function machine.

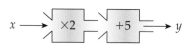

The points on the red line move up 2 squares for every one square across.

The **equation** of the red line is $y = 2x$
The equation of the blue line is $y = 2x + 5$

$y = 2x$ and $y = 2x + 5$ both have a 2 in front of the x. They are parallel.

● The number in front of the x tells you how many squares to go up for one square across.

● If two straight lines have the same number in front of the x then they are parallel.

Example

a Copy and complete this sentence.
'The points on the red line move ☐ squares up for every one square across.'

b Copy this function machine.
Use your sentence to write the rule linking the x- and y-coordinates.

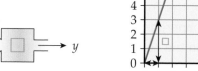

c What is the equation of the line?

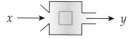

---

a 'The red line moves *three* squares up for every one square across.'

b
$$x \longrightarrow \boxed{\times 3} \longrightarrow y$$

c The equation of the line is $y = 3x$.

Exercise 6e

1 **a** For each of these graph lines copy and complete this sentence.

'The points on the line move ☐ squares up for every one square across.'

i

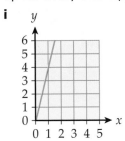

ii

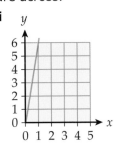

iii

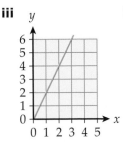

iv

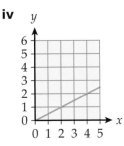

b Write the rule that links the x- and y-coordinates in the graphs above.

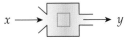

c Write the equation of each of the lines.

$y = $ ....

2 Look at these graphs.

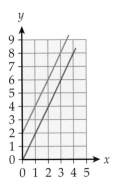

a Write the rule that links the x- and y-coordinates for the red line on this graph.

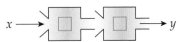

b What is the equation of the red line?

$y = $ ....

c Write the rule that links the x- and y-coordinates for the blue line.

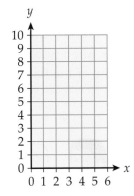

d What is the equation of the blue line?

Problem solving

3 Without plotting coordinates, draw the line of the equation $y = 3x + 1$ on a copy of this grid.

Here are some hints to help you.

— First write the rule linking the x- and y-coordinates.

— Copy and complete this sentence.

'The points move ☐ squares up for every one square across.'

— Start drawing the line where it crosses the y-axis.

4 Draw a set of axes each from 0 to 8.

Plot a graph of the line with equation $y = 7 - x$.

6f Interpreting real life graphs

⬤ On a distance–time graph
  ▶ the *x*-axis represents the time taken to travel.
  ▶ the *y*-axis represents the distance travelled.
  ▶ horizontal lines represent a pause in the journey.
  ▶ diagonal lines represent constant speed.
  ▶ a steeper line represents a faster speed.

A distance–time graph tells you about a journey.
Gabriella cycles around Oxford.
She starts at 9:00 a.m. and returns back home at 2:00 p.m.
This distance–time graph shows her journey.

At this stage Gabriella is moving again.
The distance from home goes from 40 km back to 0 km.
She is going back to where she started.
It takes her 2 hours to cycle the 40 km back home.
Her speed on the return journey is 40 km ÷ 2h = 20 km/h.

At these two stages time keeps moving but Gabriella does not.
She is **at rest** or, in other words, she has stopped.

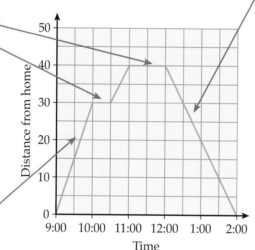

The graph line is straight.
This means that Gabriella is cycling at a **constant** speed.
She cycles 30 km in 1 hour so her speed is 30 km/h.

This graph shows how the depth of water increases in a flask when water is poured into it. It is affected by the shape of the flask.

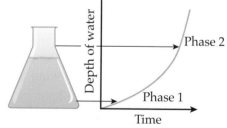

During phase 1, the depth increases slowly to start with. This is where the flask is wider. As the flask narrows, the depth increases at a faster rate.

During phase 2, the depth increases at a steady rate. The line is quite steep as the neck of the flask is quite narrow.

Exercise 6f

1 These graphs show three more of
  Gabriella's cycle rides.

A

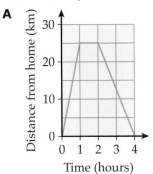

B

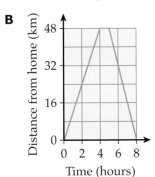

C

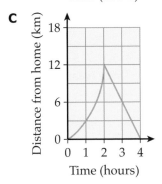

a At what speed is Gabriella cycling during
  the first part of cycle rides A and B?

1 b On which cycle ride does Gabriella not
    take a rest before she returns home?

  c For how long did Gabriella stop during
    cycle ride B?

  d Explain what is happening to
    Gabriella's speed during the first part
    of cycle ride C.

  e During which of her three cycle rides
    does Gabriella cycle over 50 km
    altogether?

2 The graphs show how the depth of liquid
  changes in three flasks as liquid is poured
  into them.
  Match the flasks to the graphs.

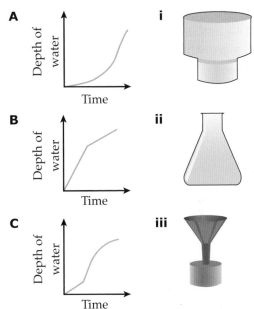

Problem solving

3 Gabriella goes on another cycle ride.
  She starts cycling at 10:00 a.m.
  She cycles for two hours at 10 km/h.
  She rests for 30 minutes.
  She travels another 5 km at the same speed.
  She then takes 1 hour to return home.
  Draw the graph of Gabriella's cycle ride.
  To draw the axes you will need to work out the total time taken and the distance travelled.

It is Guy's birthday.
On every birthday his grandad marks his height on the garage wall.

You can display this data on a **line graph**.
You join the **data points** with straight lines.
It shows the record of Guy's growth.

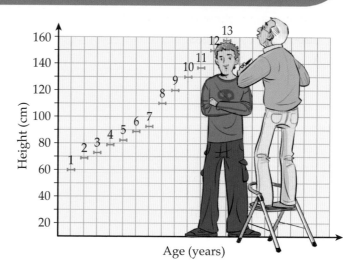

Age (years)

> A line graph shows a **trend** over a period of time.
> ▶ You always plot time on the **horizontal** axis.

Guy has a sister called Terri.
On this line graph, the record of Terri's growth is also displayed.
You need a **key** to say which data set the different points belong to.
You can compare the data for the two **time series**.

> You can put more than one set of data on a graph.

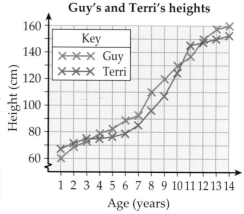

Guy's and Terri's heights

Key
××× Guy
××× Terri

Age (years)

p.144 ❭

Example

These line graphs show the **mean** average maximum temperature in London, England and in Sydney, Australia.

a Which months are the hottest for London?
b Which months are the hottest for Sydney?
c What is the range in temperatures for London and Sydney?
d Which city is generally warmer?

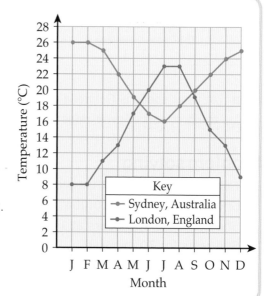

Key
● Sydney, Australia
● London, England

Month

- - - - - - -

a The hottest months for London are July and August.
b The hottest months for Sydney are January and February.
c The range for London = 23°C – 8°C = 15°C
   The range for Sydney = 26°C – 16°C = 10°C
d In general Sydney is warmer, its lowest temperature is 16°C, whereas for London it is 8°C.

Exercise 6g

1 The number of people visiting the Lagoon Café is recorded each hour.
The line graph shows the results.

Visitors to Lagoon Café

a How many people were in the café at 4 p.m.?

b At what time were 19 people recorded in the café?

c At what time was the café most busy? Approximately how many visitors were there at that time?

d The staff can have two tea breaks each day.
What would be the best times to have tea breaks?

2 This graph shows the temperature of an office at the top of a building and the temperature in the boiler room in the basement.

2 The temperature is recorded over ten hours.

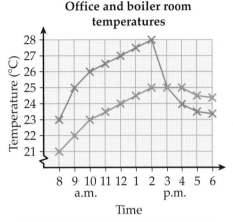

Office and boiler room temperatures

Key ✕✕ Office ✕✕ Boiler room

a What is the maximum temperature recorded in the boiler room?

b What is the maximum temperature recorded in the office?

c What is the temperature in the office at 10 a.m.?

d At what time does the boiler switch off?

e At what time is the temperature the same in the office and in the boiler room?

f At what time is a temperature of 22°C recorded in the office?

Problem solving

3 a The data records the temperature during a seven-hour period one spring day.
Copy these axes.
Plot the data from the table.
Join the points with straight lines to form a line graph.

Time	Temperature (°C)
08:00	12
09:00	14
10:00	16
11:00	18
12:00	19
13:00	20
14:00	17
15:00	15

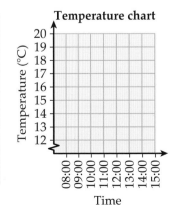

Temperature chart

b Describe the changes in temperature.

6 MySummary

Check out

You should now be able to ...

Test it ➡

Questions

✓ Identify and draw horizontal and vertical lines on a graph.	6	1
✓ Construct tables of values for graphs.	6	2
✓ Draw and understand straight line graphs.	6	2, 3
✓ Read and interpret real life graphs.	6	4
✓ Understand and draw time series graphs.	6	5

Language	Meaning	Example
Coordinates	Coordinates are two numbers which show the position of a point. They are written in brackets, separated by a comma.	(4, 7) This is 4 units right and 7 units up from (0, 0). (-3, -2) This is 3 units left and 2 units down from (0, 0)
Vertical	A vertical line is a line going straight up. A vertical line is parallel to the y-axis and has the equation $x = $ something.	
Horizontal	A horizontal line is a line going straight across. A horizontal line is parallel to the x-axis and has the equation $y = $ something.	
Equation	An equation is where an expression is equal to another expression.	$x = 3$, $y = -2$ and $y = 2x - 1$ are all equations of lines.
Trend	A trend is the general direction for a set of data.	The trend for a set of data would increase, decrease or stay the same.

1 Write the equations of lines A, B, C and D

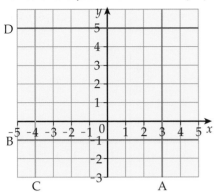

2 For the equation $y = 2x + 1$

a copy and complete the table

x	0	1	2	3	4
2x					
+1	+1	+1	+1	+1	+1
y					

b draw axes with x from 0 to 5 and y from 0 to 10 then draw the graph.

3

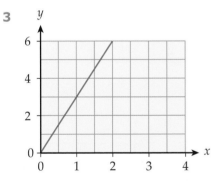

a Write the rule that links the x- and y-coordinates in the graph above.

b What is the equation of the line?

4 The graph shows Jim's journey to work.

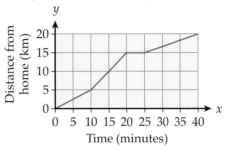

a At what speed was Jim travelling during the first 10 minutes of his journey?

b How far is Jim's journey to work?

c What happens 20 minutes into Jim's journey?

5 The time-series shows the takings in the previous hour by a newsagent, for example between 7 and 8 a.m. £300 was made.

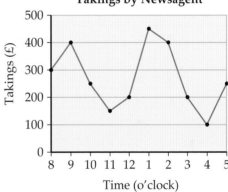

a What takings were made between 2 and 3 p.m.?

b During which hour did the newsagent take the most money?

c When do you think the newsagent is the quietest?

What next?

Score	0 – 2		Your knowledge of this topic is still developing. To improve look at Formative test: 3A-6; MyMaths: 1093, 1153, 1168 and 1184
	3 – 4		You are gaining a secure knowledge of this topic. To improve look at InvisiPen: 262, 264, 275, 276 and 277
	5		You have mastered this topic. Well done, you are ready to progress!

6a

1 Copy these axes.

Plot each set of coordinates.

Join each set with a straight line.

a (5, 5)   (3, 5)   (0, 5)
   (-2, 5)   (-6, 5)

b (-4, 5)   (-4, 1)   (-4, 0)
   (-4, -3)   (-4, -6)

c (-5, -4)   (-1, -4)   (0, -4)
   (1, -4)   (5, -4)

d (3, 6)   (3, 4)   (3, 0)
   (3, -3)   (3, -5)

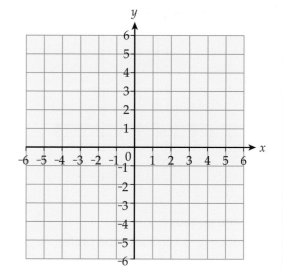

2 Write the equation of each of the lines in question **1**.

6b

3 Copy and complete the tables of values for these relationships.

a $y = 2x - 2$

x	0	1	2	3	4	5
2x	0	2	4			
-2	-2	-2	-2	-2	-2	-2
y	-2		2			

b $y = 5 - x$

x	0	1	2	3	4	5
+5	+5	+5	+5	+5	+5	+5
-x	0	-1	-2		-4	
y	5	4				

6c

4 Copy the axes.

Plot the points from the two tables in question **3**.

Join each set of points with a straight line.

5 **a** Draw a set of axes with x from 0 to 5 and y from 0 to 13.

b Plot these four lines on your axes.

   $y = 2x$ $y = 2x + 4$ $x = 2$ $x = 4$

c What is the mathematical name of the shape made by these lines?

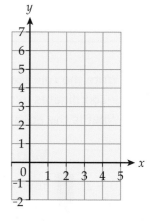

6 Write the coordinates of the point where the lines $y = 2x - 2$ and $y = 5 - x$ intersect.

7 For each of the lines on the graph, write the rule that links the x- and y-coordinates.

a

b
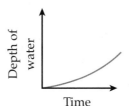

c
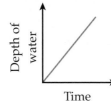

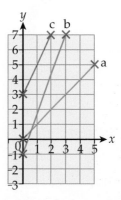

8 The graphs show how the depth of liquid changes in three flasks as liquid is poured into them.
Match the flasks to the graphs.

A

Depth of water

Time

B

Depth of water

Time

C

Depth of water

Time

i

ii

iii

9 The temperature in a vegetable cold store is recorded every hour.
The results are recorded on a line graph.
  a What is the temperature at 9 a.m.?
  b The cold store is switched off for one hour for cleaning. What time was this?
  c What is the difference in temperature between 12 p.m. and 5 p.m.?
  d How many degrees difference are there between the warmest and coolest temperatures?

Cold store temperature

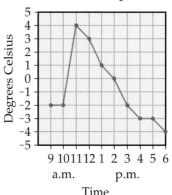

MyMaths.co.uk

113

Case study 2: Jewellery business

Katie and Jess are going to make bracelets and necklaces to sell on an online auction site. They need to ensure that they keep their costs down, to help them run a profitable business.

Katie and Jess have found out the cost of materials from two suppliers.

Each supplier quotes prices for two types of bead—long ones or round ones.

They also quote prices for waxed cord or leather thread.

diameter x length
8 mm x 16 mm beads

diameter x length
12 mm x 9 mm beads

 NATURAL BEAD COMPANY
Postage and packing: £3.50 for any size of order

8 x 16mm beads	12 x 9mm beads
8p per bead	5p per bead
£1.30p per 20	80p per 20
£2.90 per 50	£1.80 per 50
£4.80 per 100	£3.00 per 100
£8.00 per 250	£5.00 per 250

Leather thread	Waxed cord
50p per metre	10p per metre
£11.95 per 50 m	£4.95 per 100 m

Task 1

a Katie and Jess want 2000 beads of each size. Which supplier should they use? Show your workings out.

b They also want 50 m of leather thread, as well as 50 m of waxed cord. Again, decide which supplier they should use, showing clearly your workings out.

 BEAD-E-IZE
Free postage and packing. Minimum order charge of £10

8 x 16mm beads	12 x 9mm beads	Waxed cord
7p per bead	4p per bead	
£1.50p per 25	85p per 25	
£6.75 per 150	£3.75 per 150	
£19.00 per 500	£10.75 per 500	

Leather thread	Waxed cord	Leather thread
45p per metre	11p per metre	
£19.00 per 80 m	£1.95 per 20 m	
	£9.50 per 200 m	

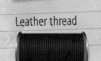

Task 2

Katie and Jess want their bracelets to be 16 cm long, with an adjustable tie. Only ¾ of this length can be used for beads.

a How many long beads would fit on a bracelet?

b How many round beads would fit on a bracelet?

c If they just make bracelets, how many bracelets could they make?

Task 3

Katie and Jess want their necklaces to be 30 cm long. Only ⅔ of this length can be used for beads.

a How many long beads would fit on a necklace?

b How many round beads would fit on a necklace?

c If they just made necklaces, how many necklaces could the girls make?

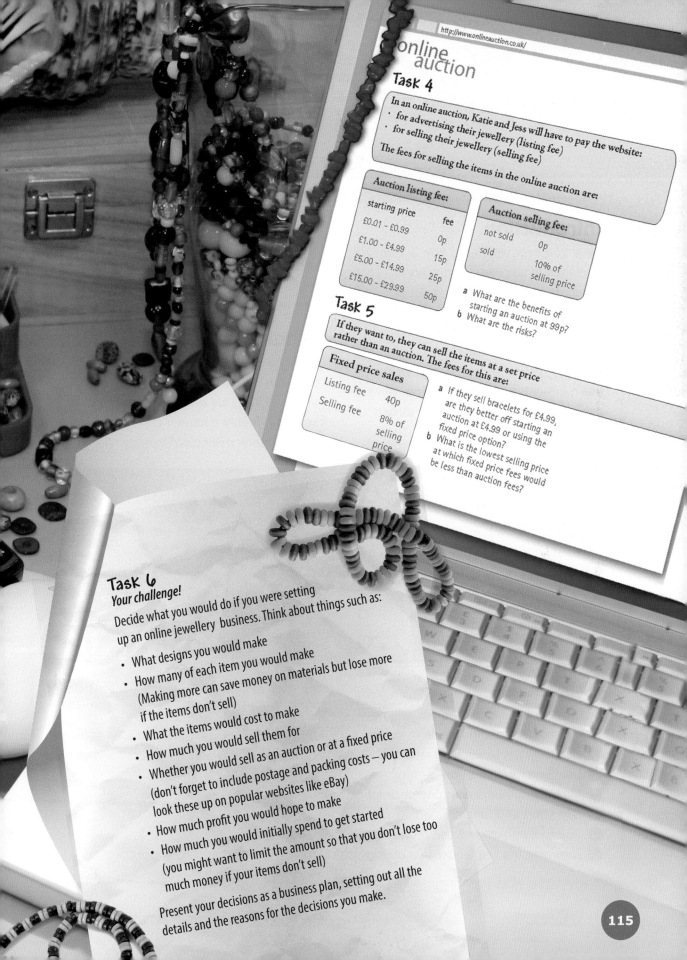

online auction

Task 4

In an online auction, Katie and Jess will have to pay the website:
- for advertising their jewellery (listing fee)
- for selling their jewellery (selling fee)

The fees for selling the items in the online auction are:

Auction listing fee:	
starting price	fee
£0.01 – £0.99	0p
£1.00 – £4.99	15p
£5.00 – £14.99	25p
£15.00 – £29.99	50p

Auction selling fee:	
not sold	0p
sold	10% of selling price

a What are the benefits of starting an auction at 99p?
b What are the risks?

Task 5

If they want to, they can sell the items at a set price rather than an auction. The fees for this are:

Fixed price sales	
Listing fee	40p
Selling fee	8% of selling price

a If they sell bracelets for £4.99, are they better off starting an auction at £4.99 or using the fixed price option?
b What is the lowest selling price at which fixed price fees would be less than auction fees?

Task 6
Your challenge!

Decide what you would do if you were setting up an online jewellery business. Think about things such as:

- What designs you would make
- How many of each item you would make (Making more can save money on materials but lose more if the items don't sell)
- What the items would cost to make
- How much you would sell them for
- Whether you would sell as an auction or at a fixed price (don't forget to include postage and packing costs – you can look these up on popular websites like eBay)
- How much profit you would hope to make
- How much you would initially spend to get started (you might want to limit the amount so that you don't lose too much money if your items don't sell)

Present your decisions as a business plan, setting out all the details and the reasons for the decisions you make.

7 Calculations

Introduction

Have you ever wondered how a computer manages to calculate so quickly? Computers are essentially a set of switches which can either be 'on' or 'off'. For that reason they read numbers in **binary code**. This uses just two symbols '1' and '0', so you can write the number 5 as 101. The computer 'sees' the number 5 as two switches turned 'on' (1) and one switch turned 'off' (0).

When the computer needs to calculate, it converts the numbers into binary and then uses patterns of logic gates (which can be either OR, NOT or AND) to add, multiply and perform other types of calculation.

What's the point?

Computers are very useful devices because they can perform lots of calculations very quickly. This enables them to do, in seconds, highly complex tasks that would take humans millions of years to do.

Objectives

By the end of this chapter, you will have learned how to …
- Use mental methods to add, subtract, multiply and divide whole numbers.
- Use columns to add and subtract whole numbers or decimals.
- Use long multiplication.
- Multiply numbers with one decimal place by a single-digit number.
- Use short and long division.
- Round numbers and use rounding to make estimates.
- Interpret the remainder in a division calculation.

Check in

1 Find the answers to these.

a	5 + 5	**b**	11 − 3	**c**	4 + 9	**d**	10 − 4
e	13 − 5	**f**	12 − 7	**g**	5 + 8	**h**	6 + 7

2 Find the answers to these.

a	5 × 2	**b**	12 ÷ 3	**c**	4 × 3	**d**	10 ÷ 1
e	15 ÷ 3	**f**	3 × 4	**g**	5 × 4	**h**	6 ÷ 2

3 Round each of these numbers to the nearest 10.

a	16	**b**	69	**c**	24	**d**	25
e	13	**f**	97	**g**	31	**h**	44

4 Round each of these amounts to the nearest £1.

a	£1.62	**b**	£0.53	**c**	£4.23	**d**	£3.91
e	£4.50	**f**	£6.29	**g**	£9.99	**h**	£7.65

Starter problem

Choose one of the methods of multiplication to investigate 13 × 21.

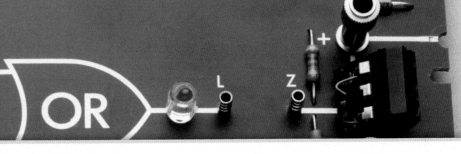

Explain how your chosen method works.

Use this method to multiply 37 × 24.

Investigate another method.

7a Addition and subtraction

You can split numbers into parts to make addition and subtraction easier.

You could also use a sketch of a number line to help you.

Example

Work out 14 + 23.

Split the number 23 into 2 tens and 3 units.

14 + 23 = 37

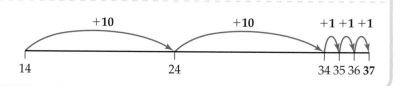

+10   +10   +1 +1 +1

14   24   34 35 36 **37**

Example

Work out 23 − 14.

Split the number 14 into 1 ten and 4 units.

23 − 14 = 9

−1 −1 −1 −1   −10

9 10 11 12 13   23

When you use the standard written method for addition and subtraction, set the calculation out in **columns**.

Example

Work these out.

a 12.6 + 8.2   **b** 26.82 − 14.3   **c** 74.8 − 25.65

a

```
  T  U  1/10
  1  2 . 6
+    8 . 2
─────────────
  2  0 . 8
```

12.6 + 8.2 = 20.8

b

```
  T  U  1/10 1/100
  2  6 . 8  2
- 1  4 . 3
──────────────────
  1  2 . 5  2
```

26.82 − 14.3 = 12.52

c

```
     T  U  1/10 1/100
    6 7  4 . 7 8  0
  - 2  5 . 6  5
───────────────────
    4  9 . 1  5
```

74.8 − 25.65 = 49.15

When adding or subtracting decimals, keep the decimal points lined up in a column.

Exercise 7a

1 Do these calculations in your head as quickly as you can.

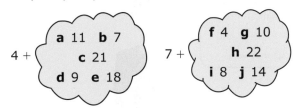

4 +
a 11 **b** 7
c 21
d 9 **e** 18

7 +
f 4 **g** 10
h 22
i 8 **j** 14

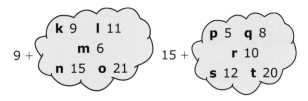

9 +
k 9 **l** 11
m 6
n 15 **o** 21

15 +
p 5 **q** 8
r 10
s 12 **t** 20

Use a number line to work out the calculations on these cards.

2

Addition card 1	
a 34 + 50	**b** 47 + 32
c 41 + 28	**d** 28 + 25
e 63 + 14	**f** 54 + 37
g 56 + 75	**h** 82 + 59

3

Subtraction card 1	
a 36 − 24	**b** 46 − 13
c 51 − 26	**d** 83 − 53
e 74 − 37	**f** 66 − 28
g 158 − 46	**h** 128 − 71

Work these out by writing the calculations in columns.

4

Addition card 2	
a 23 + 12 + 20	**b** 7 + 22 + 20
c 15 + 25 + 30	**d** 16 + 34 + 9
e 125 + 11 + 151	**f** 32 + 264 + 21
g 307 + 3 + 145	**h** 18 + 419 + 91

5

Subtraction card 2	
a 86 − 52	**b** 72 − 32
c 64 − 28	**d** 51 − 26
e 391 − 67	**f** 308 − 156
g 252 − 148	**h** 153 − 87

Problem solving

Work out these calculations involving decimals. Write the calculations in columns.

6

Addition card 3	
a 3.4 + 21.3	**b** 6.9 + 2.6
c 18.2 + 33.6	**d** 14.6 + 8.3
e 23.6 + 249.2	**f** 131.6 + 13.4
g 213.3 + 8.9	**h** 8.8 + 0.8 + 32

7

Subtraction card 3	
a 8.6 − 3.4	**b** 25.7 − 8.2
c 43.0 − 31.5	**d** 27.4 − 21.9
e 50.8 − 26.8	**f** 264.3 − 81.8
g 127.2 − 39.2	**h** 352.2 − 148.5

Did you know?

The signs + and − were first introduced in Britain in 1557 by Robert Recorde, who also designed the equals sign.

MyMaths.co.uk

Q 1020, 1028, 1345 **SEARCH**

I know that × and ÷ are the inverse of each other and that 4 × 5 = 20.

Reversing your calculation means 20 ÷ 5 = 4 and 20 ÷ 4 = 5.

● You multiply and divide by 10 and 100 by moving the digits.

	Th	H	T	U	.	$\frac{1}{10}$	$\frac{1}{100}$
Multiply by 10			2	4			
		2	4	**0**	.		
Multiply by 100			4	3			
	4	3	**0**	**0**	.		
Divide by 10			2	4			
			2		.	4	
Divide by 100		3	8	5			
			3		.	8	5

For more difficult problems you can use jottings to record your mental calculations.

● You can use **partitioning** for multiplication.

● You can use **chunking** (repeated subtraction) for division.

Example

Calculate

a 12 × 15

b 78 ÷ 6

---

a 12 × 15
= 12 × (10 + 5)   Split 15 into 10 and 5.
= 12 × 10 + 12 × 5   Multiply 10 by 12 and 5 by 12.
= 120 + 60
= 180   Add the results.

b   78   Subtract multiples of 6.
     − 6 0   10 × 6 = 60
       1 8
     − 1 8   3 × 6 = 18
        0
     10 + 3 = 13   Add the multiples.
     78 ÷ 6 = 13

Exercise 7b

You should do all the calculations in your head. You may use jottings.

Start these calculations by making an estimate.

1

Mental multiplication card 1

a	3×5	**b**	6×3
c	8×3	**d**	7×4
e	6×4	**f**	5×7
g	9×3	**h**	4×8

2

Mental division card 1

a	$20 \div 5$	**b**	$16 \div 4$
c	$18 \div 6$	**d**	$24 \div 4$
e	$30 \div 5$	**f**	$60 \div 10$
g	$35 \div 7$	**h**	$36 \div 9$

3 These calculations involve multiplying and dividing by 10 and 100.

a	8×10	**b**	$120 \div 10$
c	$280 \div 10$	**d**	41×10
e	9×100	**f**	$1500 \div 100$
g	26×100	**h**	$7100 \div 100$
i	2.8×10	**j**	$63 \div 10$
k	1.4×100	**l**	$85 \div 100$
m	0.8×10	**n**	$0.6 \div 10$
o	0.6×100	**p**	$11.5 \div 100$

4

Mental multiplication card 2

a	3×14	**b**	6×13
c	9×12	**d**	18×5
e	6×18	**f**	15×8
g	17×6	**h**	14×9

5

Mental multiplication card 3

a	21×5	**b**	23×4
c	8×22	**d**	26×4
e	3×41	**f**	35×6
g	54×3	**h**	6×37

6

Mental division card 2

a	$57 \div 5$	**b**	$84 \div 4$
c	$78 \div 6$	**d**	$84 \div 7$
e	$96 \div 6$	**f**	$96 \div 8$
g	$105 \div 7$	**h**	$108 \div 6$

7

Mental division card 3

a	$133 \div 7$	**b**	$117 \div 9$
c	$101 \div 7$	**d**	$108 \div 8$
e	$132 \div 12$	**f**	$168 \div 14$
g	$175 \div 13$	**h**	$218 \div 15$

Some of these problems have a remainder.

Problem solving

8 Use the digits 6, 7, 8, 9 to make a 3 digit number.

Multiply it by the digit you have left. What is the largest possible answer you can get?

$$\square\,\square\,\square \times \square =$$

> You can use the **column** method for **long multiplication**.

Try 247 × 53 using the grid method.

	200	40	7
50	10000		
3			

$10000 +$ _____ $+$ _____ $=$ _____

_____ $+$ _____ $+$ _____ $=$ _____ $+$

——

You should have the answer 13091.

Example

Find 247 × 53

First make an estimate.

247 × 53 ≈ 200 × 50

≈ 10 000

Now write the numbers in columns.

```
    2 4 7
  ×   5 3
  1 2 3 5 0
     2 3
  +   7 4 1
        1 2
  1 3 0 9 1
        1
```

= 247 × 50 = 247 × 5 × 10
= 247 × 3
= 247 × (50 + 3)

247 × 53 = 13 091

Example

Find 7 × 36.85

First make an estimate.

7 × 36.85 ≈ 10 × 40

≈ 400

Next, turn 36.85 into a whole number by multiplying it by 100.

36.85 × 100 = 3685

Now find 3685 × 7 using the column method.

```
    3 6 8 5
  ×       7
  2 5 7 9 5
    4 5 3
```

As 36.85 was multiplied by 100, you need to divide 25795 by 100 to get the final answer.

25795 ÷ 100 = 257.95

36.85 × 7 = 257.95

Exercise 7c

1 i Make an estimate of the answer.
  ii Work out.

    a 13×132 **b** 12×143
    c 25×125 **d** 24×160

2 Work out.

    a 123×16 **b** 12×247
    c 15×162 **d** 135×18
    e 157×23 **f** 34×186
    g 264×28 **h** 36×256

3 Copy and complete these.

a
```
      1 3 2
  ×     1 3
  + _____
    _____
```

b
```
      1 2 5
  ×     1 2
  + _____
    _____
```

c
```
      2 0 6
  ×     1 4
  + _____
    _____
```

d
```
      4 0 8
  ×     2 7
  + _____
    _____
```

4 Work out.

    a 143×15 **b** 217×13
    c 135×16 **d** 238×25
    e 239×34 **f** 439×66

5 i Make an estimate of the answer.
  ii Work out.

    a 15.2×3 **b** 14.3×4
    c 21.5×3 **d** 6×29.5

6 Work out.

    a 2×17.4 **b** 5×12.5
    c 5×23.1 **d** 6×31.6
    e 4×30.6 **f** 8×12.2

7 A teacher asks her class to work out
382×15.
Katie and Alan respond as shown below.

Who is right?
Show your workings.

Problem solving

8 Write each problem as a multiplication calculation and solve it.

  a Each box holds 32 biscuits.
    How many biscuits are there in 18 boxes?

  b Each aircraft can carry 174 passengers.
    How many passengers can seven aircraft carry?

  c A packet of crisps has a mass of 22.5 grams.
    What is the mass of six packets?

  d A lorry carries 26 crates on each trip.
    How many crates are delivered after eight trips?

  e Each steel bar is 37.4 centimetres long.
    Six bars are laid end-to-end.
    What is the total length?

7d Written division

● Use short division when dividing by a one-digit number.

Example

Work out 711 ÷ 9

Write the divisor first.

$$7\ 9$$
$$9\overline{)7\ 1\ ^81}$$

9 × 7 = 63, 71 − 63 = 8, so there is 8 left over.
9 × 9 = 81, so there is no remainder.

711 ÷ 9 = 79

● Use long division when dividing by a two-digit number.

Example

Work out 2898 ÷ 23

$$\begin{array}{r}126\\23\overline{)2898}\end{array}$$

$$\begin{array}{r}-23\\\hline 59\\-46\\\hline 138\\-138\\\hline 0\end{array}$$

1 × 23 = 23
28 − 23 = 5
2 × 23 = 46
59 − 46 = 13
6 × 23 = 138
138 − 138 = 0

2898 ÷ 23 = 126

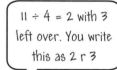

11 ÷ 4 = 2 with 3 left over. You write this as 2 r 3

● Some numbers do not divide exactly.
The amount left over is called the **remainder**.

Example

Work out 279 ÷ 12

$$\begin{array}{r}23\ \text{r}\ 3\\12\overline{)279}\end{array}$$

$$\begin{array}{r}-24\\\hline 39\\-36\\\hline 3\end{array}$$

2 × 12 = 24
27 − 24 = 3
3 × 12 = 36
39 − 36 = 3

There is a remainder of 3 when 279 is divided by 12.

$279 ÷ 12 = 23\ \text{r}\ 3$ or $279 ÷ 12 = 23\frac{3}{12} = 23\frac{1}{4}$.

Exercise 7d

1 Do these calculations in your head as quickly as you can.

a	16 ÷ 4	**b**	20 ÷ 2
c	18 ÷ 9	**d**	24 ÷ 8
e	21 ÷ 3	**f**	35 ÷ 7
g	30 ÷ 5	**h**	28 ÷ 7
i	36 ÷ 6	**j**	90 ÷ 10
k	45 ÷ 5	**l**	27 ÷ 3

2 Work these out in your head.

a What is $\frac{1}{3}$ of 30?

b What is $\frac{1}{4}$ of 24?

c What is $\frac{1}{2}$ of 32?

d What is $\frac{1}{4}$ of 80?

e What is $\frac{1}{2}$ of 46?

f What is $\frac{1}{5}$ of 45?

g What is $\frac{1}{6}$ of 72?

h What is $\frac{1}{7}$ of 63?

3 Use a suitable method to work these out.

a	$5\overline{)85}$	**b**	$6\overline{)96}$
c	$4\overline{)92}$	**d**	$8\overline{)168}$
e	$6\overline{)138}$	**f**	$7\overline{)154}$

4 Use a suitable method to work out these more difficult problems.

a	$14\overline{)308}$	**b**	$24\overline{)504}$
c	$13\overline{)299}$	**d**	$26\overline{)806}$
e	$32\overline{)736}$	**f**	$17\overline{)425}$
g	$21\overline{)567}$	**h**	$34\overline{)442}$
i	$41\overline{)1189}$	**j**	$23\overline{)1219}$

5 Use a suitable method to work out these calculations involving remainders.

a	93 ÷ 4	**b**	94 ÷ 6
c	125 ÷ 8	**d**	165 ÷ 7
e	148 ÷ 6	**f**	278 ÷ 13
g	370 ÷ 15	**h**	271 ÷ 20
i	564 ÷ 24	**j**	741 ÷ 32

Problem solving

6 Write each problem as a division calculation and solve it.

a Eleven friends share a raffle prize of £253.
How much does each person get?

b 324 hens are housed equally in six hen-houses.
How many hens are there in each hen-house?

c A coil of rope 360 metres long is cut into 15-metre lengths.
How many lengths can be cut from the coil?

d Kelly goes on holiday in 189 days.
How many weeks is this?

e Rupert is 408 months old.
How many years is this?

Did you know?

This symbol is the obelus. It is more commonly known as the division sign. It was first used as the symbol for division in 1659. It has also been used as a symbol for subtraction in some countries!

7e Estimating and approximating

In many real-life situations numbers are **rounded** rather than quoted exactly.

Most of the estimated 46 000 fans left early after more than an hour of rain.

● You can round numbers to any given power of 10.

● You should always make an **approximation** before you try to solve a problem involving any calculation.

Example

Joanne buys 348 shares at £2.89 a share.
Richard buys 227 shares at £4.65 a share.
Who spends more?

Round the number of shares to the nearest 100.

Joanne spends approximately   300 × £3 = £900
Richard spends approximately   200 × £5 = £1000
This suggests that Richard spends more.

Round the price of a share to the nearest pound.

● You can use rounding to make **estimates** in real-life situations.

Example

Peter wants to work out the amount of money taken by a football club for one football match.

Peter estimates
  There are 30 000 people at the match.
  80% pay full price of about £40.
  20% pay the concession price of £20.
  About $\frac{1}{3}$ of the people buy a drink and a hot dog for £6.

He calculates
  Admission prices   24 000 × £40 = £960 000
                       6 000 × £20 = £ 120 000
  Food prices   10 000 × £ 6 = £ 60 000
  Total   = £1 140 000

80% of 30 000 = 24 000
20% of 30 000 = 6 000
$\frac{1}{3}$ of 30 000 = 10 000

Exercise 7e

Problem solving

1 This bar chart shows the amount a family spends on food each week in six different countries.

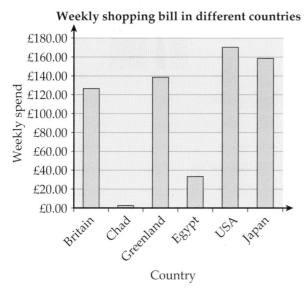

Weekly shopping bill in different countries

About how much is spent on food in each country?
Give your answers to the nearest £10.

2 Solve each of the following problems by making an approximation.

a Sam buys 43 bottles of water at 39p a bottle. Vernon buys 26 bottles of water at 62p a bottle. Who spends more?

b Phil eats two bars of chocolate a day for 12 weeks. Each bar costs 54p. Hugh eats ten cereal bars a week for four months. Each bar costs 68p. Who spends more?

> **Did you know?**
>
>
>
> The blue whale is the largest known animal to have ever existed. They almost became extinct until they were protected in 1966.

3 Solve each of these problems using rounding to estimate the answer. Do not use a calculator.

a Siobhan weighs 42 460 g.
Each day she eats two chocolate bars each weighing 240 g.
In about how many days will Siobhan eat her own weight in chocolate bars?

b A certain humpback whale weighs 27 846 kg.

James weighs 54.3 kg.
Approximately how many times heavier is the whale than James?

4 Estimate the answer to each of these problems. Show all the approximations and calculations you have used.

a Work out the amount of pocket money given to everyone in your school each week.

b Work out the amount of water used by all the people in your town in a year.

7f Using a calculator

How can you have 3.25 of an hour?

That means 3 and a quarter hours, which is 3 hours and 15 minutes.

● You need to **interpret** the **calculator** display carefully when solving problems involving money and time.

Example

Liam works out the answers to these questions on his calculator.

a 39 minutes ÷ 6   **b** 39 cm ÷ 6   **c** 39 people ÷ 6

How should he write his answers?

- -

$39 ÷ 6 = 6.5$

You need to interpret each answer carefully depending upon the quantity in the question.

a 6.5 minutes = 6 minutes and 30 seconds

b 6.5 cm = 6 cm and 5 mm

c 6.5 people = 6 groups of six people each, with 3 people left over

● You can convert a decimal **remainder** to a whole number remainder by multiplying it by the **divisor**.

Example

Convert 303 hours into days and hours.

- -

Using a calculator

    Number of days = 303 ÷ 24   There are 24 hours in a day.

               = 12.625 days

Multiply the remainder by the divisor.

    0.625 days = 0.625 × 24 hours

            = 15 hours

303 hours = 12 days and 15 hours

Exercise 7f

Problem solving

1 The school stationery shop sells the following items.

Pen	15p
Writing pad	£1.49
Calculator	£5.49
Eraser	26p
Pencil	11p

a Kasim buys three pens, two writing pads and a calculator.
What is the total cost of the items?

b Jane spends exactly £2.27.
Which items did she buy?

2 Solve each of these problems.
Give your answers in a form appropriate to the question.

a CDs are packed in bundles of 10.
How many bundles are needed to pack 244 CDs?
How many CDs will be left over?

b Seven friends share £8000.
How much do they each receive?

c The 233 staff and students in Year 9 are going to a theme park.
How many 57-seater coaches do they need?

d Gina works at a farmers' market.
She divides 320 kg of potatoes into 11 sacks.
What is the weight of potatoes in each sack?

e In a year, Valerie spends 2993 minutes brushing her teeth.
How long does she spend brushing her teeth each day?

There are 365.25 days in a year.

3 Convert these measurements of time to the units indicated in brackets.

a 2000 minutes (into hours and minutes)

b 5200 hours (into days and hours)

c 4500 seconds (into minutes and seconds)

d 320 days (into weeks and days)

e 10 000 days (into years and days)

JUNE						
SUN	MON	TUE	WED	THU	FRI	SAT
27	28	29	30	31	1	2
3	4	5	6	7	8	9
10	11	12	13	14	15	16
17	18	19	20	21	22	23
24	25	26	27	28	29	30
1	2	3	4	5	6	7

2012

4 How old would you be if you were a million hours old?
Give your answer in years, days and hours.

5 Use a calculator to work these out.
Give your answers to 2 decimal places where appropriate.

a $(7 + 2.3)^2 \div 4$

b $\dfrac{38 - 1.7^2 \times 5}{\sqrt{2.5 + 4.1}}$

c $\dfrac{82 \times (6.8 - 2.9)^2}{\sqrt{12^2 - 5^2}}$

You need to use brackets to tell the calculator to work out
$\sqrt{2.5 + 4.1} = \sqrt{(2.5 + 4.1)}$

Check out

You should now be able to ...

✓ Use mental methods to calculate with whole numbers.	5	1 – 3
✓ Use a standard column method to do addition and subtraction.	5	4
✓ Use long multiplication.	6	5
✓ Multiply decimals by a single-digit number.	5	6
✓ Use short and long division.	5	6
✓ Use rounding to estimate and approximate.	5	7, 8
✓ Use a calculator and interpret the remainder in a division calculation.	5	9, 10

Language	Meaning	Example
Column addition	Column addition is writing the numbers you are adding in columns. You start adding from the right.	137 9 + 62 208 1 1
Long multiplication	A method you can use when multiplying two numbers with two or more digits.	453 × 34 13590 1 1812 2 1 15402 1 1
Long division	A good method to use when dividing by a number with more than one digit.	12 19)228 -19↓ (1 × 9) 38 (22 – 19 = 3) -38 (2 × 19) 0 228 ÷ 19 = 12
Approximation	Rounding numbers to make a simpler calculation that is close to the exact answer	68.4 + 33.2 ≈ 70 + 30 ≈ 100

1 Use a mental method to work out these calculations.
  a 78 + 34 + 103
  b 94 − 67

2 Do these calculations in your head.
  a 7 × 8   **b** 9 × 6
  c 36 ÷ 6   **d** 14 × 10
  e 0.5 × 100   **f** 75 ÷ 100
  g 64 ÷ 10   **h** 3.5 × 100

3 Use a mental method to work out these multiplications.
  a 8 × 24   **b** 35 × 7

4 Use a written method to work out these calculations.
  a 96 + 153   **b** 327 − 54
  c 17.6 + 59.5   **d** 103.4 − 29.7

5 Work out these multiplications using a written method.
  a 135 × 12   **b** 328 × 13
  c 35 × 247   **d** 434 × 41

6 Work out these multiplications using a written method.
  a 14.7 × 9   **b** 7 × 20.9

7 Work out these divisions and leave with a remainder where necessary.
  a 136 ÷ 8   **b** 189 ÷ 9
  c 92 ÷ 6   **d** 247 ÷ 12
  e 350 ÷ 14   **f** 546 ÷ 21

8 A rectangular garden is 6.9 m by 5.2 m. Estimate its area.

9 19 bottles of water cost £15.96 and 32 bottles of cola cost £48.25.
  a Estimate the cost of 1 bottle of water.
  b Estimate the cost of 1 bottle of cola.
  c Approximately how many times more expensive is cola than water?

10 Use a calculator to work these out. Give your answer to 2 decimal places.
  a $(9.1 - 5.7)^2 \div 3$
  b $\dfrac{63 - 2.4^2 \times 1.8}{\sqrt{13^2 - 7^2}}$

11 Emily is 296 days old. How many weeks and days is this?

12 Convert.
  a 2300 hours into days and hours
  b 3 days into seconds

What next?

	Score		
Score	0 – 4		Your knowledge of this topic is still developing. To improve look at Formative test: 3A-7; MyMaths: 1002, 1020, 1021, 1028, 1041, 1043, 1345 and 1367
	5 – 9		You are gaining a secure knowledge of this topic. To improve look at InvisiPen: 121, 122, 123, 125, 126, 127 and 128
	10 – 12		You have mastered this topic. Well done, you are ready to progress!

1 Work out these additions by writing the calculations in columns.

a	198 + 331	**b**	61 + 180	**c**	272 + 94
d	37 + 73 + 152	**e**	19 + 160 + 271	**f**	337 + 148 + 22
g	218 + 29 + 267	**h**	195 + 73 + 362	**i**	88 + 357 + 457

2 Work out these subtractions by writing the calculations in columns.

a	171 − 124	**b**	368 − 198	**c**	435 − 365
d	308 − 178	**e**	430 − 124	**f**	216 − 96
g	101 − 73	**h**	360 − 225	**i**	253 − 88

3 Work out these calculations using a mental method.

Make an estimate of the answer before you start each calculation.

a	32 × 5	**b**	3 × 71	**c**	8 × 81
d	49 × 6	**e**	78 × 4	**f**	123 × 4
g	96 ÷ 3	**h**	152 ÷ 8	**i**	144 ÷ 6
j	145 ÷ 6	**k**	272 ÷ 3	**l**	763 ÷ 5

(**j**, **k** and **l** will leave a remainder.)

4 Use the standard method to complete these.

a	135 × 6	**b**	238 × 5	**c**	239 × 4
d	132 × 23	**e**	253 × 14	**f**	143 × 32
g	203 × 27	**h**	152 × 51	**i**	246 × 38
j	4037 × 6	**k**	1032 × 23	**l**	4263 × 17

5 Use a suitable method to complete these division problems.

a	138 ÷ 6	**b**	184 ÷ 8	**c**	273 ÷ 13
d	372 ÷ 12	**e**	504 ÷ 7	**f**	504 ÷ 9

(These problems will leave a remainder.)

g	107 ÷ 4	**h**	164 ÷ 7	**i**	189 ÷ 12
j	361 ÷ 14	**k**	5236 ÷ 6	**l**	9999 ÷ 8

6 Solve each of the following problems by making an approximation.

    a Aoife buys 58 trays of plants at £1.59 a tray.

       Antony buys 72 trays of plants at £1.10 a tray.

       Who spends more?

    b Nadeem eats two packets of crisps a day for a year.

       Each packet costs 43 p.

       Horratio eats one box of cereal a week.

       Each box costs £3.89.

       Who spends more over one year?

7 Estimate the answers to each of these problems using rounding. Do not use a calculator.

    a A robin weighs 18 g.

       It has to eat its own body weight in seeds each day.

       How much seed will the robin eat in a month?

    b Bird seed costs £1.23 per 250 g.

       How much would it cost to feed a robin for a year?

8 These are costs of different cat foods.

    Pouch 32 p   Tin 63 p   Biscuits £1.49   Treats 75 p

    a Axel the cat eats two pouches a day, one packet of biscuits a week and one packet of treats a month. How much does it cost to feed Axel each year?

    b Mittens the cat eats one tin a day, two packets of biscuits a month and one packet of treats each week. How much does it cost to feed Mittens each year?

9 Convert these measurements of time to the units indicated in brackets.

    a 1312 minutes   (into hours and minutes)

    b 87 hours   (into days and hours)

    c 24420 seconds   (into minutes and seconds)

10 Use a calculator to work these out.

    Give your answers to 2 decimal places where appropriate.

    a $(5 + 4.7)^2 \div 3$

    b $\dfrac{58.2 - 1.3^2 \times 3}{\sqrt{4.06 + 9.2}}$

    c $\dfrac{5.2 \times (16.3 - 4.2)^2}{\sqrt{13^2 - 5^2}}$

    d $\dfrac{\sqrt{12.7 - 5^2} + 14.3}{91 - (18.2 + 7.6)^2}$

8 Statistics

Introduction

> Watching TV is as bad for you as smoking cigarettes – every 30 minutes of watching TV shaves 11 minutes off the rest of your life!

This frightening headline certainly makes you think twice about watching TV, but statistics are not always what they seem. Politicians, advertisers and businesses often use techniques like this to represent statistics in order to support the ideas they want you to believe. Watching TV does not really shave 11 minutes off the rest of your life, but people who watch TV for most of their waking day tend to be less active and it is this lack of exercise which is unhealthy.

What's the point?

An appreciation of statistics enables you to critically analyse the sheer wealth of advertising and messaging that you receive every day, and work out what it really all means.

Objectives

By the end of this chapter, you will have learned how to ...

- Identify primary and secondary data.
- Plan how to collect data and use a suitable method to collect it.
- Construct frequency tables for discrete data.
- Interpret and draw bar charts.
- Draw pie charts.
- Find the mode, median, mean and range of a set of data.
- Construct and interpret scatter graphs.
- Construct and use stem-and-leaf diagrams.

Check in

1 Members of the netball club vote for
a new captain.
The results are shown on the bar chart.

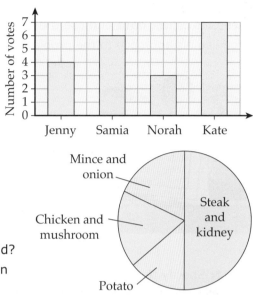

  a How many votes did the winner get?

  b Who got three votes?

  c How many votes did Jenny get?

  d How many people voted in total?

2 The pie chart shows the sale of pies at
Rovers football club.

  a Which type of pie was most popular?

  b Which type of pie sold the least?

In total sixty pies were sold.

  c How many steak and kidney pies were sold?

  d Approximately, how many mince and onion
pies were sold?

Starter problem

Tall people can jump farther.
Investigate if this is true.

Max needs to find out why the number of visitors to his theme park has been low all year.

He needs to collect **data** and use the data-handling cycle to organise his approach to the problem.

Evaluate results

Data-handling cycle

Stage 1
Specify the problem and the plan

Stage 2
Collect data from various sources

Stage 3
Process and represent data

Stage 4
Interpret and discuss data

Stage 1: Specify the problem and the plan.

The problem is that fewer people are visiting Thunder World Theme Park. Max plans to gather data and information that will help explain why this is happening.

Stage 2: Collect data from various **sources**.

⬤ **Primary data** is data that you collect yourself.

Max can carry out surveys and take measurements to gather information and data.

He will need to decide

• what questions he is going to ask

• who is he going to ask

• how he will collect and organise the data.

⬤ **Secondary data** is data that someone else has collected.

Good sources of secondary data are

• newspapers and magazines

• libraries and archives

• the Internet.

	Advantages	Disadvantages
Primary	You get exactly what you want You can trust it	Expensive and time consuming to collect
Secondary	Cheaper, saves time Lots of it	Can you trust it?

Exercise 8a

1 Max asks his staff this question.

'How can we encourage more people to visit Thunder World?'

Do you think each of these suggestions is a good idea or a bad idea?

Explain your answers.

a Charge family groups half-price.

b Give all visitors a free T-shirt.

c Pay us more and we'll work harder.

d Build some new big rides.

e Let anyone called Andrea in for free!

f Free entry for people over 65 years old.

g Open on Christmas day.

h Reduce entry charges on quiet days.

i Advertise more.

2 Max decides he has to be more organised when he collects data.

He makes a list of data-collecting tasks he will do.

Does the data come from primary or secondary sources?

a Max records the number of cars in the car park each day.

b Max checks a website: www.metoffice.gov.uk/climate/uk/

c Max visits four theme parks and takes notes.

d Max prepares a questionnaire for his staff.

e Max gets a book from the library called *Greatest Theme Parks*.

f Max asks his accountant for a spreadsheet of attendance figures.

g Max designs a data-collection sheet for visitors.

h Max gets a local bus and train timetable.

> **Did you know?**
>
>
>
> Theme parks developed from amusement parks. The oldest amusement park in the world is in Denmark and it opened in 1583.

Problem solving

3 Which stage of the data-handling cycle do these events relate to?

a 'The data shows that low attendance is caused by ...'

b 'I am going to draw a pie chart of this data.'

c 'Why are visitor numbers so low?'

d 'I'll get a spreadsheet from the Tourist Information Office.'

Evaluate results.

Stage 1 Specify the problem and the plan.

Stage 2 Collect data from various sources.

Data-handling cycle

Stage 4 Interpret and discuss data.

Stage 3 Process and represent data.

Max and his staff design a **questionnaire** and a **data-collection sheet** to find out why fewer people are visiting Thunder World.

Staff **survey** visitors as they leave Thunder World using a data-collection sheet.

Some visitors are asked to fill in a questionnaire. This takes more time, but gathers more information.

| | Male or female | Age | | | First visit? | Mark 0 to 10 0 = bad 10 = excellent |
		Under 20	21–40	Over 40		
1	M	✓				
2	M	✓			x	8
3	F				✓	6
4	M		✓		✓	5
5	F		✓		x	7
6	F	✓			✓	4
7	M	✓			✓	4
8	F			✓	x	6
9	M		✓		✓	5
10	M		✓		x	8
11	M	✓			✓	9
					x	5

NAME K. REED   M ☐ F ☑
HOME ADDRESS HIGH ROAD SCHOOL, OXFORDSHIRE
1. HOW DID YOU TRAVEL TO THUNDER WORLD?
   CAR ☐   COACH ☑   BUS ☐   TRAIN ☐   OTHER ☐
2. HOW DID YOU HEAR ABOUT THUNDER WORLD?
   FRIENDS TOLD ME
3. WHAT DID YOU ENJOY MOST AT THUNDER WORLD?
   IT WAS OK - THE ARCADE
4. HAS THE VISIT BEEN GOOD VALUE FOR MONEY?
   YES ☐   NO ☑
5. HOW HELPFUL WERE THE STAFF?

One sheet holds the data for many people.

One form is needed for each person.

When writing a questionnaire try to avoid questions which are leading, biased or open-ended. Try to use tick box responses which cover all possible answers and use a scale if you want someone's opinion.

Choosing the right **sample** is important.

Survey too few people and you won't get enough information.

Survey too many and you won't be able to cope.

The sample must also be **representative**: it must reflect a cross-section of the group you are investigating.

Max also uses secondary data that has been collected by other people and organisations. He finds it on the Internet and in books and newspapers. He has to check that it is reliable and that it relates to his investigation.

Spreadsheet from Max's accountant

Data from a website

Newspaper article

Exercise 8b

1   Tara conducts a survey on visitors as they arrive at Thunder World.

She wants to find out what types of people visit the theme park.

Think about the questions she asks and the questionnaire she uses.

What can Tara improve and what should she remove?

> c   How old are you?
> d   Have you visited Thunder World before?
> e   Have you got a girlfriend?
> f   What sort of fun-fair rides do you prefer?
> g   How much money do you have in the bank?
> h   Are you looking forward to your day here?
> i   Have you visited any other theme parks?

> a   I will survey five people.

> b   I will survey only handsome men.

2   Max is planning the first page of his visitor questionnaire.

This is what he wants to know.

> I want to know the gender (male or female) and the age of the visitors.
> I want to know
> • how they heard about Thunder World
> • the distance they travelled to the theme park
> • how they travelled to the theme park
> • if they have visited Thunder World before
> • the name, address and phone number of the visitor.

Design a 'Visitor questionnaire' to collect the data Max wants.

Problem solving

3   Ruby is in charge of the boating lake. She has noticed a number of factors that might affect visitor attendance. She makes a list.
   ● The day of the week
   ● The time of year
   ● Half-term and school holidays
   ● The weather
   a   How could each of these factors affect attendance?
   b   Ruby decides to record data each day for two weeks.
      Design a data-collection sheet she could use.
      Make it clear what data she will collect.

Stage 3: Process and represent data.

Max has collected data about 'How people travel to Thunder World'. The data is **tallied** using a **frequency** table.

Type of transport	Tally	Frequency
Car	||||| ||||| ||||| ||||| ||||| ||||| ||||| ||||| |||	43
Coach	||||| ||||| ||||| ||||| ||||| ||||| ||||| ||||| ||||| ||||| ||||| ||	57
Train	||||| ||||| |||||		16
Bus	||||| ||||| ||||| ||||| ||||| ||	27
Other	|||	3

The next data to be processed is 'The age of visitors'.

14 yrs	27 yrs	19 yrs	1 yr	6 yrs
63 yrs	28 yrs	19 yrs	48 yrs	11 yrs
41 yrs	25 yrs	27 yrs	55 yrs	17 yrs
16 yrs	15 yrs	21 yrs	74 yrs	14 yrs
12 yrs	22 yrs	24 yrs	14 yrs	16 yrs
13 yrs	23 yrs	11 yrs	12 yrs	36 yrs
18 yrs	13 yrs	19 yrs	23 yrs	44 yrs
33 yrs	17 yrs	8 yrs	10 yrs	22 yrs
15 yrs	9 yrs	23 yrs	16 yrs	19 yrs

How should I cope with all these ages? They go from 1 to 74.

You could organise them into four **groups**: 0 to 20 years, 21 to 40 years, 41 to 60 and 60+.

Each group is called a class and they have **class intervals** of 20 years.

> When grouping data, make each class interval the same size. It is useful to make the last class open-ended.

Age	Tally	Frequency
0–20	||||| ||||| ||||| ||||| |||||		26
21–40	||||| ||||| |||	13
41–60	||||	4
60+	||	2

The processed data can then be represented on a frequency diagram, a graph or a chart.

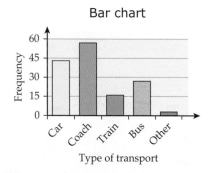
Bar chart

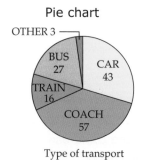
Pie chart

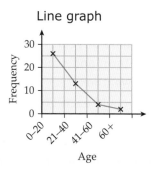
Line graph

Exercise 8c

1 As people enter the theme park they are tallied in a frequency table.

They are sorted into four classes.

a Copy the frequency table.

Tally the data into the frequency table.

Visitor	Tally	Frequency
Man		
Woman		
Boy		
Girl		

b How many people are there in the sample?

c Which is the biggest class?

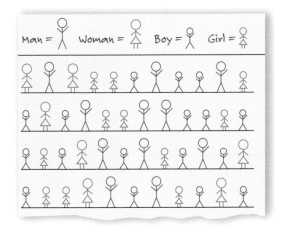

2 Visitors are asked how much money they have spent during the day.

a Copy the frequency table and complete the class intervals.

Total spent (£)	Tally	Frequency
1–5.99		
6–10.99		
11–☐		
☐–☐		
☐–☐		
26+		

b Tally the data into the frequency table.

£8	£12	£28	£14	£19
£3	£18	£22	£7	£16
£11	£21	£18	£34	£4
£14	£21	£21	£7.50	£15
£5	£8.50	£9	£9.25	£14
£12.50	£15	£5.50	£24.50	£6
£13	£10.90	£4.50	£14.60	£9.99

Problem solving

3 Visitors are asked how many kilometres they have travelled to Thunder World.

There is a wide spread of data so the data will have to be grouped.

Decide the size of each class interval and draw a frequency table to record the data.

3 km	14 km	56 km	11 km	23 km	9 km	41 km	4 km	15 km	58 km
8 km	20 km	23 km	16 km	40 km	13 km	7 km	18 km	12 km	27 km
31 km	6 km	45 km	15 km	47 km	58 km	2 km	38 km	23 km	6 km
55 km	26 km	7 km	3 km	33 km	19 km	5 km	14 km	15 km	8 km
23 km	39 km	18 km	32 km	20 km	17 km	29 km	8 km	34 km	31 km

8d Bar charts

⬤ A **bar chart** is used to display **discrete** data.

The bar chart shows how
many doughnuts are sold at
the 'Dough Bar'.
You can see that chocolate is
the most popular flavour.
Chocolate is the **mode**.
Custard is the least popular
flavour.

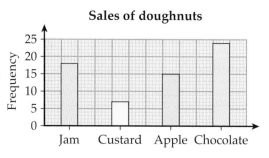

Sales of doughnuts

Discrete data is
data that can be
counted.

⬤ When drawing a bar chart, or any other chart or graph, give it a
title and label any axis.

150 people are surveyed and asked to vote for their favourite ride.

Here are the results.
26 vote for the
Haunted House.
35 vote for The Tomb.
49 vote for Typhoon.
40 vote for the
Ghost Train.

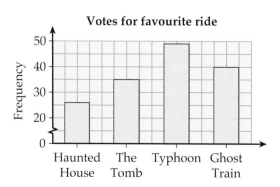

Votes for favourite ride

The vertical axis has a
broken scale. This is
used when values close
to 0 are not needed.
In this case the scale
starts at 20 because all
the rides received at
least 20 votes.

⬤ A comparative bar chart gives you more information about the
data in each group.

This bar chart shows the number of visitors to
each attraction *and* tells you the gender of the
visitors; male and female.
The Typhoon is the most popular attraction
with both males and females.
The Typhoon is the mode for both males and
females.

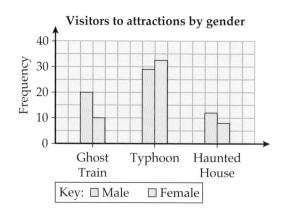

Visitors to attractions by gender

Key: ☐ Male   ☐ Female

Exercise 8d

1 The bar chart shows attendances at four of the attractions.

   a How many people visited the Spinner?

   b Which attraction is the mode?

   c Which attraction had 25 visitors?

   d How many people visited these four attractions in total?

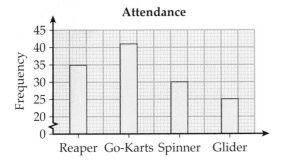

2 The staff at Thunder World vote for their new Team Leader.

Name	Tally	Frequency
Laura	卌 卌 ‖	12
Harry	卌 ‖‖	9
Carlos	卌 卌 ‖‖	14
Jenny	卌 卌 卌 ‖‖	19

   a Copy these axes.

   b Use the data collected in the frequency table to draw a bar chart.

2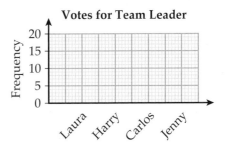

3 Visitors are asked 'How much did you enjoy your visit?'

The four choices are Poor, Fair, Good and Excellent.

The results are recorded in a frequency table.

Answer	Poor	Fair	Good	Excellent
Number of votes	11	7	29	18

   a Draw a bar chart to display this data.

   b Give the title 'Happy Visitors' to your bar chart.

Did you know?

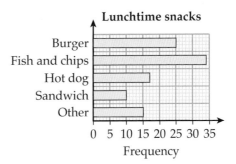

It is believed that the first bar chart was used in 1786 in a book by William Playfair.

Problem solving

4 **a** What is this survey about?

   b What is the mode?

   c How many people had hot dogs?

   d Which food item was chosen 17 times?

   e How many people were surveyed?

   f What might 'Other' mean?

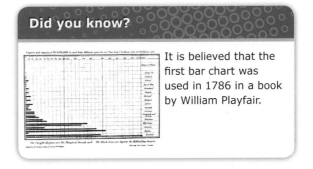

Forty people at Thunder World vote for their favourite flavour of ice cream.

The three **categories** are strawberry, vanilla and chocolate.

The results are recorded in a **frequency** table.

Flavour	Tally	Frequency
Strawberry	ⵗⵗ ⵗⵗ	10
Vanilla	ⵗⵗ	5
Chocolate	ⵗⵗ ⵗⵗ ⵗⵗ ⵗⵗ ⵗⵗ	25

You can show the results in a pie chart.

There are 40 votes and each voter is recorded as a 'slice' on the chart.

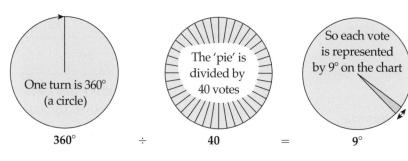

One turn is 360° (a circle)

The 'pie' is divided by 40 votes

So each vote is represented by 9° on the chart

360° ÷ 40 = 9°

Check! Do all your angles add up to 360°?

To calculate the angle for a category, use the pie chart formula

$$\text{Angle} = \frac{360}{\text{total of all frequencies}} \times \text{frequency for category}$$

Flavour	Tally	Frequency	Angle
Strawberry	ⵗⵗ ⵗⵗ	10	10 × 9° = 90°
Vanilla	ⵗⵗ	5	5 × 9° = 45°
Chocolate	ⵗⵗ ⵗⵗ ⵗⵗ ⵗⵗ ⵗⵗ	25	25 × 9° = 225°
Total		40	360°

Now you can draw the pie chart.

You show Strawberry by a **sector** that is 90°.

You show Vanilla by a sector that is 45°.

You show Chocolate by a sector that is 225°.

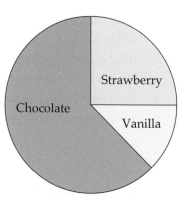

Exercise 8e

1 Thirty-six young children are asked if they believe in Santa Claus.
   They can answer 'Yes', 'No' or 'Don't know'.
   The data is collected in a frequency table.
   The angle for each category has been worked out.

Category	Tally	Frequency	Angle
Yes	卌 卌 卌 IIII	19	$19 \times 10°$ $= 190°$
No	卌 卌	10	$10 \times 10°$ $= 100°$
Don't know	卌 II	7	$7 \times 10°$ $= 70°$
Total	卌 卌 卌 卌 卌 卌 卌 I	36	360°

> There are 36 children, so divide 360° by 36 to find the angle for one child on the pie chart.
> $360° \div 36 = 10°$
> Each child is 10° of the pie chart.

a Draw a circle about 10 cm in *diameter*.

b Using a protractor, draw the angles for each category.

c Colour code the chart and provide a key for the three categories.

d Give your chart the title 'Who believes in Santa?'

2 Staff record the weather conditions at Thunder World for the 30 days of September.
   The frequency table shows the results.

Weather	Tally	Frequency
Wet	卌 卌 II	12
Hot	卌 卌 I	11
Cold	卌 II	7

a Draw a pie chart to show this information.

b Colour code each sector of the pie chart and provide a key.

c Give your pie chart the title 'September Weather Record'.

3 The fast food bar at Thunder World sold the following main meals on a busy day in July.

Meal	Frequency
Beef burger	19
Cheese burger	44
Chicken drum-sticks	21
Pizza	36

Draw a pie chart to display this data.

Problem solving

4 The twelve members of the School Council vote for an end-of-term activity.
   There are three suggestions: ice-skating, the cinema or a theme park.
   The votes are recorded in a frequency table.
   Draw a pie chart to display the data.
   Give your pie chart the title 'End-of-term activity'.

Activity	Tally	Frequency
Ice-skating	III	3
Cinema	II	2
Theme park	卌 II	7

5 In a survey 90 people were asked 'Do you eat five portions of fruit and vegetables a day? Yes or No'. The results are shown in a pie chart.
   If the angle of the Yes sector is 92°, how many people said Yes?

8f Calculating averages

One Tuesday lunchtime, Tim Ryder collects some information on the size of groups visiting Thunder World. He takes a small **sample** of data.

> An **average** is a typical value for a set of data.

The **mode**, the **median** and the **mean** are three different types of average.

> The **mode** is the most commonly occurring value.

2, 2, 2, 3, 5, 6, 8
The mode is 2.

You can have more than one mode.
In this data set, 5 and 7 are the modes.
3, 5, 5, 6, 7, 7, 8, 10

> The **median** is the middle value when you write the values in order from smallest to biggest.

2, 2, 2, 3, 5, 6, 8
The median is 3.

When there is an even number of values, the median is halfway between the two middle values.
5, 8, 10, 14, 15, 18
        ↓
        12

> You find the **mean** by adding all the values and dividing this total by the number of values.

2 + 2 + 2 + 3 + 5 + 6 + 8 = 28
28 ÷ 7 = 4
The mean is 4.

The total of the values is 28. There are 7 items.

> The **range** tells you how spread out the data is.
>   ▶ It is the difference between the largest and smallest values.

2, 2, 2, 3, 5, 6, 8   Range = 8 − 2 = 6
The range is 6.

Example

Here is a small sample of data. 6, 4, 9, 7, 1, 4, 8, 5
a   Write the values in order, starting with the smallest.
b   Find i the mode ii the median iii the mean iv the range.

- - - - - - - - - -

a   1, 4, 4, 5, 6, 7, 8, 9
b   i   The mode is 4.
    ii   The median is 5.5.   The median is half-way between 5 and 6.
    iii   1 + 4 + 4 + 5 + 6 + 7 + 8 + 9 = 44   Add all the data values
        44 ÷ 8 = 5.5   Divide by the number of data values
        The mean is 5.5.
    iv   The range is 8   9 − 1 = 8

146   **Statistics and probability** Statistics

5

Exercise 8f

1 Tim goes to the rollercoaster and records the ages of the riders.

   a Write the ages in order, from smallest to largest.

   b What is the range of ages?

   c What is the modal age?

   d What is the median age?

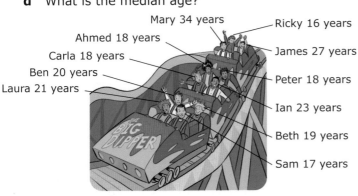

Mary 34 years
Ricky 16 years
Ahmed 18 years
James 27 years
Carla 18 years
Peter 18 years
Ben 20 years
Ian 23 years
Laura 21 years
Beth 19 years
Sam 17 years

3 Eddie throws nine darts at the target.

   a What is his total score?

   b What is the modal score?

   c What is the median score?

   d What is the mean score?

2 Tim decides that this sample is too small, so he records the ages of passengers on the next five rides.
Here are his results.

14 years	19 years	22 years	21 years	15 years
25 years	17 years	16 years	20 years	27 years
31 years	25 years	28 years	19 years	22 years
17 years	19 years	29 years	15 years	20 years
18 years	17 years	23 years	17 years	25 years

   a What is the range of the ages?

   b What is the median age?

   c What is the modal age?

4 Ten visitors are asked how many hours they stayed at Thunder World.
These are their responses.

4 hrs 5 hrs   5 hrs 3 hrs $5\frac{1}{2}$ hrs

7 hrs $6\frac{1}{2}$ hrs 6 hrs 5 hrs 2 hrs

What is the mean time spent at Thunder World?

Problem solving

5 Five boxes are set out in order of weight; the lightest box is on the left.
The heaviest box has a weight of 7 kg.

   a Use the clues to work out the weight of each box.

   b What is the total weight of the boxes?

a	b	c	d	7 kg

The median weight is 4 kg.   The mean weight is 4 kg.
The modal weight is 2 kg.   The range is 5 kg.

All weights are in whole kilograms.

⬤ A **scatter graph** shows the relationship between two sets of data.

The outside temperature and the number of ice creams sold are recorded for 20 days.

The data is displayed on two **axes**.

On Day 1 the temperature was 14 °C and eight ice creams were sold.

This **data point** is marked with a cross at (8, 14).

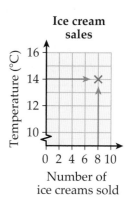

⬤ Show each data point, on a scatter graph, using a cross.

This table shows the data for all 20 days.

Day	1	2	3	4	5	6	7	8	9	10	11	12	13	14	15	16	17	18	19	20
Temp. (°C)	14	11	12	16	19	20	20	23	25	21	26	24	22	23	15	18	19	21	18	16
Sales	8	5	12	20	24	28	26	32	40	28	50	42	30	41	10	30	28	31	22	14

Displaying the data on a scatter graph helps you to see the relationship between temperature and the sale of ice creams.

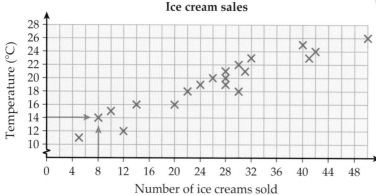

The scatter graph shows there is a strong link between the temperature and the sale of ice creams.

The scatter graph shows that the warmer it is, the more ice creams are sold.

Exercise 8g

1 Ms Kent, the librarian, notices that when the weather is cold many more students visit the library at lunchtime.
For ten days she records the temperature outside and the number of students in the library at lunchtime.

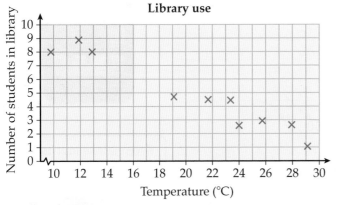

Library use

a Are Ms Kent's suspicions supported by the data?

b Looking at the graph, how many students would you expect in the library when the temperature outside is 17°C?

2 At the Go-kart track, staff are worried by the number of collisions occurring.
They record the speed of the go-karts and the number of collisions that occur.

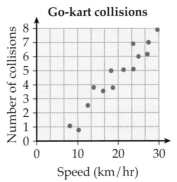

Go-kart collisions

Are these statements true or false?

a There is a link between speed and the number of collisions.

b There is no link between speed and the number of collisions.

c The results show more speed, more collisions.

d The results show less speed, more collisions.

3 Eighteen adults are attending a First Aid course.
The course lasts for eight evenings.
Many people fail to attend all parts of the course.
Will this affect their exam results?

a Copy these axes.
The table records how many times each person attended and their exam mark. Plot this data on your graph.

b Does your graph show that poor attendance resulted in a lower exam mark?

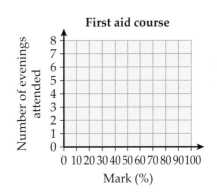

First aid course

No. of evenings attended	5	2	7	6	8	7	4	8	6	3	4	7	6	8	8	5	5	3
Mark (%)	50	10	60	65	90	70	30	85	55	30	35	65	60	95	85	45	40	15

● You can use a stem-and-leaf diagram to display ordered numerical data.

Class 9G **record** the number of text messages they each send over the weekend. The data is collected and then written out in order.
You can display the data on a **stem-and-leaf diagram**.

Number of texts				
11	15	16	16	16
16	19	20	22	23
24	24	26	27	28
29	31	32	37	39
40	44	45	52	53

50   2

The stem shows the tens digit of each number, the leaf shows the units.

```
5 | 2 3
4 | 0 4 5
3 | 1 2 7 9
2 | 0 2 3 4 4 6 7 8 9
1 | 1 5 6 6 6 6 9
```

Key 5|2 stands for 52

Remember to include a key to explain the scale.

● A stem-and-leaf diagram makes it easier to find the range and averages.

The **range** is the difference between the largest and the smallest data value.

The range is 53 – 11 = 42 texts.

Look for repeated digits in a row.

The **mode** is the most common data value.

The modal number of texts is 16.

The **modal group** is the group with the highest frequency.

The modal group is 20 to 29 texts.

Look for the longest row.

The **median** is the middle value.

There are 25 pieces of data.
The middle value is the 13th value.

The median is 26 texts.

Count along the rows.

Exercise 8h

1 In a competition, students each threw two darts at a dart board.
Their scores are shown on the stem-and-leaf diagram.

Darts competition scores

```
5 | 0 4
4 | 4 7 8
3 | 0 0 4 5 8
2 | 1 5 5 5 7 7 9
1 | 0 2 6
0 | 9
```
Key 5|0 stands for 50

   a How many people took part?
   b What was the highest score?
   c What was the lowest score?
   d What was the range of the scores?
   e How many people scored between 40 and 49?
   f Which was the modal group?
   g What was the median score?

2 Here are the results of an end-of-term science test.

8	9	16	18	20
23	25	27	31	32
34	34	34	34	35
37	38	38	39	40
41	46	47	49	49
51	53	55		

2 **Results of science test**

```
5 | _____
4 | _____
3 | _____
2 | _____
1 | _____
0 | _____
```
Key 5|5 stands for 55

   a Copy and complete this stem-and-leaf diagram.
   b What is the modal score for the test?
   c What is the range of scores?

3 Here is a record of the number of merits earned by class 9H.

12	17	19	21	24
28	33	35	36	37
37	38	39	44	47
48	49	50	54	57
62	64	66	74	76

   a Draw the stem of a stem-and-leaf diagram.
   b Put each number on the right stem.
   c Draw a key to explain the scale.
   d Use your diagram to find the range of the data.
   e What is the modal group?
   f What is the median value?

Problem solving

4 The height of students is measured at the start of the school year and again at the end of the year.
Here is a record of the increases in height, in centimetres.

Growth (centimetres)								
1.7	1.8	2.3	2.8	2.8	3.0	3.8	4.3	4.6
4.7	4.7	4.7	4.7	4.9	5.2	5.8	5.8	5.9

Record of growth

```
5 | 
4 | 
3 | 
2 | 
1 | 7  8
```
Key

Copy and complete this stem-and-leaf diagram.
The first two data values have been done for you.
Use the range and an average to describe the data.

● A **frequency diagram** displays continuous data.

● Continuous data is data that is measured.

Examples are time, temperature, weight and length.
Twenty-seven students are weighed.
Their weights, in kilograms, are recorded.

| 32 32 33 34 38 39 | 40 40 41 42 42 44 45 47 47 48 49 | 51 52 55 56 58 59 59 | 62 64 65 |

The data is organised into a frequency table.

Weight (w kg)	Tally	Frequency
$30 \leq w < 40$	⊞ |	6
$40 \leq w < 50$	⊞ ⊞ |	11
$50 \leq w < 60$	⊞ ||	7
$60 \leq w < 70$	|||	3

Each group is called a **class**.

All the class intervals are the same, 10 kg.

The data is gathered in intervals of 10.

The first **class interval** is

$$30 \leq w < 40$$

weights at least 30 kg   but less than 40 kg

w = weight

Weight (kilograms)

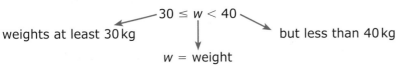

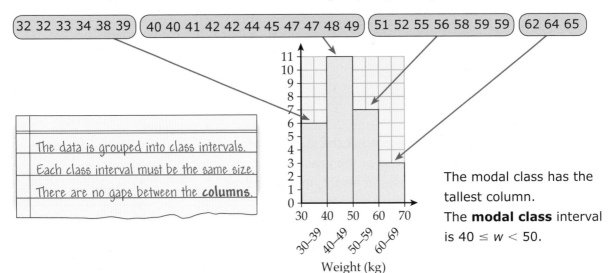

The data is grouped into class intervals.
Each class interval must be the same size.
There are no gaps between the **columns**.

The modal class has the tallest column.
The **modal class** interval is $40 \leq w < 50$.

Exercise 8i

1 The heights of students are measured at the start of the school year and again at the end of the year.

Here is a record of the increases in height, in centimetres.

Increase (centimetres)
4.5 4.8 4.9 5.0 5.1 5.4 5.4 5.4 5.7 5.9 5.9
6.1 6.3 6.5 6.8 7.3 7.4 7.6 7.7 8.2 8.5

a Use the data to find

  i the range of measurements

  ii the median of the measurements.

The data is organised in a frequency table.

Growth (g cm)	Tally	Frequency
$4 \leq g < 5$	|||	3
$5 \leq g < 6$	⸾⸾⸾⸾ |||	
$6 \leq g < 7$		
$7 \leq g < 8$		
$8 \leq g < 9$		

b Copy and complete the frequency table.

1 c Copy the axes.

Use the data to complete the frequency diagram.

d How many students grew between 4 and 6 cm?

e How many students grew between 7 and 9 cm?

f What is the modal class?

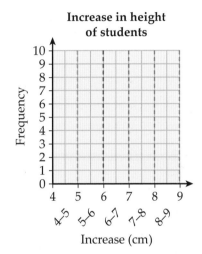

Increase in height of students

Problem solving

2 These diagrams show the amount of time students spend doing homework each night.

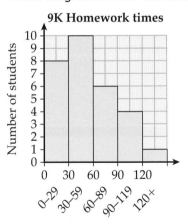

Time spent on homework (minutes)

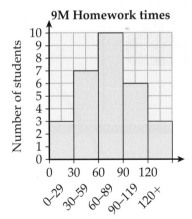

Time spent on homework (minutes)

Assignments

a How many students in 9K spend between 30 and 59 minutes each night doing homework?

b How many students in 9M spend between 60 and 119 minutes each night doing homework?

c What is the modal class for time spent doing homework for each class?

 **MyMaths**.co.uk Q 1196 SEARCH

Stage 4: Interpret and discuss data.

Max and his staff have worked through the data-handling cycle.

He has worked through a checklist and displayed the data in charts, tables and graphs.

He must now prepare a report for the Board of Directors.

In his report he needs to explain the findings of his **investigation**.

- Plan how to collect and record **data**. ✓
- Make sure you ask the right questions. ✓
- Check the results carefully. ✓
- Ensure that the **sample** is large enough and is representative. ✓

Interpreting data means explaining what you found.

To do this look back at the question you started with and make sure you are answering the question.

1   Title page

2   Contents list

To help the reader find different sections of the report.

3   Introduction

Explain what the investigation is about.

4   Results

Explain how the data was gathered. Display the data in graphs, charts and tables. Interpret the data.

5   Conclusions

Look back at the original question and answer it clearly.

Conclusions

There are two factors affecting attendance.

– Bad weather affected the number of visitors.

  Action   More indoor attractions are planned and covered walkways to be built.

– Visitors found Thunder World expensive.

  Action   Prices are to be reduced and special group and family deals advertised.

Exercise 8j

Problem solving

1 What could Max use as a title for his report?

2 **a** Write a brief statement stating the reason for Max's investigation.

b The **comparison** bar chart compares last year's attendance figures with the figures for this year.
   Does it support Max's statement that attendance figures have fallen?

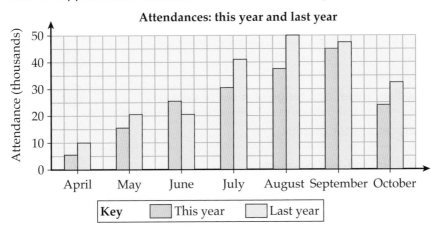

Attendances: this year and last year

| Key | This year | Last year |

c Which was the busiest month last year?

d Which was the busiest month this year?

e How many thousands of people visited Thunder World in May last year?

f How many thousands visited during May this year?

3 **a** How did Max and his staff gather data and information to help with the investigation?

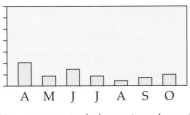

Mean average rainfall over 10 years

Rainfall records for this year

b Max presented these two bar charts.
   How might this data explain low attendance this year?

4 Max also presented this pie chart.

   a What does it say about people's attitudes towards Thunder World?

   b What might the Directors do to change this situation?

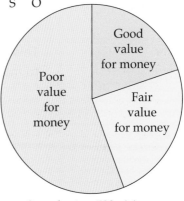

Sample size: 500 visitors

8 MySummary

Check out

You should now be able to ...

Test it ➡

Questions

✓ Plan how to collect data and use a suitable method to collect it.	4	1
✓ Construct frequency tables for discrete data.	4	2
✓ Interpret and draw bar charts.	5	3
✓ Draw pie charts.	6	4
✓ Find the mode, median, mean and range of a set of data.	5	5
✓ Construct and interpret scatter graphs.	6	6
✓ Construct and use stem-and-leaf diagrams.	6	7

Language	Meaning	Example
Class interval	One of the groups that data can be divided into.	$40 \leq a < 60$ contains ages from 40 years, but less than 60 years.
Continuous data	Continuous data can take any value between given limits.	The height of each student in your class.
Discrete data	Discrete data can take only certain definite values.	The number of siblings for each student in your class.
Primary data	Primary data is data which you collect yourself.	A questionnaire which you have written and distributed.
Secondary data	Secondary data is data that someone else has collected.	Data from the Internet, newspapers, magazines or books.
Tally	This groups items into fives, to make it easier to count.	⫴⫲ represents 7

1 Pippa is going to stand at the entrance to a supermarket and record whether the shoppers
   – are male or female and
   – have brought their own shopping bags.
   Design a data-collection sheet for her to use.

2 Pippa also asks people leaving the supermarket how much they have spent and records the answers.

£69	£34	£55	£18.42
£4.50	£9.99	£75	£25.13
£37	£48	£62	£8.45
£15	£22	£37	£18.99

Copy and complete the frequency table

Amount Spent (£)	Tally	Frequency
0–9.99		
10–19.99		
20–29.99		
30–39.99		
40–49.99		
50–59.99		
60–69.99		
70–79.99		

3 Out of the 20 people Pippa asked, 13 had brought their own shopping bags and 7 had not.
   Draw a bar chart to display this data.

4 Children have a choice of three dinners in a school canteen. The table shows what they chose to eat.

Food	Frequency
Roast Chicken	35
Chilli	15
Vegetable Lasagne	10

Draw a pie chart to show this information.

5 The age of children in a playground were

| 1 | 3 | 2 | 5 | 4 | 6 |
| 1 | 1 | 1 | 3 | 2 | 1 |

a Find the mode.
b Calculate the mean.
c Find the median.
d Calculate the range.

6 The number of sandwiches and packs of crisps sold at a cafe on different days is shown in the table.

Sandwiches	55	30	40	20	10	25	50
Crisps	25	15	20	5	2	15	20

a Draw a scatter diagram for this data.
b Describe the correlation.

7 Here are the scores of students in a maths test.

| 4 | 18 | 23 | 28 | 31 | 32 | 32 | 34 |
| 36 | 38 | 40 | 42 | 43 | 43 | 43 | 47 |

Draw a stem-and-leaf diagram to display this data.

What next?

Score	0 – 3		Your knowledge of this topic is still developing. To improve look at Formative test: 3A-8; MyMaths: 1192, 1193, 1196, 1200, 1203, 1205, 1206, 1207, 1212, 1213, 1215 and 1248
	4 – 6		You are gaining a secure knowledge of this topic. To improve look at InvisiPen: 411, 414, 415, 422, 423, 426, 427, 431, 441 and 448
	7		You have mastered this topic. Well done, you are ready to progress!

1 Decide whether each source of data is primary or secondary.

   a Surveying the students in your class about their favourite food.

   b Data from a newspaper about popular takeaway companies.

2 Andrea surveys the students in her class. She wants to find out their age, gender and if they are vegetarian. Design a data-collection sheet for her to use.

3 Students on a field trip are asked to vote for what they want to eat on the final night of their visit. Copy and complete this frequency table from the data.

Burgers   Burgers   Fish & chips
Chinese   Fish & chips   Fish & chips
Curry   Fish & chips   Kebab   Burgers
Chinese   Burgers   Fish & chips
Burgers   Curry   Vegetarian   Burgers   Curry
Curry   Fish & chips   Fish & chips   Burgers
Fish and chips   Burgers   Burgers   Fish & chips
Curry   Vegetarian   Burgers
Vegetarian   Kebab   Burgers   Fish & chips
Fish & chips   Chinese   Fish & chips

Food	Tally	Frequency
Burgers		
Fish & chips		
Kebab		
Chinese		
Vegetarian		
Curry		

4 **a** Draw a bar chart from the frequency table in question **3**.

   b How many people voted in total?

   c What was the modal choice of food?

5 Andrea wants to display the data from question **3** as a pie chart.

   a Complete the sentence: 'Each student is _____ of the pie chart.'

   b Draw the pie chart. Use a colour code or key to explain each sector.

6 These are the sizes of shoes sold in one day in the men's shoe department.

   a Write out the shoe sizes in order, smallest to largest.

   b What is the modal size?

   c What is the median size?

   d What is the range of sizes?

Shoe sizes				
6	8	8	7	10
8	10	9	9	12
7	10	11	8	8
9	9	8	9	9
6	10	11	7	8

7 Leon and Ben play for the school basketball team.

   In matches Leon has scored 4, 10, 4, 5, 7 and 6.

   In matches Ben has scored 5, 9, 8 and 6. Who has the best mean score?

8 Ms DaCosta uses taxis to travel around.
The scatter diagram shows the relationship between distance and cost.
a What distance was the longest
trip she took?
b What is the most she has paid
for a journey?
How much might she expect to
pay if she travels
c 3.5 km?   d 10 km?

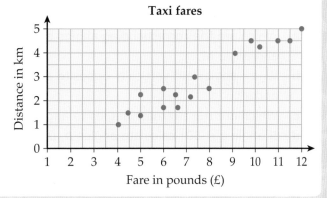

Taxi fares

9 The BusCo bus company records the number of passengers
on the Route 13 bus for one day. The bus makes 30 trips.
The stem-and-leaf diagram shows the data.
a Which was the modal group?
b What was the median number of passengers?
c What was the range of passenger numbers?

Passengers on Route 13

```
5 | 2 3 5
4 | 1 3 3 5 6 9
3 | 0 0 2 4 6 6 7 8 8 9
2 | 0 3 7
1 | 4 5 5 5 5 8
0 | 5 7
```

| Key 5 | 5 = 55 |

10 Thirty students took a history test. Their marks are shown
in the table.

48	44	43	41	40	39	39	39	36	34
31	31	29	28	28	27	26	25	25	23
22	21	20	19	18	18	17	16	15	11

Draw a stem-and-leaf diagram to display the data.

11 The data from question **10** is organised in a
frequency table.
a Copy and complete the frequency table.
b Draw a frequency diagram.

Marks, m	Frequency
$10 \leq m < 20$	7
$20 \leq m < 30$	
$30 \leq m < 40$	
$40 \leq m < 50$	

12 The BusCo bus company recorded the number of passengers on the Route 13 bus
on the same day during the previous year. During the 30 trips the largest number
of passengers was 42 and the median was 27.
Does the data support the claim that the number of passengers using the Route
13 bus has increased?

MyAssessment 2

These questions will test you on your knowledge of the topics in chapters 5 to 8.

They give you practice in the types of questions that you may see in your GCSE exams.

There are 90 marks in total.

1   a   Which are the corresponding angles to angle a
        and angle b?   (2 marks)

    b   Which angles are vertically opposite angles v
        and x?   (2 marks)

    c   Which are the alternate angles to angles c and d?   (2 marks)

    d   If angle $a = 50°$ calculate angles b, u, v, w and x.   (5 marks)

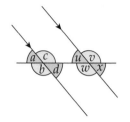

2   a   Find the size of the angles marked with letters.   (2 marks)

    b   What names do we give to these triangles?   (2 marks)

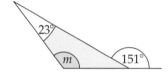

3   This is an isosceles trapezium.

    a   Give three properties of an isosceles trapezium.   (3 marks)

    b   Find the sizes of angles x, y and z.   (2 marks)

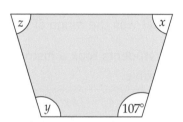

4   a   Draw x- and y-axes from -5 to +5 on square grid paper and plot
        the points (-5, 4) (-3, 4) (-1, 4) (1, 4) and (3, 4).   (2 marks)

    b   What is the equation of the line that joins these points together?   (1 mark)

    c   Draw the line that corresponds to the equation $x = -3$ on your graph.   (2 marks)

    d   What is the coordinate of the point where the two lines cross?   (2 marks)

5   Use the same axes as above.

    a   Complete the table of values for the equation $y = x - 3$ (3 marks)

x	-2	-1	0	1	2	3	4	5
y								

    b   Plot these coordinates on your graph and join the points with a
        straight line.   (3 marks)

    c   What are the coordinates of the point where the straight line meets
        the line $y = 0$?   (2 marks)

    d   Complete this sentence.

        'The points move … square up for every … square across'   (2 marks)

6 This perfume bottle is filled at a steady rate.
Draw a sketch of the height of the perfume versus time. 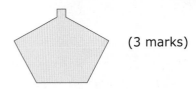 (3 marks)

7 Work out these calculations using a mental method.
    a 21 + 13 + 7   **b** 86 − 38   **c** 87.6 + 124.2   **d** 543.7 − 349.1 (4 marks)

8 Work out these calculations using a mental method.
Make an estimate of the answer before you start each calculation.
    a 18 × 7   **b** 6 × 46   **c** 78 ÷ 3   **d** 216 ÷ 9   (4 marks)

9 Work out these calculations using a written method.
    a 145 × 26   **b** 43.7 × 9   **c** $16\overline{)464}$ **d** 572 ÷ 12   (8 marks)

10 Solve each of these problems using your calculator.
    a Convert 256 hours into days and hours.   (4 marks)
    b The cost of 46 seats on a coach at £5.68 per person.   (2 marks)
    c The annual salary of a worker who works 40 hours per week for
       48 weeks at £13.56 per hour.   (3 marks)

11 What is the difference between **primary** and **secondary** data?   (2 marks)

12 Design a questionnaire to collect this information.
    a How did you travel to school today?   (2 marks)
    b How old are you?   (2 marks)

13 The masses (in grams) of 20 plum tomatoes were recorded as follows.
    52 49 46 51 46 45 41 40 60 37
    50 46 46 51 44 42 51 52 42 39
    a Construct a frequency table to show this data using class intervals
       36–40, 41–45, 46–50, 51–55 and 56–60.   (3 marks)
    b Draw a bar chart to represent this information.   (3 marks)
    c Determine the mode, median and range for this data.   (3 marks)
    d Calculate the mean mass for this set of tomatoes.   (2 marks)

14 In a local health clinic study the results of weight (kg) versus blood pressure
(mm of mercury) was studied in eight men with these results.

Weight (kg)	67.2	66.8	76.2	75.0	89.8	100.4	55.8	72.8
Blood pressure (mm of mercury)	70	65	80	75	85	90	60	70

    a Draw a scatter graph for this data. The *x*-axis is taken from
       50 to 110 kg and the *y*-axis from 50 to 100 mm of mercury.   (5 marks)
    b Draw the best straight line through the points.   (1 mark)
    c Comment on the correlation.   (2 marks)

9 Transformations and symmetry

Introduction

Since the 15th century artists have used the ideas of perspective to draw pictures of three dimensional objects and images. The use of construction lines which meet at a 'vanishing point' allows the artist to accurately draw and position smaller objects so that they appear to be in the distance and therefore give the illusion of depth to the picture.

What's the point?

The construction lines and vanishing points used by artists are based upon the mathematics used to construct enlargements.

Objectives

By the end of this chapter, you will have learned how to ...

- Recognise reflection and rotational symmetry of 2D shapes.
- Reflect shapes in mirror lines.
- Use vectors to translate shapes in any direction.
- Rotate shapes about a centre of rotation.
- Enlarge shapes using whole number and fractional scale factors.
- Enlarge shapes through a centre of enlargement.
- Use and draw scale drawings.

Check in

1 Which of these shapes have at least one line of symmetry?

a   b   c   d

2 The triangle A has moved to a new position shown by triangle B.
Comment on whether it has
a been enlarged b been reduced c remained unchanged in size.

3 The jagged shape has been rotated. Estimate how many
degrees it has turned each time.

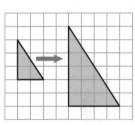

a  b  c   d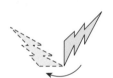

4 What do you notice about the lengths of the sides of the
two triangles?

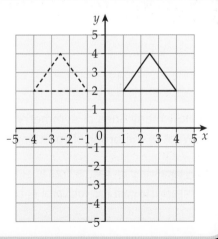

Starter problem

A shape (object) is reflected in the y-axis. There is a
quick way to predict the coordinates of each vertex
of the new shape (image).
Investigate rules for finding the image coordinates
for this and other transformations.

9a Reflection and rotation symmetry

● A **line of symmetry** divides a shape into two identical halves.

● A shape has **reflection symmetry** if it has at least one line of symmetry.

● A shape has **rotational symmetry** if it rotates onto itself more than once in a full turn.

● The **order of rotational symmetry** is the number of times a shape looks exactly like itself in a complete turn.

You can find the line of symmetry by using a mirror or by folding the shape.

You can use tracing paper to find the order of rotational symmetry.

This flower has rotational symmetry of order 4.

Example

The diagram shows a regular hexagon.
a Draw on the lines of reflection symmetry.
b State the order of rotational symmetry.

a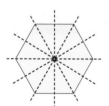

b order 6

▲ This crab has one vertical line of symmetry, but no rotation symmetry.

Example

a How many lines of symmetry does a parallelogram have?
b What is the order of rotational symmetry for a parallelogram?

a A parallelogram has no lines of symmetry.
b A parallelogram has rotational symmetry order 2.

Exercise 9a

1 You see these symbols inside a lift.
Draw each symbol and draw any lines of symmetry.
State the order of rotational symmetry in each case.

a   b   c

d   e   f

2 This shape has two lines of reflection symmetry and rotational symmetry of order 2.

2 lines of   Rotational
symmetry   symmetry
         of order 2

Draw these shapes and describe their symmetry in a similar way.

a   b

c   d

3 The lines of reflection symmetry of a rhombus are along the diagonals.
The angle shown is 50°.
Calculate the four interior angles of the rhombus.

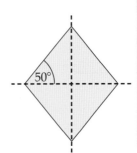

4 Draw each quadrilateral and give its mathematical name.
On each diagram, draw any lines of symmetry and state the order of rotational symmetry.

a   b   c

d   e

f   g

Problem solving

5 a Place a mirror on a copy of these two squares to form these shapes.

b Draw these shapes and describe what they all have in common.

6 Can you draw a shape that has
- rotational symmetry but no reflection symmetry
- reflection symmetry but no rotational symmetry?
Give examples of each case.

9b Reflection

> When you **reflect** an **object** in a **mirror line** its position changes but its size and angles remain the same.

The position of the **image** depends on the position of the mirror line.

‹ P.94

> A vertical mirror line changes only the x-coordinates.

> A horizontal mirror line changes only the y-coordinates.

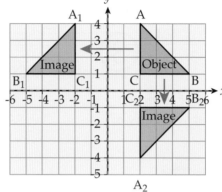

A $(2, 4) \rightarrow A_1 (-2, 4)$
B $(5, 1) \rightarrow B_1 (-5, 1)$
C $(2, 1) \rightarrow C_1 (-2, 1)$

A $(2, 4) \rightarrow A_2 (2, -4)$
B $(5, 1) \rightarrow B_2 (5, -1)$
C $(2, 1) \rightarrow C_2 (2, -1)$

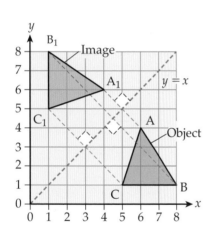

> The diagonal line $y = x$ swaps the x- and y-coordinates.

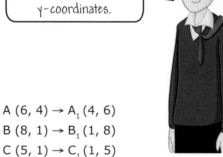

A $(6, 4) \rightarrow A_1 (4, 6)$
B $(8, 1) \rightarrow B_1 (1, 8)$
C $(5, 1) \rightarrow C_1 (1, 5)$

Example

These are the coordinates of a triangle ABC and its image after a reflection, $A_1B_1C_1$.
A$(1, 5) \rightarrow A_1(11, 5)$, B$(4, 1) \rightarrow B_1(8, 1)$, C$(1, 1) \rightarrow C_1(11, 1)$

a Has the triangle been reflected in a vertical mirror line or a horizontal mirror line? Explain your answer.

b What is the equation of the mirror line?

- - - - - - -

a Triangle ABC has been reflected in a vertical mirror line because only the x-coordinates have changed.

b First plot triangles ABC and $A_1B_1C_1$ on a grid. The mirror line is vertical and is halfway between the object and image.
The equation of the mirror line is $x = 6$.

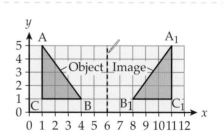

Exercise 9b

1 a Copy this diagram.

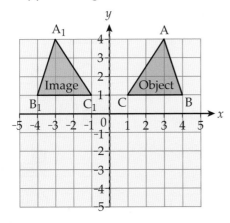

b Draw the mirror line on your diagram.
c What is the equation of the mirror line?
d Reflect triangle $A_1B_1C_1$ in the x-axis.
  Label the image $A_2B_2C_2$.
e What are the coordinates of the
  vertices of triangle $A_2B_2C_2$?
f Reflect ABC in the x-axis.
  Label the image $A_3B_3C_3$.
g What are the coordinates of the
  vertices of triangle $A_3B_3C_3$?
h Describe the reflection that takes
  triangle $A_2B_2C_2$ to $A_3B_3C_3$.

2 a Copy this diagram.

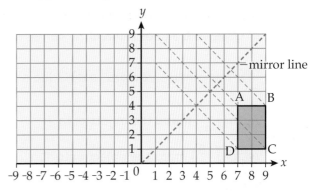

b Reflect rectangle ABCD in the mirror line.
  Label the vertices of the image $A_1B_1C_1D_1$.
c What is the equation of the mirror line?
d Reflect rectangle $A_1B_1C_1D_1$ in the y-axis.
  Label the image $A_2B_2C_2D_2$.
e What are the coordinates of the
  vertices of rectangle $A_2B_2C_2D_2$?

3 a Reflect the point A(5, 8) in the y-axis.
  What are the coordinates of its image?
b Reflect the point B(2, 6) in the x-axis.
  What are the coordinates of its image?
c Reflect the point C(3, 5) in the line
  $y = x$.
  What are the coordinates of its image?

Problem solving

4 a Reflect the point A in the line $y = 3$.
  What are the coordinates of its image?
b Reflect the point B in the line $y = 2$.
  What are the coordinates of its image?
c Reflect the point C in the line $y = x$.
  What are the coordinates of its image?

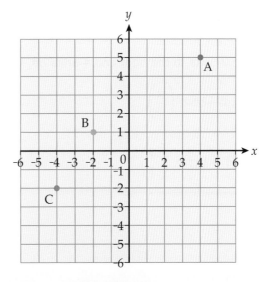

9c Translation

- When you **translate** an **object** its position changes but its size and angles remain the same.

- You can use **vectors** to describe a translation.

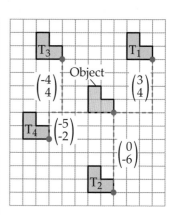

Vector $\begin{pmatrix} 3 \\ 4 \end{pmatrix}$ **maps** the object onto T_1. | To the right 3 and up 4.

Vector $\begin{pmatrix} 0 \\ -6 \end{pmatrix}$ maps the object onto T_2. | No change left or right and *down* 6.

Vector $\begin{pmatrix} -4 \\ 4 \end{pmatrix}$ maps the object onto T_3. | To the *left* 4 and up 4.

Vector $\begin{pmatrix} -5 \\ -2 \end{pmatrix}$ maps the object onto T_4. | To the *left* 5 and *down* 2.

- Vectors are written in columns, $\begin{pmatrix} x \\ y \end{pmatrix}$.

The top number gives the horizontal movement.
negative to the left ← positive to the right →
The bottom number gives the vertical movement.
negative downward ↓ positive upwards ↑

> Be careful not to confuse vectors and coordinates. Vectors move an object and coordinates say where it is.

Example

a Translate the green triangle by the vector $\begin{pmatrix} 2 \\ 4 \end{pmatrix}$ and label it A.

b Use a vector to describe the translation that maps the red triangle
  i onto the blue triangle
  ii onto the green triangle.

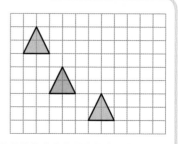

---

a Move 2 units to the right and 4 units up.

b **i** Red → Blue: $\begin{pmatrix} -2 \\ 3 \end{pmatrix}$

  ii Red → Green: $\begin{pmatrix} 3 \\ -2 \end{pmatrix}$

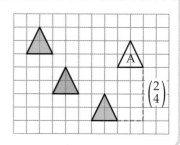

Exercise 9c

1 a Copy this diagram.

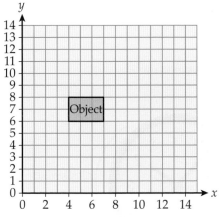

b Draw the images of the rectangle after translations by these vectors.

i $T_1: \begin{pmatrix} 6 \\ 3 \end{pmatrix}$ **ii** $T_2: \begin{pmatrix} 0 \\ 5 \end{pmatrix}$

iii $T_3: \begin{pmatrix} 0 \\ -3 \end{pmatrix}$ **iv** $T_4: \begin{pmatrix} -2 \\ 4 \end{pmatrix}$

v $T_5: \begin{pmatrix} 5 \\ -6 \end{pmatrix}$ **vi** $T_6: \begin{pmatrix} 7 \\ 0 \end{pmatrix}$

2 Use vectors to describe these translations.

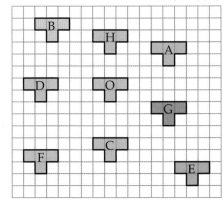

2 a O → D   **b** F → C
c C → F   **d** F → H
e G → A   **f** O → A
g C → H   **h** B → A
i E → C   **j** D → O
k D → A   **l** A → G
m B → O   **n** O → H

3 a Copy the grid.

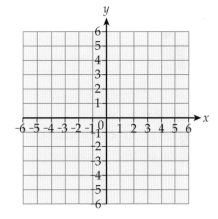

b Plot the points (1, 1), (1, 5) and (4, 2). Join them up to draw a triangle. Label your triangle A.

c Translate triangle A by $\begin{pmatrix} -4 \\ -3 \end{pmatrix}$. Label this triangle B.

d Translate triangle B by $\begin{pmatrix} 6 \\ -1 \end{pmatrix}$. Label this triangle C.

Problem solving

4 A robot is given instructions to move using vectors. These four instructions are given to the robot.

$\begin{pmatrix} 6 \\ 3 \end{pmatrix}$ $\begin{pmatrix} 1 \\ -9 \end{pmatrix}$ $\begin{pmatrix} -1 \\ 4 \end{pmatrix}$ $\begin{pmatrix} -5 \\ 2 \end{pmatrix}$

Does the robot return to its starting place? Explain your answer.

MyMaths.co.uk   Q 1127   SEARCH

● When you **rotate** an object its position changes but its size and angles remain the same.

● To rotate an object you need to know the angle, the direction and the **centre of rotation**.

You need to remember which way is clockwise and which way is anticlockwise.

clockwise

The pentagon P is rotated clockwise about the centre of rotation at O.

After a rotation of 90° **clockwise** the image is R_1.

After a rotation of 180° clockwise the image is R_2.

After a rotation of 270° clockwise the image is R_3.

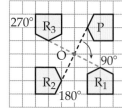

The **angle of rotation** is the angle between the two lines from the centre of rotation to a point on the object and the same point on the image.

Example

a   Copy the diagram and rotate the shape through 90° **anticlockwise** about the centre of rotation at O.

b   Copy the diagram again and rotate the shape through 180° about the centre of rotation at O.

a

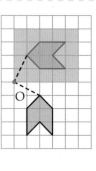

Using tracing paper draw the outline of the shape and use the point of your pencil to fix the centre of rotation.

b

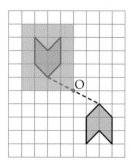

Then rotate the tracing paper through the given angle in the given direction and copy the image of the shape.

Exercise 9d

1 Copy these diagrams.
Rotate the shapes about the centre of rotation marked on each diagram through the angle and direction given.

a

90° clockwise

b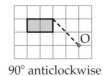

90° anticlockwise

c

180°

d

270° clockwise

2 A rotation transforms shape X on to shape Y.

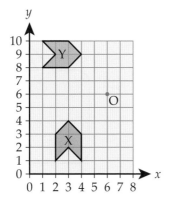

a What are the coordinates of the centre of rotation?

b What is the direction of the rotation?

c What is the angle of the rotation?

3 Copy this diagram.
Rotate the triangle through 90° clockwise about the centre marked on the diagram.

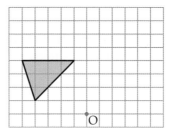

4 **a** Copy the grid.

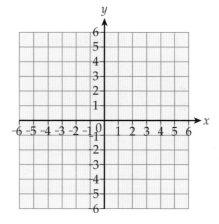

b Plot the points (1, 1), (1, 5) and (4, 2). Join them up to draw a triangle and Label it A.

c Rotate triangle A 90° clockwise about the origin and label it B.

d Rotate triangle A 180° about the origin and label it C.

Problem solving

5 Copy the pink rectangle and mark the centre of rotation on your diagram.
Use a protractor and tracing paper to rotate the rectangle through 120° anticlockwise.
Measure the distance from each vertex of the object to the centre of rotation and make sure that it is the same distance from the centre of rotation to the matching vertex on the image.

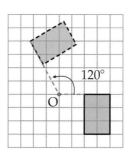

🔘 Enlarging an object changes its size but its angles stay the same.

The green triangle is an **enlargement** of the pink triangle.

The vertical side of the object is 3 units long.
The vertical side of the image is 9 units long.

The horizontal side of the object is 2 units long.
The horizontal side of the image is 6 units long.

The sides of the image are three times longer than the sides of the object.

$$\frac{9}{3} = \frac{6}{2} = 3$$

So you say that the **scale factor** is 3.

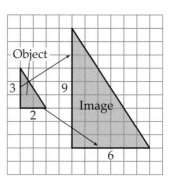

🔘 The scale factor tells you how many times bigger or smaller to draw each side of the object.

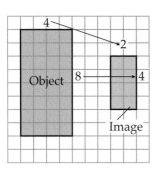

In this diagram the pink rectangle has been **reduced**.
The sides of the image are half the length of the object.

$$4 \div 8 = \frac{1}{2} \text{ and } 2 \div 4 = \frac{1}{2}$$

The scale factor is $\frac{1}{2}$.

Remember that multiplying by $\frac{1}{2}$ is the same as dividing by 2.
$8 \times \frac{1}{2} = 4$ and $8 \div 2 = 4$

Example

a Enlarge this shape by a scale factor of 4.
b What is the scale factor that would reduce the large rectangle to the small rectangle?

a Make each length four times as long.
   $1 \times 4 = 4$
   $2 \times 4 = 8$

b The vertical sides of the large rectangle are 4 units long.
   The vertical sides of the small rectangle are 1 unit long.
   The sides of the image are 4 times smaller than the object.
   The scale factor is $\frac{1}{4}$.

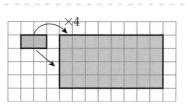

Dividing by 4 has the same effect as multiplying by $\frac{1}{4}$.

Exercise 9e

1 Enlarge these shapes by the scale factors given.

a

Scale factor 2

b

Scale factor 3

c

Scale factor 4

d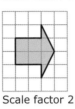

Scale factor 2

2 What is the scale factor of enlargement in each of these diagrams?

a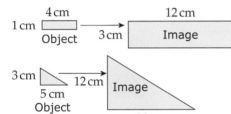

4 cm
1 cm Object 3 cm 12 cm Image

b

3 cm
5 cm Object 12 cm Image 20 cm

3 Copy and complete these equations.
   a $10 \div 2 = 10 \times \square$
   b $6 \times \square = 6 \div 3$
   c $15 \div 5 = 15 \times \square$

4 Copy this diagram.
   a Reduce the triangle by a scale factor of $\frac{1}{4}$.

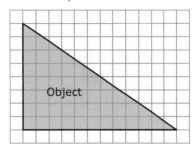

Object

   b What is the scale factor that would enlarge the small triangle to the large triangle?

Problem solving

5 Dinesh is trying to enlarge a photograph by a scale factor of 3. Here are the original and three of his attempts.

a 15 cm
5 cm

b 30 cm
15 cm

c 10 cm
6 cm

d 45 cm
15 cm

Which are the original photograph and the true enlargement?

● When you enlarge a shape using a **centre of enlargement**, use lines which meet at the centre.

This is how to draw an enlargement with a **scale factor** of 2 using a centre of enlargement.

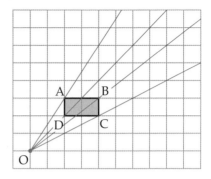

Draw lines from the centre of enlargement through each vertex of the object ABCD.

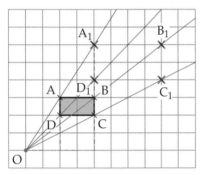

For each line, draw another point that is twice as far from the origin as the point on the object.

The scale factor is 2. For a scale factor of 3 the image is three times as far from the centre as the object.

Join all the new points to draw the image.

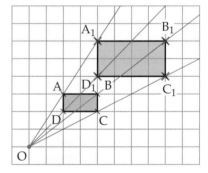

Finally you should check that the image is an enlargement of the object with scale factor 2.

$$\frac{D_1A_1}{DA} = \frac{2}{1} = 2$$

$$\frac{A_1B_1}{AB} = \frac{4}{2} = 2$$

● For any point on the object and the equivalent point on the image

Scale factor = $\dfrac{\text{Distance from centre of enlargement to image point}}{\text{Distance from centre of enlargement to object point}}$

Exercise 9f

1 Copy each diagram carefully.
Use the lines to enlarge the square by
a scale factor of 2. Label the image
$A_1B_1C_1D_1$.

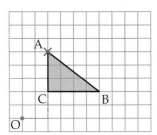

2 **a** Draw lines through the vertices of the
object and extend them.
b Use the lines to enlarge the triangle by
a scale factor of 3.

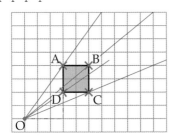

3

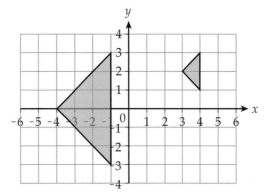

a The smaller triangle has been
enlarged. What is the scale factor
of the enlargement?
b Find the coordinates of the centre
of enlargement.

4

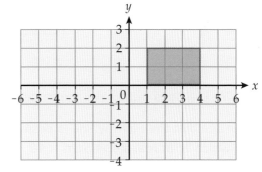

Enlarge the rectangle by a scale factor of
2 from the centre of enlargement (6, 3).

Problem solving

5 The object is the larger triangle.
a What is the scale factor of enlargement?
b Copy the diagram carefully.
Use lines to show the position of the
centre of enlargement.

> Make sure you draw the two
> triangles in exactly the same
> position in relation to each
> other as in the diagram.

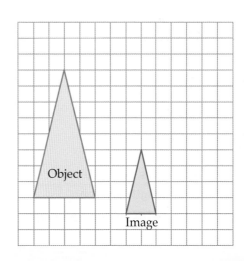

> You can use a scale drawing to give an accurate plan of an object that may be too large or too small to show using real-life measurements.

A hockey pitch is 91m long and 55m wide. This is a scale drawing of the hockey pitch. It is 9.1cm long and 5.5cm wide.

The scale is 1cm : 10m.

So 5.5cm represents
5.5 × 10m = 55m
and 9.1cm represents
9.1 × 10m = 91m

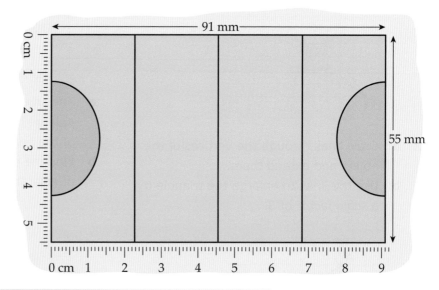

> Scale drawings must have the same scale for all measurements.

You can see that the halfway line is positioned at just over 4.5cm which is, in real life, 4.5cm × 10 = 45m.

Example

A triangle has sides of 20m, 25m and 30m.
A scale drawing is to be made using a scale of 1cm : 5m.
What lengths should the sides be in the drawing?

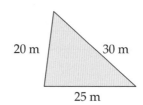

| 5m → 1cm |
| 20m → 4cm |
| 25m → 5cm |
| 30m → 6cm |

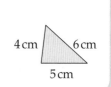

Example

a Measure the sides of this rectangle to the nearest millimetre.

b The scale of the drawing is 1cm : 10cm. What length are the sides of the actual rectangle?

a length = 3.2cm   width = 1.8cm
b 3.2cm × 10 = 32cm
The length of the rectangle is 32cm.
1.8cm × 10 = 18cm
The width is 18cm.

Exercise 9g

1 Use the scales to say what lengths should be used to make each drawing.

a

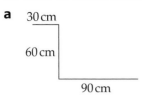

30 cm

60 cm

90 cm

Scale 1 cm : 3 cm

b

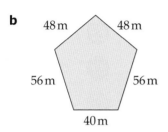

48 m   48 m

56 m   56 m

40 m

Scale 1 cm : 8 m

c

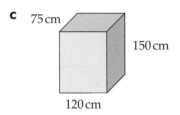

75 cm

150 cm

120 cm

Scale 1 cm : 15 cm

d

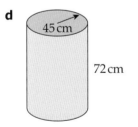

45 cm

72 cm

Scale 1 cm : 9 cm

2 The scale for this drawing is 1 cm : 4 m. The measurements have been left off the drawing.

a Measure the length of each side of the shape to the nearest millimetre.

b What length are the sides of the actual shape?

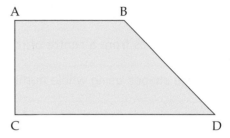

A   B

C   D

3 Draw straight lines to these scales.

a 20 m to a scale of 1 cm : 5 m

b 100 m to a scale of 1 cm : 20 m

c 200 km to a scale of 1 cm : 50 km

d 15 m to a scale of 1 cm : 5 m

e 36 m to a scale of 1 cm : 3 m

Did you know?

Architects use scale drawings in their work. Architectural drawings allow designers, builders and clients to review plans as well as providing a record of the finished building.

Problem solving

4 This is a sketch plan of Rob's bedroom.
Draw a plan of Rob's room to a scale of 2 cm : 1 m.

You can use squared paper. You do not need to position the bed or the table exactly, but place the window in the correct position.

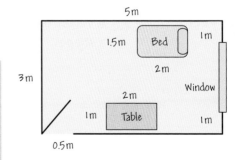

5 m

1.5 m   Bed   1 m

3 m

2 m

2 m   Window

2 m

1 m   Table   1 m

0.5 m

MyMaths.co.uk

Q 1103, 1117   SEARCH

Check out

You should now be able to ...

✓ Recognise reflection and rotational symmetry of 2D shapes.	5	1
✓ Reflect shapes in mirror lines.	5	2
✓ Use vectors to translate shapes in any direction.	5	3
✓ Rotate shapes from a centre of rotation.	5	4
✓ Enlarge shapes using whole number and fractional scale factors.	5	5
✓ Enlarge shapes from a centre of enlargement.	6	6
✓ Use and draw scale drawings.	6	7

Language	Meaning	Example
Clockwise/ Anticlockwise	These are directions you can turn. It is the same/opposite direction to the hands on a clock.	clockwise anticlockwise
Line of symmetry	A line which divides a shape into two halves which are the mirror image of each other.	A rectangle has 2 lines of symmetry.
Mirror line	A line in which you reflect a shape.	
Order of rotational symmetry	The number of times a shape looks exactly the same as itself during a complete turn.	A rectangle has rotational symmetry order 2.
Scale factor	Tells you by how many times to change each side of the shape.	A scale factor 2 tells you to draw each side twice as long.
Vector	A vector tells you how far to move a shape.	$\begin{pmatrix} 4 \\ -5 \end{pmatrix}$ move shape 4 units right move shape 5 units down

1 Describe
  a the reflective symmetry
  b the rotational symmetry
    of this shape.

2 Copy the quadrilaterals on squared paper
  and reflect the shapes in the mirror lines.

a   b

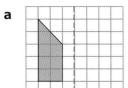

3 Copy the diagram and translate
  by the vector $\begin{pmatrix} 3 \\ -4 \end{pmatrix}$.

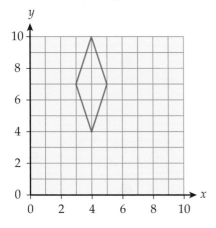

4 Copy the triangle on squared paper and
  rotate the triangle 90° clockwise about
  the point.

5 a Copy the shape on squared paper then
    enlarge it by scale factor 3.

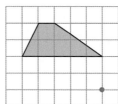

  b What is the scale factor that would reduce
    the enlarged shape to the original?

6 Copy the trapezium on squared paper
  then enlarge by scale factor 2 using the
  dot as the centre of enlargement.

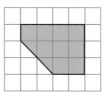

7 A rectangular room is 5 m by 3 m. Draw a
  scale diagram of the room using the scale
  2 cm : 1 m.

What next?

Score		
	0 – 3	Your knowledge of this topic is still developing. To improve look at Formative test: 3A-9; MyMaths: 1099, 1103, 1113, 1114, 1115, 1116, 1117, 1125 and 1127
	4 – 6	You are gaining a secure knowledge of this topic. To improve look at InvisiPen: 361, 362, 363, 366 and 372
	7	You have mastered this topic. Well done, you are ready to progress!

MyMaths.co.uk

9a

1 a Describe the reflection and rotation symmetry of the shape.

b Shade two more squares on the shape so that it has rotation symmetry of order 4.

c How many lines of symmetry does the shape in part **b** have?

9b

2 a Reflect the triangle A, in the x-axis.
Label the image B.

b Reflect the new image B in the y-axis.
Label this new image C.

c What are the coordinates of image C?

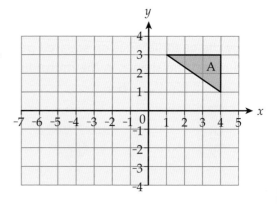

9c

3 Write down the vector which translates the YELLOW dot to the positions of the other coloured dots.

Write, yellow to black $\rightarrow \begin{pmatrix} 4 \\ 5 \end{pmatrix}$

yellow to green $\rightarrow$ ....
yellow to white $\rightarrow$ ....
yellow to brown $\rightarrow$ ....
yellow to purple $\rightarrow$ ....
yellow to blue $\rightarrow$ ....
yellow to orange $\rightarrow$ ....
yellow to red $\rightarrow$ ....

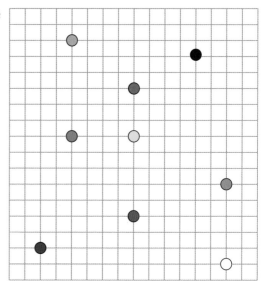

9d

4 a Copy the 'T' shape and position the centre of rotation O.
Rotate the 'T' shape through 180°.
Label the image T_1.

b Reflect the image, T_1 in the blue dotted mirror line.
Label the image T_2.

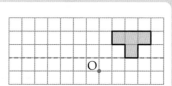

5 **a** What is the perimeter of the shape?

b Reduce the shape by a scale factor of $\frac{1}{2}$.

c What is the perimeter of the reduced image?

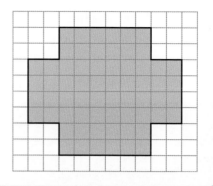

6 Copy the trapezium carefully.

Position the centre of enlargement in exactly the right place.

By drawing lines from the centre O, enlarge the shape by a scale factor of 2.

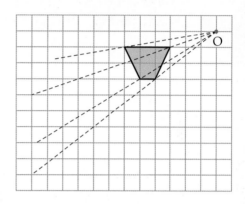

7 Draw straight lines to these scales.

a 36 m to a scale of 1 cm : 6 m

b 200 m to a scale of 1 cm : 40 m

c 40 km to a scale of 2 cm : 5 km

d 100 m to a scale of 3 cm : 25 m

e 28 m to a scale of 3 cm : 7 m

8 **a** Measure the lengths of this 'L' shape to the nearest millimetre.

b Calculate the true perimeter of this shape if the scale of the drawing is 1 cm : 4 m.

The Earth's climate has always changed due to natural causes such as change of orbit, volcanic eruptions and changes in the sun's energy, but now there is real concern that human activity is upsetting the balance by adding to 'greenhouse gases'.

Greenhouse gases

This diagram shows some of the main factors behind global warming.

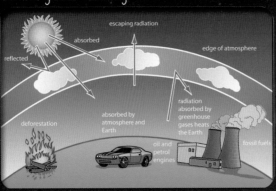

[**Task 1**]

The pie chart shows the contribution made to the warming effect by the main greenhouse gases.

- ■ carbon dioxide
- ☐ methane
- ☐ nitrous oxide
- ☐ others

a Which greenhouse gas causes about ¼ of the warming effect?

b Roughly what fraction of the warming effect is caused by carbon dioxide (CO_2)?

[**Task 2**]

THE DAILY NEWS

What's News ▷

GREENHOUSE GASES UP BY 25%

A recent report says that in the last 60 years, CO_2 concentrations have increased by around 25%.

a Does the graph show the same increase in CO_2 levels as the report? Show your workings out.

b In the year 1000 AD, CO_2 concentration was around 280 ppm (parts per million). By what percentage has it increased?

Global temperature change

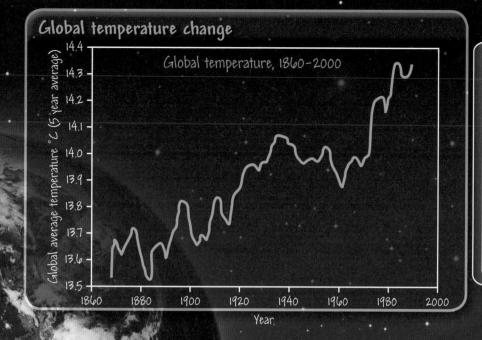

Global temperature, 1860–2000

Global average temperature °C (5 year average)

Year

Task 3

a Describe in words what the graph shows.

b Estimate the global temperature in
   i 1880
   ii 1980

c Calculate the percentage change in temperature, giving the answer on your calculator display to 1 decimal place.

Task 4

Here are the monthly temperatures for Oxford in 1908 and 2008.

1908	Jan	Feb	Mar	Apr	May	June	July	Aug	Sep	Oct	Nov	Dec
max °C	5.5	8.6	8.3	10.4	17.6	20.5	21.5	20	17	16.1	11.1	6.5
min °C	-0.4	2.7	1.5	2.4	9	9.8	12.2	10.7	9.4	8.1	5	1.6

2008	Jan	Feb	Mar	Apr	May	June	July	Aug	Sep	Oct	Nov	Dec
max °C	10.3	10.5	10.6	13.1	18.7	20.1	21.7	20.8	17.6	14.3	9.9	6.5
min °C	4.7	1.7	3.5	4.7	9.5	11.1	12.8	13.9	10	6.3	4.6	1.3

a Write down the range in
   i maximum temperatures,
   ii minimum temperatures, for each year.

b Calculate the median of
   i maximum temperatures,
   ii minimum temperatures, for each year.

c Use your results from a and b to compare the temperatures in Oxford in 1908 and 2008. Are your findings in agreement with the graph in Task 3?

d Why might using data for just two year in a single city not be adequate to make any firm conclusions about global warming?

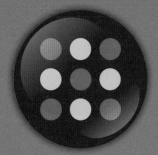

10 Equations

Introduction

You might think that equations exist only in maths textbooks, but …

… Astronomers use equations to describe the movements of planets and the paths of asteroids. Nuclear physicists use equations to calculate the half-lives of dangerous radioactive isotopes. Biologists use equations to predict the likely growth or decline of populations of endangered animals. The police force use equations to determine the cause of accidents by calculating speeds and braking distances of the vehicles involved.

What's the point?

Equations are used in all walks of life to model complex real-life situations.

Objectives

By the end of this chapter, you will have learned how to …

- Understand what an equation is.
- Calculate the unknown value in equations.
- Use balancing to solve equations.
- Solve equations with unknowns on both sides.
- Write equations from real-life situations.

Check in

1   Collect these numbers together and work out the answers.

   a 5 + 4 + 7 + 3 + 2 + 1   **b** 4 + 4 − 5   **c** 6 + 7 − 9 + 1 − 2

   d 5 − 6 − 1 + 8 + 2   **e** 9 − 9 + 3 − 4   **f** 10 − 1 + 4 − 9

2   Write the expressions which are the outcomes of these function machines.

   a

   b
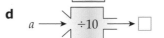

   c
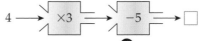

   d
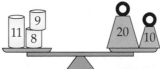

3   What is the output of this function
   machine?

4   Will these scales balance?
   Explain your answer.

Starter problem

In this diagram the equation $3x + 2 = 17$
has been changed in different ways, but all
of these ways still give the same solution
of $x = 5$.

Describe each change to the equation.

Continue each change for at least one
more step.

Invent some changes of your own.

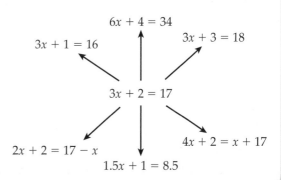

$6x + 4 = 34$

$3x + 3 = 18$

$3x + 1 = 16$

$3x + 2 = 17$

$2x + 2 = 17 − x$

$1.5x + 1 = 8.5$

$4x + 2 = x + 17$

These two expressions have the same **value**.

$$5 \times 4 \quad = \quad 18 + 2$$

$5 \times 4 \qquad 18 + 2$

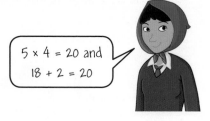

5 × 4 = 20 and
18 + 2 = 20

An **equality** has two sides, one left and one right of the equals sign.

These two expressions do not have the same value.

$$2 \times 6 \quad \neq \quad 5 + 6$$

You can write this as an **inequality**.

$$2 \times 6 \quad > \quad 5 + 6$$

$2 \times 6 \qquad 5 + 6$

2 × 6 = 12 but
5 + 6 = 11

⬤ An inequality has one side greater than the other.

These two expressions do not have the same value

$$12 - 8 \quad \neq \quad 12 \div 2$$

You can write,

$$12 - 8 \quad < \quad 12 \div 2$$

$12 - 8 \qquad 12 \div 2$

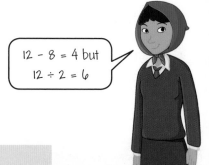

12 – 8 = 4 but
12 ÷ 2 = 6

⬤ < means 'less than' and > means 'greater than'.

Example

a Choose one of these signs, > or < or =, to link the calculations in each of these pairs.
  i 12×2 and 5×5 **ii** $14 - 7$ and $14 \div 2$
  iii $36 \div 4$ and $16 \div 2$ **iv** $12 - 5$ and $64 \div 8$

b Copy these and fill in the missing numbers to make the statements true.
  i $8 + 10 = 9 \times \square$ **ii** $5 \times \square = 12 + 3$
  iii $20 - 6 = 7 \times \square$ **iv** $56 \div \square = 19 - 12$

a i 12 × 2 = 24 and 5 × 5 = 25
      12 × 2 < 5 × 5
  iii 36 ÷ 4 = 9 and 16 ÷ 2 = 8
      36 ÷ 4 > 16 ÷ 2

  ii 14 – 7 = 7 and 14 ÷ 2 = 7
      14 – 7 = 14 ÷ 2
  iv 12 – 5 = 7 and 64 ÷ 8 = 8
      12 – 5 < 64 ÷ 8

b i 8 + 10 = 9 × ☐
      18 = 9 × **2**
  iii 20 – 6 = 7 × ☐
      14 = 7 × **2**

  ii 5 × ☐ = 12 + 3
      5 × **3** = **15**
  iv 56 ÷ ☐ = 19 – 12
      56 ÷ **8** = 7

Exercise 10a

1 Do these pairs of calculations make equations?

Use = for an equation and · for not an equation.

a 20 ÷ 4 and 25 ÷ 5

b 30 − 15 and 2 × 8

c 50 ÷ 2 and 31 − 6

d 10 + 4 and 12 − 5

e 36 ÷ 9 and 7 − 2

f 45 + 15 and 12 × 5

g 80 ÷ 4 and 2 × 10

h 240 ÷ 10 and 36 − 12

i 44 ÷ 8 and 5 × 6

2 Are these scales balanced?

a
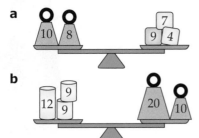

b
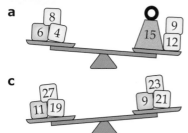

3 Are these statements true or false?

a 14 = 7 + 7

b 23 < 12 + 12

c 21 × 2 > 31 + 12

d 25 ÷ 5 > 10 ÷ 2

e 100 ÷ 5 < 2 × 9

f 6 × 6 = 9 × 4

g 28 ÷ 2 = 10 + 4

h 90 × 4 = 180 × 29

i 16 × 5 < 9 × 9

4 Copy these and fill in the missing numbers to make the statements true.

a 10 + 2 = 6 + ☐

b 15 − 1 = 7 × ☐

c 20 ÷ 2 = 2 × ☐

d 25 − 5 = 16 + ☐

e 40 ÷ 10 = 16 − ☐

f 24 + 6 = 6 × ☐

g 5 + 55 = 3 × ☐

h 100 ÷ 4 = 5 × ☐

i 47 + 13 = 12 × ☐

Problem solving

5 Find the weight you need to make these scales balance.

a
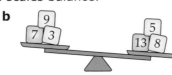

b

c

d
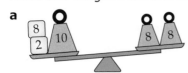

6 Move one weight from one side to the other to make the scales balance.

a

b
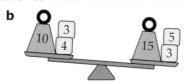

10b Solving equations

An **inverse operation** is what you do to get back to where you started.

If you add 10 to 6 you get 16.

$$6 + 10 = 16$$

To get back to 6 you must subtract 10.

$$16 - 10 = 6$$

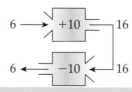

⚫ When you solve an equation you find the value which is **unknown**.

You can use inverse operations on the equation $30 = 5 \times x$ to find the unknown value of x.

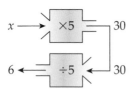

So $x = 6$

When you solve an equation you must always keep it balanced.

$$x + 15 = 31$$
$$x + 15 - 15 = 31 - 15$$
$$x = 16$$

> The inverse of
> ×5 is ÷5 ...

> ... so working backwards gives the answer 30 ÷ 5 = 6

> The inverse of +15 is −15, so subtract 15 from both sides.

⚫ An equation is balanced when one side is equal to the other.
   To keep the equation balanced you must always do the same to both sides.

Example

a What is the inverse of each of these operations?

  i   ×7

  ii −12

  iii ÷3

b Use an inverse operation to find the value of a.

 $a \longrightarrow +16 \longrightarrow 21$

c Solve this equation. $x - 13 = 25$

---

a i The inverse of ×7 is ÷7.

b

  ii The inverse of −12 is +12.

  iii The inverse of ÷3 is ×3.

  c $x - 13 = 25$
     $x - 13 + 13 = 25 + 13$
     $x = 38$

> The inverse of −13 is +13 so add 13 to both sides.

$a = 5$

Exercise 10b

1 What is the inverse of each of these operations?

i 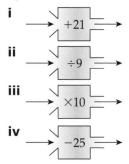 +21

ii ÷9

iii ×10

iv −25

2 Use inverse operations to find the value of each unknown.

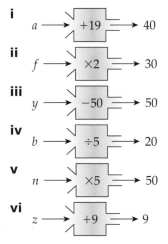

i $a \longrightarrow +19 \longrightarrow 40$

ii $f \longrightarrow ×2 \longrightarrow 30$

iii $y \longrightarrow -50 \longrightarrow 50$

iv $b \longrightarrow ÷5 \longrightarrow 20$

v $n \longrightarrow ×5 \longrightarrow 50$

vi $z \longrightarrow +9 \longrightarrow 9$

3 Solve these equations.

a $n + 17 = 20$ **b** $v + 32 = 41$

c $q - 20 = 10$ **d** $k + 27 = 35$

e $p - 5 = 45$ **f** $t - 20 = 0$

4 Solve these equations.

a $12 + t = 20$ **b** $19 + b = 41$

c $q - 16 = 5$ **d** $h + 30 = 45$

e $5 + p = 45$ **f** $d - 13 = 17$

5 Sammy and Gavin are asked to solve the equation $8x = 56$.

Sammy says:

The answer is 7, because 8 × 7 = 56

Gavin says:

The answer is 48, because 8 + 48 = 56

Who is right?
Explain your answer.

6 Find the value of the unknown in each of these equations.

a $2 × f = 20$ **b** $10 × p = 30$

c $m ÷ 8 = 2$ **d** $6 × t = 24$

e $3 × g = 45$ **f** $v ÷ 5 = 10$

g $5a = 20$ **h** $10b = 60$

i $\frac{t}{4} = 2$ **j** $\frac{c}{5} = 3$

k $7q = 21$ **l** $\frac{z}{10} = 6$

Problem solving

7 Ten CDs weigh 150 g.

a What is the weight of three CDs?

b What is the weight of one CD?

You can write an equation for these scales because the two sides **balance**.

$$n + n + 2 = 10$$
$$\text{or} \quad 2n + 2 = 10$$

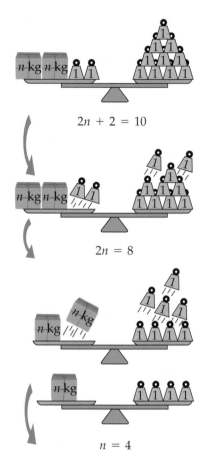

$2n + 2 = 10$

$2n = 8$

$n = 4$

Work out the weight of the parcels by taking 2 kg away from the **left-hand side**.

Keep the scales balanced by taking 2 kg away from the **right-hand side** as well.

$$2n + 2 - 2 = 10 - 2$$
$$2n = 8$$

There are two parcels so divide both sides by 2.

$$2n \div 2 = 8 \div 2$$
$$n = 4$$

So one parcel has a weight of 4 kg.

● For the equation to remain balanced you must always do the same to both sides.

Example

a   Write an equation for these scales.
b   Solve the equation by balancing.

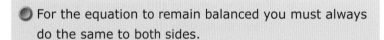

a   The equation is $3x + 1 = 10$.
b
$$3x + 1 = 10$$
$$3x + 1 - 1 = 10 - 1 \qquad \text{Subtract 1 from both sides.}$$
$$3x = 9$$
$$3x \div 3 = 9 \div 3 \qquad \text{Divide both sides by 3.}$$
$$x = 3$$

● When you **solve** an equation you find the **unknown** value.

Exercise 10c

1   Calculate the unknown value in each of these problems.

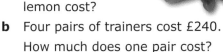

   a   Three lemons cost 60p. How much does one lemon cost?

   b   Four pairs of trainers cost £240. How much does one pair cost?

   c   Ten pencils laid end to end have a length of 150 cm. What is the length of one pencil?

   d   Two ingots of gold have a mass of 25 kg. What is the mass of one ingot?

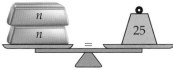

2   Solve these equations by balancing.

   a $3x = 12$ **b** $5n = 20$
   c $10k = 70$ **d** $4f = 60$
   e $6t = 12$ **f** $7q = 21$
   g $20h = 100$ **h** $9d = 45$

3   **i**   Write an equation for each of these scales.

   a
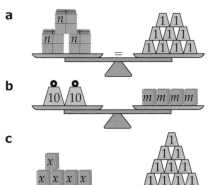

   b

   c

3

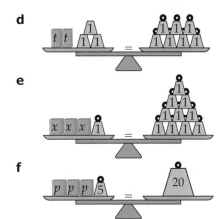

   d

   e

   f

   ii   Find the mass of one parcel on each of the scales by solving the equations.

4   Solve these equations.

   a $3x + 4 = 19$ **b** $2m + 6 = 24$
   c $5t - 4 = 11$ **d** $10y - 3 = 27$
   e $4g + 5 = 17$ **f** $3h + 7 = 22$
   g $8r + 3 = 35$ **h** $5n - 6 = 24$
   i $2e + 20 = 40$ **j** $5p + 13 = 33$
   k $10d + 7 = 37$ **l** $7f - 5 = 9$

5   Josie is trying to solve the equation
    $4x - 3 = 29$
    She says:

   > If I subtract 3 from both sides, I get $4x = 26$. Now divide both sides by 4, so $x = 6\frac{1}{2}$

   Is she right?
   If not, where has she gone wrong?

Problem solving

6   **a**   Write the equation which describes this picture.
    b   Solve the equation by balancing to find how many litres a bucket holds when it is full.

10d Balancing equations 2

‹ p.40

These scales have symbols on both sides.
You can write this as an equation.

$c + c + c + 1 = c + c + 6$
or $\qquad 3c + 1 = 2c + 6$

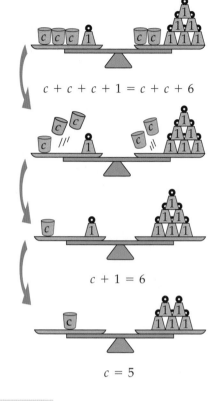

$c + c + c + 1 = c + c + 6$

To work out the weight of one tin take two tins
away from the **right-hand side**.

Keep the scales **balanced** by taking two tins away
from the **left-hand side** as well.

$$3c + 1 - 2c = 2c + 6 - 2c$$
$$c + 1 = 6$$

Now take 1 kg away from both sides.

$$c + 1 - 1 = 6 - 1$$
$$c = 5$$

$c + 1 = 6$

So one tin has a weight of 5 kg.

$c = 5$

> When there are unknowns on both sides, eliminate the unknowns
> from the side with the smallest amount of unknowns.
> Remember to do the same to both sides.

Example

Write an equation for these scales.
Find the weight of one parcel by solving the equation.

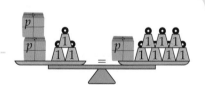

$p + p + 3 = p + 7 \qquad$ Subtract p from both sides.
$p + 3 = 7$
$\qquad p = 4 \qquad$ Subtract 3 from both sides.

Example

Write an equation for these scales.
Find the weight of one box by solving the equation.

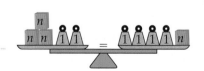

$n + n + n + 2 = n + 4 \qquad$ Subtract n from both sides.
$n + n + 2 = 4$
$\qquad n + n = 2$ or $2n = 2 \qquad$ Subtract 2 from both sides.
$\qquad\qquad n = 1 \qquad\qquad$ Divide both sides by 2.

Algebra Equations

6

Exercise 10d

1 i Write an equation for each of these scales.

ii Find the weight of one parcel on each of the scales by solving the equations.

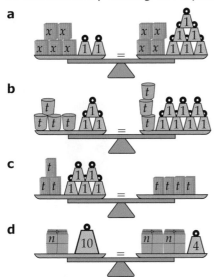

a

b

c

d

2 Solve these equations.

a $n + n + n + 10 = n + n + 3$

b $x + x + 16 = x + 20$

c $y + y + y + y + 9 = y + y + y + 15$

d $h + h + 15 = h + h + h + 8$

e $2n + 20 = n + 35$

f $5t + 7 = 4t + 13$

g $8k + 12 = 9k + 7$

h $6y + 15 = 5y + 23$

i $10b + 13 = 9b + 20$

j $12v + 9 = 11v + 30$

3 i Write an equation for each of these scales.

ii Find the weight of one parcel on each of the scales by solving the equations.

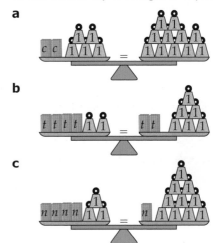

a

b

c

4 Solve these equations.

a $n + n + n + 6 = n + 14$

b $h + h + h + h + 9 = h + 21$

c $t + t + t + 25 = t + 55$

d $m + m + m + m + m + 20 = m + m + 40$

e $2k + 9 = k + 12$

f $4t + 2 = t + 11$

g $5t + 6 = 3t + 24$

h $6d + 10 = d + 25$

i $7x + 2 = 3x + 18$

j $3x + 19 = 6x + 4$

k $2x + 20 = 5x - 1$

l $4x - 7 = 6x - 13$

Problem solving

5 Andy has 3 full tubes and 15 loose mints.

Jo has 5 full tubes and 3 loose mints.

There are the same number of mints in each tube.

Andy and Jo have the same number of mints.

How many mints are there in a tube?

How many mints do Andy and Jo each have?

You can write an **expression** for the perimeter of this rectangle.

Emily wrote:

$x + 2x + x + 2x = 6x$

‹ p. 46

2x cm

x cm

x cm

2x cm

Shakila was told that the perimeter of the rectangle is 24 cm.

That means $6x = 24$. Solving my equation gives $x = 4$.

So the rectangle has a width 4 cm and length 8 cm.

Example

Match two of these calculations to make an equation.

10×5 $45 + 6$ $200 \div 4$ 25×3

$10 \times 5 = 50$
$45 + 6 = 51$
$200 \div 4 = 50$
$25 \times 3 = 75$
Answer: $10 \times 5 = 200 \div 4$

Example

a Write an expression for the perimeter of this square using y.

b The perimeter is 12 cm.
Write an equation and solve it to find the length of one side, y.

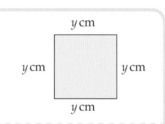

y cm

y cm

y cm

y cm

a Perimeter = $y + y + y + y = 4y$

b $4y = 12$
  $y = 3$
The length of one side of the square is 3 cm.

Example

a Write an equation using the amounts of money in this story.
Ivy has £x in her wallet. She spends £5. She is left with £15.

b Solve your equation to find how much Ivy had at the start.

a $x - 5 = 15$

b $x = 20$
Ivy had £20 at the start.

Exercise 10e

1 Match these calculations in pairs to make equations.

$42 + 7$ 5×20 $42 \div 1$ $90 \div 2$

$90 \div 3$ 5×6 $9 + 5$

6×7 3×20 3×15 7×7

$17 + 83$ 2×7 15×4

2 i Write an expression for the perimeter of each shape. Use the symbols given.

ii The perimeter of each shape is 60 cm. Write an equation and solve it to find the length of the sides of each shape.

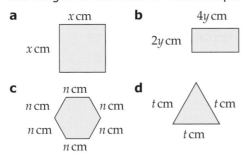

a x cm x cm

b $4y$ cm $2y$ cm

c n cm n cm n cm n cm n cm n cm

d t cm t cm t cm

3 Write an equation for each of these stories. Solve the equations to answer the questions. Show your working.

a Sanjay has £y in his wallet. He spends £15. He is left with £35. How much money did Sanjay have at the start?

3 b Jessie's dad is double her weight.
He has a weight of 70 kg.
Jessie has a weight of x kg.
What is Jessie's weight?

c Jack has £120 in his bank account.
He receives p pounds for his birthday.
He now has £210.
How much money did Jack receive for his birthday?

d It costs £5 to enter the bowling club.
Each game costs £c.
Kim plays five games.
The total cost is £20.
How much does each game cost?

Problem solving

4 a Write an equation for these scales.
Use t for the weight of one tin.

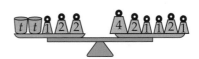

b Solve the equation to find the weight of one tin.

c Use your answer to find the weight of five tins.

Check out

You should now be able to ...

✓ Understand what an equation is.	5	1, 2
✓ Calculate the unknown value in equations.	5	3
✓ Use balancing to solve equations.	6	4, 5
✓ Solve equations with unknowns on both sides.	6	6
✓ Write equations from real-life situations.	6	7

Language	Meaning	Example
Equation	An equation is true for particular values. For any equation, the left-hand side is equal to the right-hand side.	$2x - 5 = 13$ True for $x = 9$
Expression	An expression is a group of terms but no equals sign.	$2a - 3b$
Inequality	An inequality is where one side is greater than the other.	$7 < 8$ is the same as $8 > 7$
Solve	To solve an equation means to find the value of the unknown.	Solve $2x - 5 = 13$ $2x - 5 + 5 = 13 + 5$ $2x = 18$ $2x \div 2 = 18 \div 2$ $x = 9$
Unknown	The letter in an equation represents the unknown value.	In the equation $2x - 5 = 13$ the unknown is represented by the letter x.

1 Do these pairs of calculations make equations? Use = for an equation and ≠ for not an equation.

 a 5×7 and $70 \div 2$

 b $24 + 17$ and 8×5

 c 14×3 and $50 - 9$

2 Write > or < in-between the calculations to make inequalities.

 a $25 \div 5$ 4×2

 b $42 \div 3$ 3×4

 c 5×11 7×8

3 Solve these equations.

 a $a + 16 = 29$

 b $b - 14 = 31$

 c $3 + c = 13$

 d $2 \times d = 30$

 e $e \div 5 = 9$

 f $3f = 27$

 g $\dfrac{g}{2} = 8$

4 Solve these equations by balancing.

 a $3x + 6 = 27$

 b $5x - 7 = 48$

 c $6x + 4 = 10$

 d $32 = 3x - 4$

5 a Write an equation for these scales.

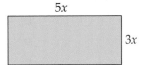

 b Solve the equation to calculate the value of p.

6 Solve these equations.

 a $n + n + 7 = n + n + n + 5$

 b $m + m + m + m = m + 18$

 c $3q + 7 = 13$

 d $5x - 12 = 4x - 10$

 e $4x - 13 = x + 5$

 f $6x - 8 = 4x - 2$

7 The perimeter of this rectangle is 32 cm

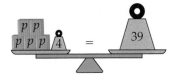

 a Write an equation for the perimeter of the rectangle.

 b Solve the equation.

 c Find the lengths of each side of the rectangle.

What next?

Score		
	0 – 3	Your knowledge of this topic is still developing. To improve look at Formative test: 3A-10; MyMaths: 1154, 1158 and 1182
	4 – 6	You are gaining a secure knowledge of this topic. To improve look at InvisiPen: 231, 232, 233, 234, 235 and 237
	7	You have mastered this topic. Well done, you are ready to progress!

1 **a** Are these scales balanced?

b What could you do to the left-hand side to make the scales balance?

c What could you do to the right-hand side?

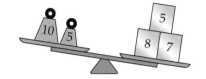

2 Copy these and complete them with >, < or = to make the statements true.

a $90 \div 3 \square 30$ **b** $32 \div 8 \square 9$ **c** $12 \square 33 \div 11$

d $19 - 6 \square 6 + 7$ **e** $24 \square 5 \times 4$ **f** $35 \div 5 \square 7$

3 Copy these and fill in the missing numbers to make the statements true.

a $15 = 3 \times \square$ **b** $12 = \square \times 3$ **c** $25 = 5 \times \square$

d $10 = 40 \div \square$ **e** $15 + \square = 21$ **f** $36 = \square \times 6$

g $12 + 3 = 6 + \square$ **h** $21 - 4 = 9 + \square$ **i** $32 \div 4 = 2 \times \square$

j $26 - 5 = 7 \times \square$ **k** $45 \div 9 = 5 \times \square$ **l** $28 + 8 = 6 \times \square$

4 Find the value of the unknown in each of these equations.

a $b + 22 = 29$ **b** $t - 30 = 40$ **c** $f - 19 = 9$

d $m + 56 = 63$ **e** $g - 18 = 2$ **f** $k - 6 = 0$

g $2t = 16$ **h** $5t = 30$ **i** $10j = 70$

j $\dfrac{t}{2} = 5$ **k** $\dfrac{t}{5} = 4$ **l** $6d = 36$

m $\dfrac{u}{10} = 2$ **n** $8n = 24$ **o** $\dfrac{v}{3} = 5$

5 **i** Write an equation for each of these scales.

ii Find the weight of one parcel on each of the scales by solving the equations.

a

b

c

6 Solve these equations.

a $5x + 34 = 19$ **b** $3b + 7 = 19$ **c** $8t - 5 = 11$

d $6s - 3 = 21$ **e** $7q + 7 = 35$ **f** $8r - 6 = 18$

g $8j - 7 = 25$ **h** $20a - 2 = 18$ **i** $2z + 30 = 50$

j $9f - 4 = 14$ **k** $11q + 3 = 36$ **l** $12k + 15 = 39$

7 i Write an equation for each of these scales.

  ii Find the weight of one parcel on each of the scales by solving the equations.

  a 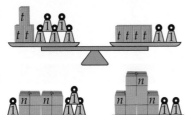   **b**

  c

8 Solve these equations.

  a $d + d + d + 7 = d + d + 15$ **b** $c + c + c + c + 10 = c + c + c + 20$

  c $v + v + v + 35 = v + 55$ **d** $m + m + m + 30 = m + 40$

  e $3e + 3 = e + 19$ **f** $5f + 6 = 2f + 18$

  g $6h + 4 = 2h + 24$ **h** $8u + 12 = u + 26$

9 i Write an expression for the perimeter of each shape.
   Use the symbols given.

  ii The perimeter of each shape is 40 cm.
   Write an equation and solve it to find the length of the sides of each shape.

  a $3n$ cm
   n cm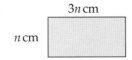

  b $4x$ cm
   $3x$ cm $3x$ cm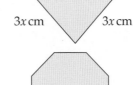

  c
   all sides are p cm

  d
   all sides are h cm

10 The perimeter of this hexagon is 56 cm.

  a Write an expression for the perimeter using y.

  b Write an equation and solve it to find the value of y.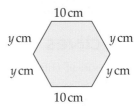

  10 cm
  y cm y cm
  y cm y cm
  10 cm

11 Powers and roots

Introduction

When you look up at the night sky you might see the M31 Galaxy, more commonly known as the Andromeda Galaxy. It is about 24 000 000 000 000 000 000 000 km from the Earth. Astronomers write the distance of the galaxy in **standard index form** as 2.4×10^{19} km. The light from the M31 galaxy has taken about 2.3 million years to reach the Earth, so you are effectively looking back in time!

What's the point?

Scientists and astronomers have to work with very large numbers. Standard index form was invented so that a number like the distance of the M31 galaxy can be written down in a much easier and clearer way than writing lots of zeros.

Objectives

By the end of this chapter, you will have learned how to …

- Identify and understand square numbers.
- Calculate and estimate square roots.
- Know the meaning of an index.
- Find numbers written in index form.
- Multiply and divide numbers by powers of 10.
- Write numbers in standard form.

Check in

1 Work out these multiplications.

   a 6 × 5   **b** 4 × 8   **c** 3 × 9   **d** 7 × 6

   e 8 × 9   **f** 3 × 7   **g** 12 × 9   **h** 7 × 4

2 Work out these divisions.

   a 36 ÷ 6   **b** 14 ÷ 2   **c** 35 ÷ 7   **d** 70 ÷ 10

   e 84 ÷ 12   **f** 32 ÷ 8   **g** 16 ÷ 4   **h** 49 ÷ 7

3 Work out these multiplications.

   a 6 × 100   **b** 5.4 × 10   **c** 3.2 × 100   **d** 6.7 × 1000

   e 8.97 × 10   **f** 3.72 × 100   **g** 2.734 × 1000   **h** 7.4 × 1000

4 Work out these divisions.

   a 36 ÷ 10   **b** 124 ÷ 10   **c** 345 ÷ 100   **d** 72.1 ÷ 10

   e 94 ÷ 100   **f** 87 ÷ 100   **g** 4829 ÷ 1000   **h** 29 ÷ 1000

Starter problem

You are given a calculator but the square root key is not working.

Find $\sqrt{70}$ to 2 decimal places.

These chocolates have been arranged into squares.

1	4	9	16	25
$1 \times 1 = 1$	$2 \times 2 = 4$	$3 \times 3 = 9$	$4 \times 4 = 16$	$5 \times 5 = 25$

The total number of chocolates in the third square is $3 \times 3 = 9$.

● 9 is a **square number** because it is made by multiplying a number by itself, like multiplying the side of a square by itself.

You can write 3×3 as 3^2.
So, $5^2 = 5 \times 5 = 25$
The graph shows the first five square numbers.

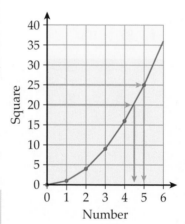

● You can use the graph to estimate the **square roots** of numbers.

The graph shows that the square root of 25 is 5...

... and the square root of 20 is about 4.5

● The square roots of numbers that are not square numbers are not whole numbers.

Exercise 11a

1 Copy and complete these statements about square roots.

The first one has been done for you.

  a   16 is the ......$square$...... of 4.

       4 is the $\underline{square\ root}$ of 16.

  b   10 is the .... of 100.

       100 is the .... of 10.

  c   9 is the .... of 3.

       3 is the .... of 9.

  d   5 is the .... of 25.

       25 is the .... of 5.

2 Copy and complete these statements.

  a $6^2 = 6 \times \square = 36$

  b $8^2 = 8 \times \square = \square$

  c $0^2 = \square \times \square = \square$

  d $9^2 = \square \times \square = \square$

  e $7^2 = 7 \times \square = \square$

  f $10^2 = \square \times \square = \square$

3 Copy and complete these statements.

  a $\sqrt{9} = \square$ b $\sqrt{16} = \square$

  c $\sqrt{36} = \square$ d $\sqrt{49} = \square$

  e $\sqrt{81} = \square$ f $\sqrt{4} = \square$

  g $\sqrt{1} = \square$ h $\sqrt{64} = \square$

  i $\sqrt{100} = \square$ j $\sqrt{0} = \square$

4 Without using a calculator, find

  a 5^2 b 3^2 c 12^2

  d 2^2 e $\sqrt{121}$ f $\sqrt{400}$

  g 9^2 h $\sqrt{144}$ i $\sqrt{625}$

5 Use your calculator to find

  a 17^2 b 26^2 c 4.7^2

  d $\sqrt{2601}$ e $\sqrt{729}$ f 9.3^2

  g 3.1^2 h $\sqrt{1681}$ i $\sqrt{1024}$

6 Use your calculator to find the answers. Round your answers to one decimal place.

  a $\sqrt{150}$ b 2.96^2 c $\sqrt{260}$

  d 11.27^2 e $\sqrt{2}$ f 9.27^2

  g 21.63^2 h $\sqrt{300}$ i $\sqrt{3}$

Problem solving

7 a Copy this graph carefully onto 2 mm graph paper.

      Make the curve as smooth as possible.

      Complete the graph for numbers up to 10 and their squares up to 100.

      Use your answers to question 1 to help.

      Join the points with a smooth curve.

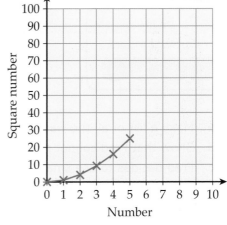

  b   Use your graph to estimate these square roots.

      i $\sqrt{30}$ ii $\sqrt{70}$ iii $\sqrt{90}$

      iv $\sqrt{55}$ v $\sqrt{86}$ vi $\sqrt{50}$

  c   Use your graph to estimate these values.

      i 3.5^2 ii 7.5^2 iii 6.8^2 iv 1.5^2 v 9.2^2 vi 0.7^2

8 Copy and complete these calculations.

  a $4^2 + \square^2 = 20$ b $5^2 - \square^2 = 24$ c $6^2 - \square^2 = 27$ d $1^2 + \square^2 = 2$

  e $2^2 \times \square^2 = 36$ f $10^2 \div \square^2 = 25$ g $13^2 - 12^2 = \square^2$ h $15^2 + 8^2 = \square^2$

9 Which two whole numbers do these square roots lie between?

  a $\sqrt{39}$ b $\sqrt{62}$ c $\sqrt{78}$ d $\sqrt{122}$

Fred wants to make a small patio from 12 square paving slabs.

Each slab has an area of 1 m².

There are different ways to make the patio.

1×12 or 12×1   2×6 or 6×2   3×4 or 4×3

I want my patio to be square. So I need to find √12.

√12 is between 3 and 4 as 3² = 9 and 4² = 16. You'll have to use a calculator.

√12
3.464 10 16 15

On my calculator I pressed √ 1 2 = .

So √12 = 3.46 m to the nearest centimetre.

It won't work, you'd have to cut your 1 m² slabs into too many pieces to make your 12 m² square patio.

Example

a Make a list of all the ways that Fred can arrange slabs for a patio of 36 m².

b Show that Fred cannot make a square patio using exactly 40 whole slabs.

c Fred decides to use smaller slabs. Each slab is square with sides of 50 cm.
What is the area of Fred's square patio if he uses 121 of these slabs?

a 1 × 36, 2 × 18, 3 × 12, 4 × 9 and 6 × 6

b The sides of the square cannot be a whole number
because 6 × 6 = 36 and 7 × 7 = 49.
40 is between 36 and 49 so √40 is between 6 and 7.

c √121 = 11
11 slabs × 50 cm = 550 cm = 5.5 m
Area = 5.5 × 5.5 m² = 30.25 m²

Exercise 11b

1 a Which of these piles of slabs will Fred be able to arrange into square patios without cutting any of the slabs?

i
15 slabs

ii
25 slabs

iii
48 slabs

iv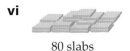
100 slabs

v
64 slabs

vi
80 slabs

b For the other three piles of slabs, use factors to show all the ways that the slabs can be arranged into rectangular patios.

> Which two numbers multiplied together would make the total number of paving slabs?

2 Show or explain why Fred cannot make a square from 30 whole slabs.

3 a Are these statements true?
b Explain your answers.

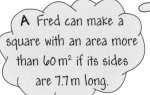
A Fred can make a square with an area more than 60 m² if its sides are 7.7 m long.

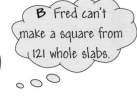
B Fred can't make a square from 121 whole slabs.

4 A square garden with an area of 225 m² is fenced.
a How long is each side of the garden?
b The gardener has 55 m of fencing. Will she be able to put a fence all the way around the garden?

Area = 225 m²

Problem solving

5 a Taylor's birthday cake has a red ribbon around it. The area of the top of the cake is 130 cm². How long is the ribbon, to the nearest centimetre? Don't include the bow!

Did you know?

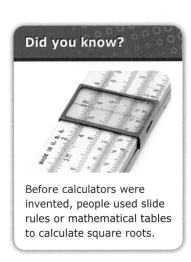

Before calculators were invented, people used slide rules or mathematical tables to calculate square roots.

Any number multiplied by itself can be written using an index or power.

You can write square numbers using the power 2.

$7^2 = 7 \times 7 = 49$

Example

Find the values of each of these expressions.

a 5^3 **b** 2^7 **c** 3^4

a $5^3 = 5 \times 5 \times 5 = 125$
b $2^7 = 2 \times 2 \times 2 \times 2 \times 2 \times 2 \times 2 = 128$
c $3^4 = 3 \times 3 \times 3 \times 3 = 81$

Example

Simplify each of these using indices.

a $9 \times 9 \times 9 \times 9 \times 9$ **b** $7 \times 7 \times 7 \times 7 \times 7 \times 7$ **c** $6 \times 6 \times 6 \times 6$

a $9 \times 9 \times 9 \times 9 \times 9 = 9^5$ Count the number of 9s.
b $7 \times 7 \times 7 \times 7 \times 7 \times 7 = 7^6$
c $6 \times 6 \times 6 \times 6 = 6^4$

You can also simplify an expression using indices.

Any letter multiplied by itself can be written using an index or power.

Example

Simplify each of these using indices.

a $a \times a \times a$ **b** $y \times y \times y \times y \times y$ **c** $p \times p \times p \times p \times p \times p$

a $a \times a \times a = a^3$ Count the number of as.
b $y \times y \times y \times y \times y = y^5$
c $p \times p \times p \times p \times p \times p = p^6$

You can multiply numbers written in index form.

4 is the same as saying 4^1.

Example

Simplify these, writing your answers using indices.

a $5^3 \times 5^2$ **b** $4^5 \times 4$

a $5^3 \times 5^2 = (5 \times 5 \times 5) \times (5 \times 5) = 5^5$ $3 + 2 = 5$
b $4^5 \times 4 = (4 \times 4 \times 4 \times 4 \times 4) \times 4 = 4^6$ $5 + 1 = 6$

When multiplying numbers in index form, add the indices. This works only when the numbers are the same.

Exercise 11c

1 Find the values of each of these.

    a 3^2 **b** 4^3

    c 2^5 **d** 7^3

    e 10^5 **f** 5^4

    g 2^{10} **h** 1^{101}

2 Molly and Nick have been asked to find the value for 3^2.

    Molly says   Nick says

    $3 \times 2 = 6$

    $3 \times 3 = 9$

    Who is correct?

    Explain your answer.

3 Simplify each of these by using indices. Do not work out the values.

    a $4 \times 4 \times 4 \times 4 \times 4$

    b $7 \times 7 \times 7$

    c $9 \times 9 \times 9 \times 9 \times 9 \times 9 \times 9$

    d $5 \times 5 \times 5 \times 5 \times 5 \times 5 \times 5 \times 5$

    e $6 \times 6 \times 6 \times 6$

    f 12×12

4 Simplify each of these by using indices.

    a $a \times a \times a$

    b $q \times q \times q \times q \times q$

    c $r \times r \times r \times r \times r \times r \times r$

    d $z \times z$

    e $d \times d \times d \times d$

    f $f \times f \times f \times f \times f \times f \times f \times f$

5 Simplify each of these using indices.

    a $3^2 \times 3^3$ **b** $8^5 \times 8^2$

    c $4^8 \times 4^2$ **d** $7^6 \times 7$

    e $5^4 \times 5^3$ **f** 12×12^3

6 Chris is asked to simplify $4^3 \times 5^2$. He says:

    $4 \times 5 = 20$ and $3 + 2 = 5$. The answer must be 20^5.

    Is he correct?

    Explain your answer.

7 Simplify each of these using indices.

    a $a^3 \times a^4$ **b** $f^5 \times f^2$

    c $d^2 \times d^3$ **d** $g \times g^4$

    e $z^2 \times z^4$ **f** $b^5 \times b^3$

    g $s^6 \times s^4$ **h** $t^3 \times t^9$

Problem solving

8 Simplify each of these using indices.

    a $9^2 \times 9^3 \times 9^4$ **b** $7^4 \times 7 \times 7^3$

    c $2^3 \times 2^3 \times 2^3$ **d** $4^2 \times 2^4$

    e $x^4 \times x^5 \times x^6$ **f** $y^9 \times y^2 \times y^4$

    g $z^2 \times z^2 \times z^2$ **h** $3^4 \times p^2 \times 3^2 \times p^3$

Did you know?

10^{100}

The number 10^{100} is called the googol. It is the number 1 followed by one hundred zeros. The number was named by nine-year-old Edwin Sirotta. Edwin came up with the name for his uncle, the mathematician Edward Kasner.

11d Standard form

> You can write all powers of ten using index notation.

1 million	(mega)	= 1 000 000	= 10 × 10 × 10 × 10 × 10 × 10	= 10^6
1 thousand	(kilo)	= 1000	= 10 × 10 × 10	= 10^3
1 hundred		= 100	= 10 × 10	= 10^2
1 ten		= 10	= 10	= 10^1
1 unit		= 1		= 10^0
1 tenth		= $\frac{1}{10}$	= $\frac{1}{10^1}$	= 10^{-1}
1 hundredth	(centi)	= $\frac{1}{100}$	= $\frac{1}{10^2}$	= 10^{-2}
1 thousandth	(milli)	= $\frac{1}{1000}$	= $\frac{1}{10^3}$	= 10^{-3}

> You use a negative index to mean one over the power. So 10^{-2} means $\frac{1}{10^2}$.

Example

Write these numbers in full.

a 2.4×10^4 **b** 5.32×10^7 **c** 4.5×10^{-3} **d** 7.9×10^{-5}

a $2.4 \times 10^4 = 2.4 \times 10\ 000 = 24\ 000$

b $5.32 \times 10^7 = 5.32 \times 10\ 000\ 000 = 53\ 200\ 000$

c $4.5 \times 10^{-3} = 4.5 \div 1000 = 0.0045$

d $7.9 \times 10^{-5} = 7.9 \div 100\ 000 = 0.000079$

> To write a number in standard form, re-write the number between 1 and 10 multiplied by a power of 10.

Example

Write these numbers in standard form.

a 490 000   **b** 6 480 000 000   **c** 0.00000057   **d** 0.0000153

First divide each number by a power of 10 so that it becomes a decimal between 1 and 10.

a $490\ 000 \div 100\ 000 = 4.9$

  $490\ 000 = 4.9 \times 100\ 000 = 4.9 \times 10^5$

b $6\ 480\ 000\ 000 \div 1\ 000\ 000\ 000 = 6.48$

  $6\ 480\ 000\ 000 = 6.48 \times 1\ 000\ 000\ 000 = 6.48 \times 10^9$

c $0.00000057 \div 0.0000001 = 5.7$

  $0.00000057 = 5.7 \times 0.0000001 = 5.7 \times 10^{-7}$

d $0.0000153 \div 0.00001 = 1.53$

  $0.0000153 = 1.53 \times 0.00001 = 1.53 \times 10^{-5}$

Exercise 11d

1 Sarah and Oliver are choosing the numbers written in standard form from the list.

A 4.6×10^5 **B** 38×10^3

C 3.6×10^{-2} **D** 6×10^7

E 5.4×100000

Sarah says   Oliver says

Numbers A, C, D and E are all written in standard form because they all start with a number between 1 and 10.

The numbers A, B, C and D are all written in standard form because they are all multiplied by a power of 10.

Each student has chosen an incorrect number from the list.

a Which is Sarah's incorrect number? Explain your answer.

b Which is Oliver's incorrect number? Explain your answer.

2 Write these numbers in full.

a 6.4×10^4 **b** 3.1×10^7

c 5.2×10^5 **d** 9.6×10^3

e 4.39×10^7 **f** 6.53×10^6

g 1.53×10^5 **h** 5.24×10^8

i 4.23×10^3 **j** 7.325×10^9

3 Write these numbers in standard form.

a 740 000   **b** 9300

c 1 900 000   **d** 49 300 000

e 9270   **f** 264 000 000

g 6 830 000   **h** 78 000

i 135 000   **j** 64 910 000 000

4 Write these numbers in full.

a 5.3×10^{-2} **b** 3.1×10^{-4}

c 2.4×10^{-5} **d** 3.74×10^{-3}

e 9.53×10^{-7} **f** 7.48×10^{-6}

g 3.29×10^{-5} **h** 4.7×10^{-8}

i 3.65×10^{-9} **j** 1.584×10^{-3}

5 Write these numbers in standard form.

a 0.0046   **b** 0.0000027

c 0.05   **d** 0.00528

e 0.0000034   **f** 0.00000041

g 0.0000089   **h** 0.0000006

i 0.0000167   **j** 0.000000921

Did you know?

The distance between Earth and the sun varies. This is because Earth's orbit is elliptical. The average distance between Earth and the sun is approximately 9.3×10^7 miles.

Problem solving

6 The table shows the approximate population of six capital cities from around the world. Write these capital cities in order, starting with the least populated.

City	Population
San José (Costa Rica)	3.3×10^5
Ottawa (Canada)	900 000
St. Helier (Jersey)	2.8×10^4
Tokyo (Japan)	1.32×10^7
Oslo (Norway)	575 000
London (England)	8.2×10^6

11 MySummary

Check out
You should now be able to ...

	Check out		Test it Questions
✓	Identify and understand square numbers.	5	1, 2
✓	Calculate and estimate square roots.	5	1, 3, 4
✓	Know the meaning of an index.	6	5, 6, 7
✓	Simplify expressions using indices.	6	8, 9
✓	Multiply and divide numbers by powers of 10.	6	10
✓	Write numbers in standard form.	6	11

Language	Meaning	Example
Index notation	Using powers to show how many times a number has been multiplied by itself.	$5 \times 5 \times 5 \times 5 = 5^4$
Square number	A number which is equal to another number multiplied by itself.	49 is a square number because $49 = 7 \times 7$ 7 squared is written as 7^2
Square root	The square root of a number is the number you multiply by itself to get the number.	The square root of 144 is written as $\sqrt{144}$ $\sqrt{144} = 12$ as $12 \times 12 = 144$
Standard form	A way to write very large or very small numbers. A number in standard form starts with a number between 1 and 10 and is multiplied by a power of 10.	A large number in standard form looks like: $13\,400\,000\,000 = 1.34 \times 10^{10}$ A small number in standard form looks like: $0.00000056 = 5.6 \times 10^{-7}$

1 Without using a calculator, find

  a 3^2 **b** 1^2 **c** 10^2

  d $\sqrt{36}$ **e** $\sqrt{81}$ **f** $\sqrt{64}$

2 Which of these are square numbers?

1	2	4	6
8	9	12	16

3 This square has an area of $49\,cm^2$.
What is the length of each of its sides?

Area = $49\,m^2$

4 A square has an area of $144\,cm^2$.
What is its perimeter?

5 Find the value of each of these.

  a 4^3 **b** 5^4 **c** 3^6

6 Simplify each of these using indices.

  a $2 \times 2 \times 2 \times 2$

  b $6 \times 6 \times 6$

  c $7 \times 7 \times 7 \times 7 \times 7 \times 7$

  d 5

7 Simplify each of these using indices.

  a $d \times d \times d$

  b $e \times e \times e \times e \times e$

  c $f \times f \times f \times f \times f \times f \times f$

8 Simplify these, write your answer
using indices.

  a $3^2 \times 3^5$

  b $7^3 \times 7^9$

  c 11×11^4

9 Simplify these, write your answer
using indices.

  a $r^6 \times r^5$

  b $s^4 \times s^9$

  c $t^{13} \times t$

  d $y^2 \times z^3$

10 Write these numbers in full.

  a 5.6×10^2

  b 2×10^5

  c 9.4×10^6

11 Write these numbers in standard form.

  a 4000

  b $76\,000$

  c $83\,000\,000$

What next?

Score			
	0 – 4		Your knowledge of this topic is still developing. To improve look at Formative test: 3A-11; MyMaths: 1033, 1051 and 1053
	5 – 9		You are gaining a secure knowledge of this topic. To improve look at InvisiPen: 181, 182 and 183
	10 – 11		You have mastered this topic. Well done, you are ready to progress!

1 Copy and complete these statements about square numbers.

a $1^2 = 1 \times \square = 1$ b $10^2 = 10 \times \square = \square$

c $0^2 = \square \times \square = \square$ d $11^2 = \square \times \square = \square$

e $4^2 = 4 \times \square = \square$ f $12^2 = \square \times \square = \square$

2 Copy and complete these statements about square roots.

a $\sqrt{16} = \square$ b $\sqrt{4} = \square$ c $\sqrt{1} = \square$

d $\sqrt{81} = \square$ e $\sqrt{49} = \square$ f $\sqrt{144} = \square$

3 Without using a calculator, estimate the square roots of these numbers.

a $\sqrt{26}$ b $\sqrt{10}$ c $\sqrt{40}$

d $\sqrt{60}$ e $\sqrt{108}$ f $\sqrt{150}$

g $\sqrt{200}$ h $\sqrt{120}$ i $\sqrt{75}$

4 Use your calculator to find the answers to these.

a 19^2 b 23^2 c 32^2

d 5.4^2 e 8.31^2 f 14.1^2

g $\sqrt{441}$ h $\sqrt{1296}$ i $\sqrt{1369}$

j $\sqrt{2.89}$ k $\sqrt{9.3025}$ l $\sqrt{44.3556}$

5 Use your calculator to find the answer.
Round your answer to one decimal place.

a 3.77^2 b 1.234^2 c 0.999^2

d $\sqrt{3}$ e $\sqrt{10}$ f $\sqrt{17}$

g $\sqrt{200}$ h $\sqrt{1000}$ i $\sqrt{1700}$

6 a Use a calculator to decide whether you can make a square from 625 square tiles.

b Explain how you know.

7 A square garden with an area of 196 m² is to be fenced.

a What is the length of each side of the garden?

b The gardener has 50 m of fencing.
How many more metres of fencing will he need to put a fence all the way around the garden?

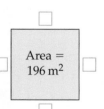

Area = 196 m²

8 Rini wants to make the largest square possible from 500 square tiles.
How many tiles will she have left over?

9 Find the values of each of these.

   a 5^2 **b** 3^3 **c** 2^4

   d 4^3 **e** 10^7 **f** 5^5

   g 4^4 **h** 2^9 **i** 7^3

10 Simplify each of these by using indices. Do not work out the values.

   a $7 \times 7 \times 7 \times 7$ **b** $10 \times 10 \times 10 \times 10 \times 10$

   c $3 \times 3 \times 3 \times 3 \times 3$ **d** $4 \times 4 \times 4 \times 4 \times 4 \times 4 \times 4 \times 4$

   e $2 \times 2 \times 2 \times 2 \times 2 \times 2 \times 2$ **f** 3

   g $6 \times 6 \times 6 \times 6 \times 6 \times 6$ **h** $12 \times 12 \times 12 \times 12 \times 12 \times 12 \times 12 \times 12$

11 Simplify each of these by using indices.

   a $y \times y \times y \times y \times y$ **b** $z \times z \times z \times z$

   c $t \times t \times t \times t \times t \times t \times t$ **d** $g \times g \times g$

   e $p \times p \times p \times p \times p \times p \times p \times p \times p$ **f** q

   g $r \times r \times r \times r$

12 Simplify each of these using indices.

   a $4^3 \times 4^5$ **b** $5^4 \times 5^5$ **c** $7^5 \times 7^6$

   d $9^7 \times 9$ **e** $6^3 \times 6^7$ **f** $12^2 \times 12^4$

13 Write these numbers in full.

   a 3.1×10^3 **b** 1.8×10^5 **c** 7.83×10^7

   d 1.29×10^5 **e** 2.89×10^6 **f** 8.39×10^8

   g 1.002×10^3 **h** 7.62×10^6 **i** 8.804×10^5

14 Write these numbers in standard form.

   a $9\,300\,000$ **b** $46\,000$ **c** $940\,000$

   d $4\,700\,000$ **e** $86\,900$ **f** $63\,800\,000$

   g $300\,400$ **h** $627\,000$ **i** $909\,900\,000$

15 Write these numbers in full.

   a 4.7×10^{-4} **b** 2.8×10^{-3} **c** 3.45×10^{-6}

   d 8.13×10^{-5} **e** 5.49×10^{-6} **f** 9.1×10^{-7}

   g 1.234×10^{-6} **h** 7.007×10^{-3} **i** 9.631×10^{-1}

16 Write these numbers in standard form.

   a 0.055 **b** 0.00038 **c** 0.0092

   d 0.000023 **e** 0.0000000445 **f** 0.000000962

   g 0.1667 **h** 0.000102 **i** 0.0000007

MyMaths.co.uk

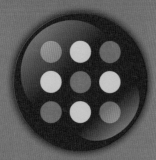

12 Constructions

Introduction

How do you build a pyramid? The Great Pyramid of Giza is one of the seven wonders of the ancient world. It was completed in approximately 2560 BC and took about 20 years to build. At its time, and for the next 3000 years, it was the tallest building in the world!

What's the point?

To construct any complex building requires accurate scale drawings and mathematical calculations for all the dimensions.

Objectives

By the end of this chapter, you will have learned how to …

- Use a protractor to draw acute and obtuse angles.
- Construct a triangle given two angles and the side between them (ASA).
- Use a ruler and compasses to construct the perpendicular bisector of a line.
- Use a ruler and compasses to bisect an angle.
- Construct a triangle given two sides and the angle between them (SAS).
- Construct a triangle given three sides (SSS).
- Use bearings to specify a direction.

Check in

1 Draw lines of length
   a 3 cm   **b** 4.2 cm   **c** 7.4 cm   **d** 5.6 cm   **e** 18 mm   **f** 29 mm

2 Measure the three sides of each triangle. Give your answer in   **i** cm   **ii** mm.
   iii Write the mathematical name of each triangle.

a
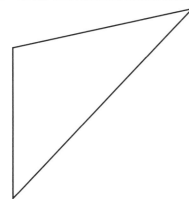

b
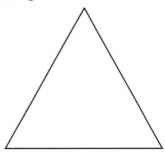

Starter problem

Construct an equilateral triangle with sides of length 8 cm.
Construct the perpendicular bisector of each side and you
should notice that all three bisectors meet at a point.
Using this point as the centre, draw a new circle.

Investigate other types of triangles.

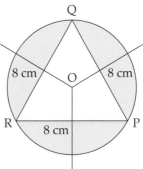

● You use a protractor to draw angles.

Make sure you use the scale which starts at zero.

60° is an acute angle.

Step 1

Draw a line.

Step 2

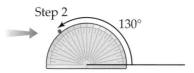

Measure 60° and mark angle.

Step 3

Draw angle.

130° is an obtuse angle.

Step 1

Draw a line.

Step 2

Measure 130° and mark angle.

Step 3

Draw angle.

● You can construct a triangle given two angles and the side between them.

Example

Construct triangle ABC.

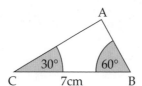

Side CB = 7 cm
∠C = 30°
∠B = 60°

Step 1

7 cm

Draw side CB.

Step 2

Measure ∠C (30°) and mark angle.

Step 3

Draw angle.

Step 1

Measure ∠B (60°) and mark angle.

Step 2

Draw angle so that it intersects line AC.

Step 3

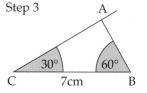

Label triangle.

Exercise 12a

1 Read the scale on each protractor to measure each angle.

  i What is the size of each angle?

  ii Is it an acute or obtuse angle?

a

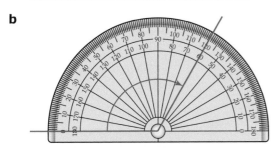

b

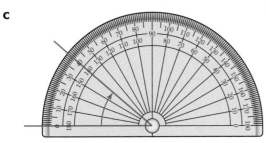

c

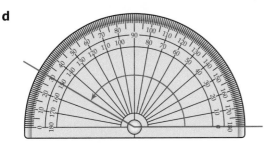

d

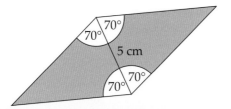

2 Use a ruler and a protractor to construct these acute angles.

  a 50°   **b** 35°

  c 10°   **d** 83°

3 Use a ruler and a protractor to construct these obtuse angles.

  a 150°   **b** 125°

  c 100°   **d** 174°

4 Use a ruler and a protractor to construct these triangles.

a

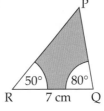

b

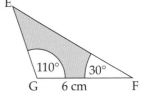

c

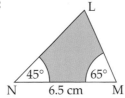

d

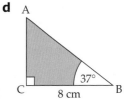

e

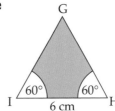

f

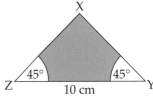

Problem solving

5 Construct these quadrilateral using a ruler and protractor.

a

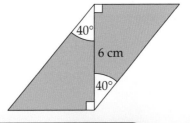

b

12b Perpendicular lines

🔘 When a line meets or crosses another line at 90° the lines are perpendicular.

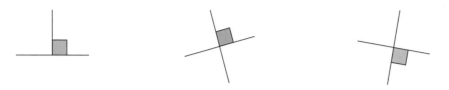

🔘 You can draw perpendicular lines using a set square and ruler or using a protractor and ruler.

1 Using a ruler and a set square.

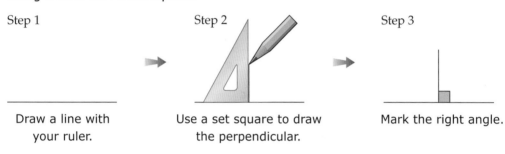

Step 1

Draw a line with your ruler.

Step 2

Use a set square to draw the perpendicular.

Step 3

Mark the right angle.

2 Using a ruler and a protractor.

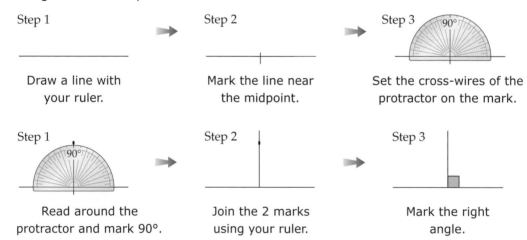

Step 1

Draw a line with your ruler.

Step 2

Mark the line near the midpoint.

Step 3

Set the cross-wires of the protractor on the mark.

Step 1

Read around the protractor and mark 90°.

Step 2

Join the 2 marks using your ruler.

Step 3

Mark the right angle.

Exercise 12b

1 In each picture an angle is marked between a pair of lines.
Write whether each of the lines are perpendicular or not.

a

b

c

d

e

f

g

h

2 Use a set square or protractor to decide which 2 lines are perpendicular to the red line.

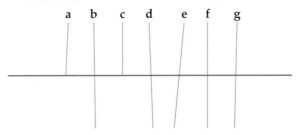

a b c d e f g

3 a Draw a horizontal line 8 cm long.
Label it RS.
Mark the midpoint of this line.
Draw a line perpendicular to RS.
Mark the right angle.

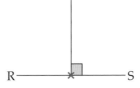

R ———×——— S

b Draw a vertical line 6 cm long.
Label it KL.
Mark the midpoint of this line.
Draw a line perpendicular to KL.
Mark the right angle.

K
×
L

Problem solving

4 On plain paper, use a protractor or set square to draw a
a right-angled triangle
b square
c rectangle.

○ A **bisector** cuts a line exactly in half.
○ A **perpendicular** line is at right angles (90°) to another line.

Follow these steps to bisect a line AB.

Do not rub out your
construction lines.

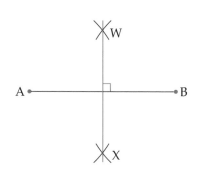

Step 1

Open your compasses so that the radius is
more than half the length of the line AB.

Step 2

Place the point of   Draw two **arcs**, one above
the compasses at A.   and one below the line.

Step 3

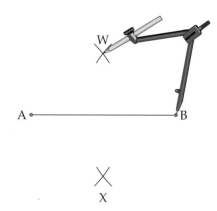

Do not adjust the compasses.
Place the point of the compasses at B.
Draw two more arcs that **intersect** the first
at W and X.

Step 4

Draw a line though W and X.
This line bisects AB and is perpendicular to AB.
It is the **perpendicular bisector** of the line AB.

○ The **perpendicular bisector** of a line cuts the line exactly in
half and is at right angles to the line.

Example

What mistakes have been made in constructing these perpendicular bisectors?

a

b

a   The radius of the compasses is less than half the   b   The radius of the compasses has not been kept
    length of the line.   the same.

6

Exercise 12c

1 a Draw a line 8 cm long.
Construct the perpendicular bisector.
Measure to check that the line is cut
exactly in half.
Measure to check that the bisector
is perpendicular (at right angles) to
the line.

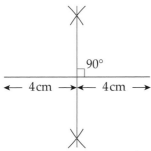

b Repeat part **a** for lines of these
lengths.

i 5 cm   **ii** 10 cm

iii 7.5 cm   **iv** 11.5 cm

2 a Follow these steps to construct a
perpendicular bisector on one arm
of an angle.

Step 1

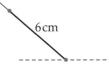

Draw a base line and mark a point.
Draw a line at an angle of
40° from the point.

Step 2

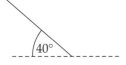

Mark another point 6 cm along the line.

2   **Step 3**

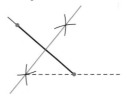

Construct the perpendicular
bisector of the line.

b Draw these lines and construct their
perpendicular bisectors.

i A line 8 cm long at an angle of 30°

ii A line 7.5 cm long at an angle of 75°

iii A line 6 cm long at an angle of 90°

iv A line 9 cm long at an angle of 105°

3 Draw a circle, centre O and radius 4 cm.
Draw a line AB between any two points on
the edge of the circle and construct the
perpendicular bisector of AB.
Does the bisector go through O, the
centre of the circle?

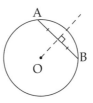

4 Draw a large triangle.
Bisect each side of the triangle.
Do all the bisectors intersect at one point?

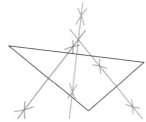

> Make the
> sides between
> 7 cm and
> 12 cm long.

Problem solving

5 a Draw a line AB that is 7 cm long and follow steps 1 to 4 on the previous page.
Then join A, W, B and X to create a four sided shape.

b What is the name of the quadrilateral?
Explain how you know which shape it is.

MyMaths.co.uk   🔍 1089   **SEARCH**

12d Angle bisectors

⬤ Bisect means to cut in two.
When you bisect an angle you cut it exactly in half.

The red line bisects this angle of 50°.
Half of 50° is 25°.

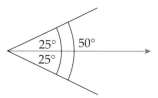

Follow these steps to bisect an angle of 70°.

Step 1

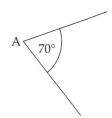

This is the angle to be bisected.

Step 2

Place the point of the **compasses** at A.
Draw two **arcs**, one on each arm of the angle.

Step 3

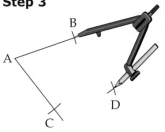

Draw two more arcs, one from B and one from A, that **intersect** at D.

Step 4

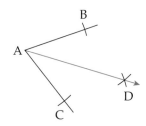

Draw a line from A through D.
This line bisects the angle.
It is the **angle bisector** of the angle.

⬤ Use your protractor to check you have bisected the angle correctly.

Example

Bisect an angle of 140°.

Step 1

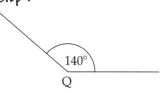

Draw an angle of 140° using a protractor.

Step 2

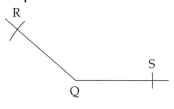

Put the point of the compasses at Q.
Draw an arc on each arm.

Step 3

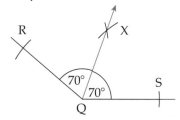

Draw two more arcs, one from R and one from S, that intersect at X.
Draw the angle bisector from Q through X.

Geometry and measures Constructions

Exercise 12d

Draw each angle using a protractor and a ruler.

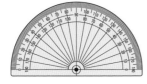

1 Bisect each angle.

a

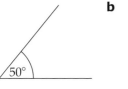

50°

b

70°

c

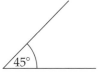

45°

d

30°

2 Bisect each angle.

a

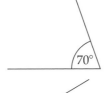

110°

b

105°

2 c

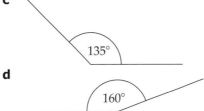

135°

d

160°

3 Use a pair of compasses to bisect each angle.

  a 58°   **b** 134°

  c 87°   **d** 163°

Use your protractor to measure the bisected angles.

Is each bisector exactly half of each angle?

If you didn't have a pair of compasses, can you think of a way to bisect an angle?

Problem solving

4 Draw a large triangle.

Bisect each angle of the triangle.

Do all the bisectors intersect at one point?

Make the sides between 6 cm and 12 cm long.

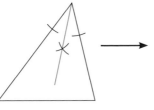

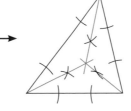

5 a Draw a line AB, 8 cm long, and construct its perpendicular bisector XY.

Label the midpoint of AB as M.

b Bisect the angle BMX and angle AMX.

c What is the angle between the two angle bisectors.

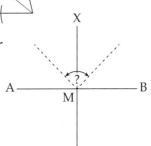

12e Constructing triangles

> You can **construct** a triangle when you know two sides and the angle between them (SAS).

Example

Construct the triangle PQR using a ruler and protractor.
PQ = 6 cm, angle QPR = 35° and PR = 6 cm

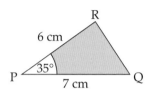

Draw the **base** 7 cm long.

Mark an angle of 35° with a protractor.

Draw a line through the mark and measure and mark 6 cm along the line.

Join the end of the base to the **apex** to complete the triangle.

> You can construct a triangle when you know all three sides (SSS).

Example

Construct the triangle ABC with sides
AB = 8 cm, AC = 6 cm and BC = 5 cm.

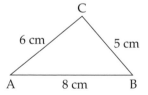

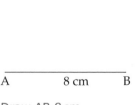

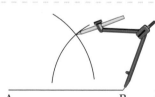

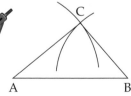

Draw AB 8 cm

Draw an arc, centre A and radius 6 cm

Draw an arc, centre B and radius 5 cm to cross the first arc.

Label the crossing point C and draw in lines AC and BC

Exercise 12e

1   These are SAS triangles.

You are given two sides and the angle between them. Construct the triangles.

Label each triangle with its mathematical name. It may be scalene, right-angled, isosceles or equilateral.

a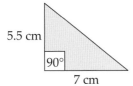

5.5 cm

90°

7 cm

b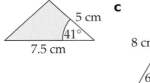

5 cm

41°

7.5 cm

c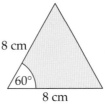

8 cm

60°

8 cm

d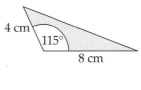

4 cm

115°

8 cm

2   These are SSS triangles.

You are given three sides. Construct the triangles.

a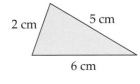

2 cm   5 cm

6 cm

b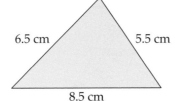

6.5 cm   5.5 cm

8.5 cm

c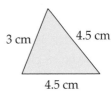

3 cm   4.5 cm

4.5 cm

d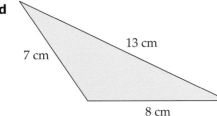

7 cm   13 cm

8 cm

e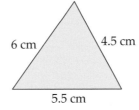

6 cm   4.5 cm

5.5 cm

f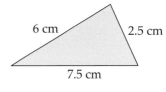

6 cm   2.5 cm

7.5 cm

Problem solving

3   Construct these triangles and measure their angles.

   a   ABC with AB = 6 cm
                  BC = 8 cm
         and AC = 10 cm

   b   XYZ with XY = 12 cm
                 YZ = 5 cm
         and XZ = 13 cm

4   How many different ways can you find to construct these triangles?

a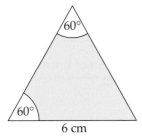

60°

60°

6 cm

b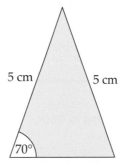

5 cm   5 cm

70°

![MyMaths.co.uk]   Q 1090   SEARCH

12f Bearings

> The angle of turn from north is called a **bearing**.

Jack is standing on Broom Hill looking north.

He turns **clockwise** through an angle of 50°.
He can see the church tower.

He turns clockwise through an angle of 130°.
He can see the gate.

> To give an accurate bearing
> - use the 360° scale
> - measure clockwise from north
> - use three digits, even when the bearing is less than 100°

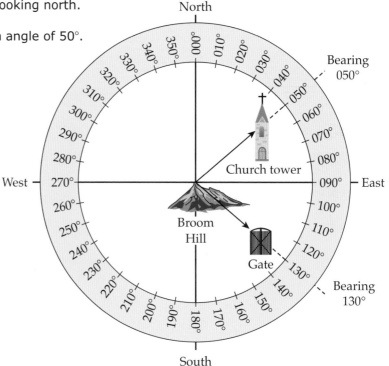

You can use a 180° protractor to measure bearings.

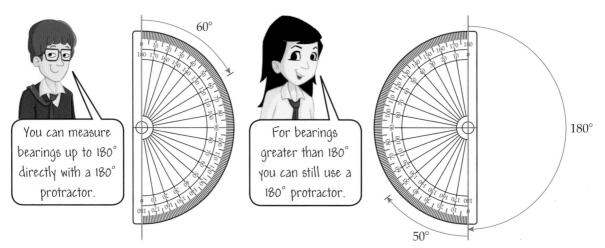

You can measure bearings up to 180° directly with a 180° protractor.

For bearings greater than 180° you can still use a 180° protractor.

This angle measures 60°.
The **three-figure bearing** is 060°.

Use the protractor to measure the part of the angle past 180°.
Add this to 180° to find the bearing.
180° + 50° = 230°
The bearing is 230°.

Exercise 12f

Ruth is standing in the middle of a field.

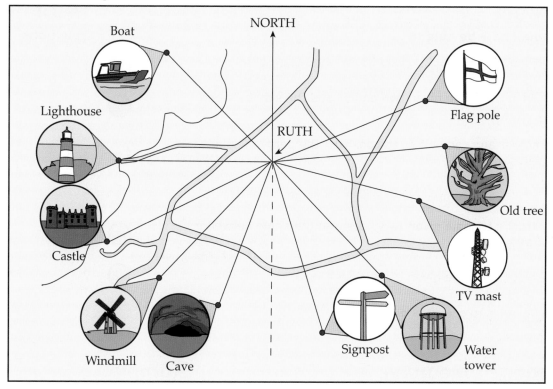

1   What will Ruth see on a bearing of
    a 085°   **b** 200°
    c 105°   **d** 315°
    e 225°?

2   On what bearing is Ruth looking when she
    can see these landmarks?
    a The water tower **b** The lighthouse
    c The old tree   **d** The castle
    e The signpost

3   A **compass** shows
    the main points
    of direction.
    What will Ruth
    see if she looks to
    a the west
    b the south-east
    c the north-west
    d the south-west?

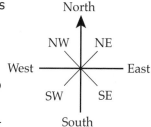

4   Copy this table. Use the information on this page to complete the table.

Direction	N					SW	W	NW
Bearing	000°	045°	090°	135°	180°			

Problem solving

5   Heather can see Mandy on a bearing 057° and Tony on a bearing 290°.
    What is Heather's bearing as seen by
    a Mandy   **b** Tony?

Draw a sketch
to help you.

Check out

You should now be able to ...

✓ Use a protractor to draw acute and obtuse angles.	5	1
✓ Construct a triangle given two angles and the side between them (ASA).	5	2
✓ Use a ruler and compasses to construct the perpendicular bisector of a line.	6	3, 4
✓ Use a ruler and compasses to bisect an angle.	6	5
✓ Construct a triangle given two sides and the angle between them (SAS).	5	6
✓ Construct a triangle given three sides (SSS).	5	7
✓ Use bearings to specify a direction.	6	8

Language	Meaning	Example
Bearing	A bearing is a clockwise measure of turn from north using three digits.	North Lighthouse Bearing 142° Boat
Bisector	A bisector is a line that divides an angle or another line in half.	angle bisector
Perpendicular	Two lines are perpendicular if they meet at right-angles (90°).	

1   Use a ruler and protractor to draw
    these angles.
    a   55°   **b**   145°
    c   170°   **d**   225°

2   Construct these triangles.

    a
    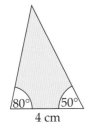
    80° 50°
    4 cm

    b
    35°
    6 cm

3   **a**   Draw a horizontal line 9 cm long,
              label it AB.
    b   Draw a line perpendicular to AB.

4   **a**   Draw a vertical line 6 cm long.
    b   Construct the perpendicular bisector.

5   **a**   Use your protractor to draw an angle
              of 66°.
    b   Use a pair of compasses to construct
              the angle bisector.

6   Construct these triangles.

    a
    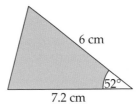
    6 cm
    52°
    7.2 cm

    b
    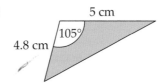
    5 cm
    105°
    4.8 cm

7   Construct
    this triangle.
    10 cm
    8 cm
    6 cm

8   What is the bearing of A from North in
    each diagram?

    a   A **b**   N

    N

    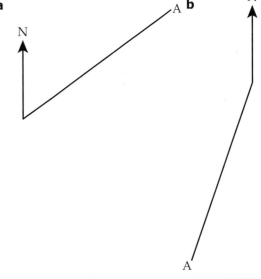

    A

What next?

Score	0 – 3		Your knowledge of this topic is still developing. To improve look at Formative test: 3A-12; MyMaths: 1081, 1086, 1089 and 1090
	4 – 6		You are gaining a secure knowledge of this topic. To improve look at InvisiPen: 371, 373 and 374
	7 – 8		You have mastered this topic. Well done, you are ready to progress!

MyMaths.co.uk

12a

1 Measure each angle and say whether it is acute or obtuse.

a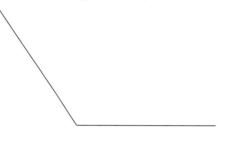

b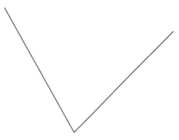

2 Draw these angles accurately.

a 70°   b 140°   c 25°   d 108°

3 Construct these triangles accurately using a ruler and protractor.

a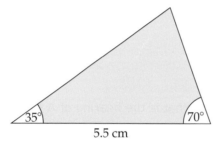

b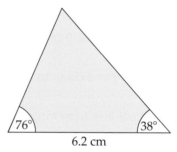

12b

4 Draw a horizontal line 6 cm long.
Draw a line perpendicular to your line.

5 Draw a vertical line 7 cm long.
Draw a line perpendicular to your line.

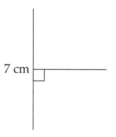

12c

6 a Draw line RS.
b Using a pair of compasses, draw a perpendicular bisector for line RS.

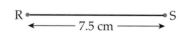

7 a Draw angle EFG.

b Using a pair of compasses, bisect angle EFG.

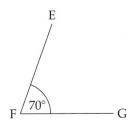

8 Using a ruler, compasses and protractor, construct these triangles (SAS).

a

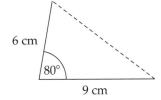

b

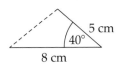

9 Using a ruler, compasses and protractor, construct these triangles (SSS).

a

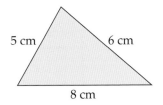

b

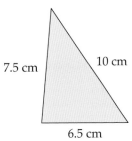

10 Measure each bearing, clockwise from north. Give each answer as a three-figure bearing.

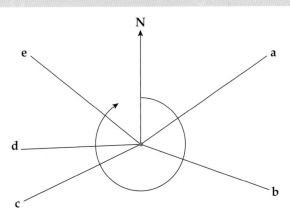

Case study 4: Garden design

Sensory gardens are designed to stimulate the senses - sight, sound, smell, touch and even taste - and are thought to have a beneficial effect on people who visit them. Whilst they must be designed for all users, this case study considers their accessibility for wheelchair users.

Raised flowerbeds are easier to reach for a person in a wheelchair.

Cross section of a raised bed

PLAN FOR A SENSORY CORNER

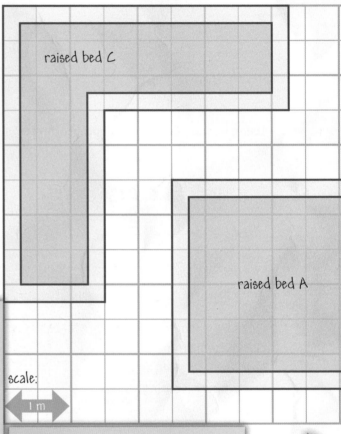

raised bed C

raised bed A

scale:

1 m

Task 1

Look at the scale drawing of the garden.

Calculate the area in m² of
a) bed A   b) bed B (to 1 d.p.)

By considering different shapes, calculate the area of
c) bed C (to 1 d.p.) d) bed D (to 1 d.p.)

Task 2

Look at the cross-section diagram of a raised bed. Each bed is to be filled with soil to 5 cm from the top of the wall. Calculate the volume of soil needed to fill

a)   bed A   b)   bed B
c)   bed C   d)   bed D

Give your answers in m³ to 1 d.p. where appropriate.

Wide paths and few sharp corners make it easier to get around.

232

...ants have different feels, different scents and ...ake different sounds as the wind blows. They ...o attract insects which add to the sounds.

Task 4

The area surrounding the beds and the path will be paved. Calculate the area that is to be paved, giving your answer in m² to 1 d.p.

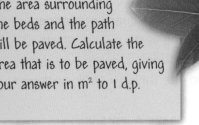

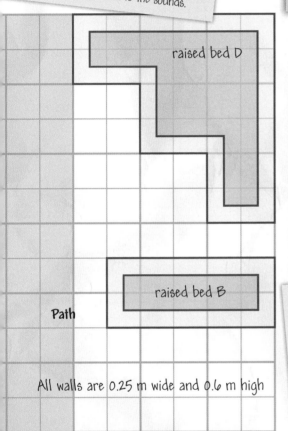

raised bed D

raised bed B

Path

All walls are 0.25 m wide and 0.6 m high

Task 5

The path is made extra wide to fit a wheelchair comfortably.

a) Looking at the scale drawing, how wide is the path?

b) The path is to be sloped to provide access for wheelchair users.

It will have a gradient of 1:20, starting at X and rising up to Y.

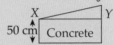

i) At what height above bed A will the path be in the middle?

ii) At what height above bed D will the path be, at the end of the path Y?

Water features add sound and touch to a garden.

Task 3 (challenge)

Look again at the cross-section diagram of a raised bed.

Calculate the volume of concrete needed to make the **foundations** of

a) bed A b) bed B

Calculate the volume of concrete needed to make the **walls** of

c) bed A d) bed C

Give your answers in m³ to 1 d.p.

2.

These questions will test you on your knowledge of the topics in chapters 9 to 12.
They give you practice in the types of questions that you may see in your GCSE exams.
There are 85 marks in total.

1 Copy this diagram onto square grid paper.

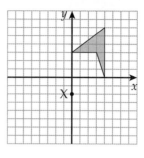

  a Reflect the shape in the *x*-axis which
  acts as a mirror line. (2 marks)

  b Rotate this shape through 180° clockwise
  about the point X. (2 marks)

  c Translate this shape 4 units up. (1 mark)

  d What do you notice about the original
  shape and this translated shape? (2 marks)

2 Copy these shapes onto square grid paper.

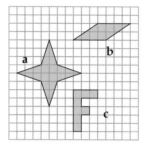

  i Draw any lines of symmetry on each shape. (3 marks)

  ii State the order of rotational symmetry in
  each case. (3 marks)

3 The quadrilateral ABCD is enlarged to give the
quadrilateral A′B′C′D′.
Copy the diagram onto square grid paper.

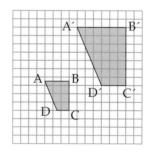

  a By drawing lines find the point of intersection.
  Mark this point O. (4 marks)

  b Measure the lines OA and OA′ and OB, OB′
  to determine the scale factor. (3 marks)

4 Are these equations true or false?

  a $13 \times 7 > 14 \times 6$ (1 mark) **b** $48 \div 6 < 49 \div 7$ (1 mark)

  c $92 \times 3 = 4 \times 69$ (1 mark) **d** $625 < 24 \times 26$ (1 mark)

5 Solve these equations.

  a $d - 15 = 6$ (1 mark) **b** $\frac{e}{7} = 3$ (1 mark)

  c $7f + 12 = 33$ (2 marks) **d** $5g - 4 = 46$ (2 marks)

6 Solve these equations.

  a $12a + 4 = 8a + 16$ (2 marks) **b** $2v + 7 = v + 10$ (2 marks)

  c $5t + 3 = 7t - 15$ (2 marks) **d** $7u + 2 = 13u - 4$ (2 marks)

7 I collect 2 boxes (*b*) of apples together with 5 loose apples. I have 53 apples altogether. Write an equation for this problem and solve it to find the number of apples in a box. (2 marks)

8 a Draw an *x*-axis from 0 to 10 and a *y*-axis from 0 to 100 on square grid paper. (2 marks)
  b On your graph plot the square numbers from 1 up to 10. (3 marks)
  c Join up the points with a smooth curve. (2 marks)
  d Use your graph to estimate
   i $\sqrt{20}$ (1 mark) **ii** 8.5^2 (1 mark) **iii** $\sqrt{72}$ (1 mark) **iv** 2.8^2 (1 mark)

9 a A hectare of land covers an area of 10 000 square metres. If this land area was square, how long would each side be? (2 marks)
  b An acre of land covers an area of 4046 square metres. If this land area was square, how long would each side be? (2 marks)
  c By what size factor (to 2 dp) is a hectare bigger than an acre? (2 marks)

10 Write these expressions in index notation.
  a $b \times b \times b \times b$ (1 mark)   **b** $4 \times y \times y \times y \times y$ (1 mark)
  c $3 \times g^2 \times 2 \times g^4$ (1 mark)

11 Draw a horizontal line 10 cm long. Construct the perpendicular bisector of this line. Leave on your construction arcs. (3 marks)

12 i Copy these angles accurately onto plain paper using a ruler and a protractor. (4 marks)
  ii Using a pair of compasses bisect each angle. Leave on your construction arcs. (4 marks)

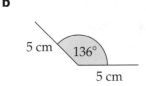

13 a Draw this triangle using a ruler and protractor. (3 marks)
  b Bisect each angle accurately to find the middle of the triangle. (4 marks)
  c Measure one of the centre angles. (2 marks)

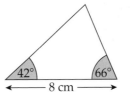

14 A short sailing course starts at a point S. The boats sail on a bearing of 140° for 300 m before rounding a buoy at A to sail on a new bearing of 045°. They continue on this bearing for 800 m before reaching a second buoy B. From here they head straight for home at S.
  a Draw an accurate diagram of the course using a scale of 1 cm = 50 m. (3 marks)
  b Determine the bearing of S from B. (2 marks)

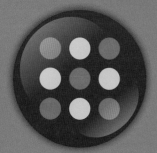

13 Sequences

Introduction

There is a famous story told across many cultures of a wise man and a king. The wise man serves the king over many years and is rewarded with any prize he wishes to name. The man asks only for a chessboard and for one grain of rice to be placed on the first square, double this amount on the second square, double this amount on the third square and so on ... The king agrees to this prize.

Was this a good prize to choose?

What's the point?

If the king had known a bit about sequences he would not have agreed to the prize!

Objectives

By the end of this chapter, you will have learned how to ...

- Identify and use term-to-term rules.
- Generate sequences using term-to-term rules.
- Find and use position-to-term rules.
- Find and use the nth term.

Check in

1 Do these calculations in your head.

   a 5 + 7 + 7 + 7 + 7   **b** 1 × 2 × 2 × 2 × 2

   c 80 − 6 − 6 − 6 − 6   **d** 400 ÷ 2 ÷ 2 ÷ 2 ÷ 2

   e 16 + 9 + 9 + 9   **f** 41 − 3 − 3 − 3 − 3

2 Complete the mapping for this rule.

In		Out
1	→	1
2	→	☐
3	→	☐
4	→	☐
5	→	☐
6	→	☐

in → ×3 → −2 → out

3 Write the first five multiples of

   a 3   **b** 7   **c** 5   **d** 4   **e** 11   **f** 9

Starter problem

A very bright girl receives £3 a week in pocket money.

She decides to renegotiate her pocket money with her father.

'Dad, could I just have 50p pocket money this week?'

'Of course', says her father.

'And next week can I have 20p more?'

'I don't see why not', replies her dad.

'And maybe just 20p more each week from then on?'

'OK – sounds like I'm getting a good deal here – are you sure?'

Investigate the new pocket money scheme. After how many weeks will the girl receive more than £3 a week pocket money?

Mark starts with £2 and then saves three pounds each week thereafter.

Week 1   Week 2   Week 3   Week 4   ....
£2   £5   £8   £11

His savings grow by £3 each week.
The savings can be written as a **sequence**.

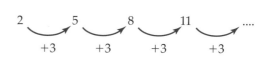

You get the next term in this sequence by adding 3.

This is the **rule** that **generates** the next **term** in the sequence.

This pattern uses a different rule.

1   3   9

This is the sequence.

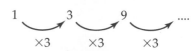

You get the next term in this sequence by multiplying by 3.

So the next term will be 3 × 9 = 27.

 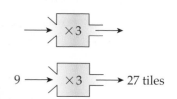

The next drawing in the pattern has 27 tiles.

⬤ A rule that allows you to find the value of the next term in a sequence is called a **term-to-term rule**.

Example

a What is the term-to-term rule for this pattern of beads?

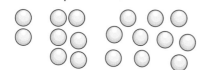

b Use this rule to add two more terms to this sequence.
21, 18, 15, ...

⟶ −3 ⟶

a The sequence for this pattern is 2, 6, 10, ...
The rule is +4.

b 21 ⤵ 18 ⤵ 15 ⤵ 12 ⤵ 9
       −3   −3   −3   −3

6

Exercise 13a

1 For each pattern
   i   write the sequence
   ii write the term-to-term rule.

   a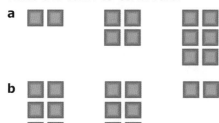

   b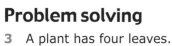

   c

1   **d**

2 For each sequence
   i   write the term-to-term rule
   ii use the rule to find the next
       three terms of the sequence.
     a 6, 11, 16, 21, ...
     b 7, 16, 25, 34, ...
     c 25, 21, 17, 13, ...
     d 13, 21, 29, 37, ...
     e 3, 6, 12, 24, ...
     f 960, 480, 240, 120, ...

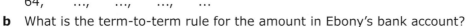

Problem solving

3 A plant has four leaves.
It grows four new leaves each week.
   a Write the sequence for this plant for the first six weeks.
   b What is the term-to-term rule for the sequence?

4 Ebony has £64 in her bank account.
Every week she spends half of the money left in her bank account.
   a Copy and complete this sequence for the money in her bank account
       for the first five weeks.
       64,   ...,   ...,   ...,   ...
   b What is the term-to-term rule for the amount in Ebony's bank account?

5 This is a special pattern.
   a Count the number of beads in each pattern and write
       the numbers as a sequence.
   b Write the differences between the terms as the
       sequence moves on.
   c How many beads are there in the next drawing?

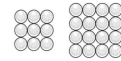

Chloe records the growth of a plant.

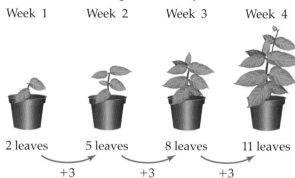

Week 1   Week 2   Week 3   Week 4

2 leaves   5 leaves   8 leaves   11 leaves

+3   +3   +3

Each week the plant grows three more leaves.

Week		Number of leaves	Multiples of 3
1	→	2	3
2	→	5	6
3	→	8	9
4	→	11	12

> The number of leaves goes up by three each time, so I looked at the 3 times table. The actual number of leaves is always 1 less.

The rule that connects the week number and the number of leaves is multiply by 3 then subtract 1.

Week number → ×3 → −1 → Number of leaves

> ● To find the **position-to-term** rule
> ▶ First find the number that is added each time in the term-to-term rule.
> ▶ Second find the difference between multiples of this number and the sequence.

Karl saves some of his pocket money each week.

Week		Amount of money
1	→	£15
2	→	£25
3	→	£35
4	→	£45

a What is the rule that connects the week number and the amount of money saved?

b How much will Karl have saved by the 10th week?

Week 1   Week 2   Week 3   Week 4

£15   £25   £35   £45

+10   +10   +10

a Karl saves £10 each week and he started with £5. The amount of money is always £5 more than the multiples of 10.

The rule is multiply the week number by 10 then add 5.

Week number → ×10 → +15 → Money saved

b

10 → ×10 → +15 → £105

By the tenth week Karl has saved £105.

Exercise 13b

1 Susan makes this **pattern** using tiles.

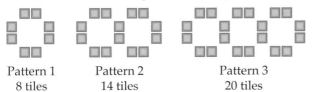

Pattern 1 — 8 tiles
Pattern 2 — 14 tiles
Pattern 3 — 20 tiles

a How many tiles are added to the previous pattern to make the next pattern?

b Copy and complete this **mapping** to show the number of tiles needed for each pattern.

Pattern number	Number of tiles
1	8
2	☐
3	☐
4	☐
5	☐

c State the rule that connects the pattern number and the number of tiles needed.

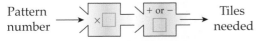

d Use your rule to calculate the value of these terms.
  i tenth term   **ii** thirtieth term
  iii fiftieth term   **vi** hundredth term

2 For each of these sequences, work out the rule which connects the position of the term and the value of the term.
You can use mappings and write your rules in this format.

a 6, 11, 16, 21, …
b 5, 7, 9, 11, …
c 9, 13, 17, 21, …
d 3, 8, 13, 18, …

Did you know?

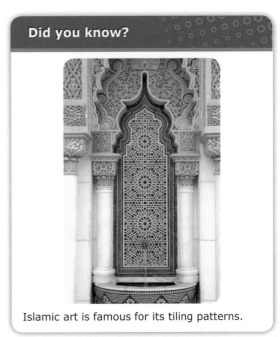

Islamic art is famous for its tiling patterns.

Problem solving

3 A seedling grows in a greenhouse.
Here is a record of its growth.

Day	1	2	3	4
Height (cm)	5.0	5.5	6.0	6.5

a How much does the plant grow each day?

b Copy and complete the rule that connects the height of the plant and the number of days' growth.

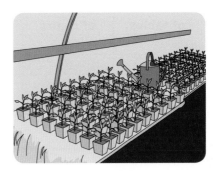

⬤ The *n*th term is a formula for the position-to-term rule.

Steve lays matchsticks in a pattern.

3 matchsticks   5 matchsticks   7 matchsticks   9 matchsticks

+2   +2   +2

Steve adds two more matchsticks each time to make his pattern.

Term	Number of matchsticks	2 times table
1	3	2
2	5	4
3	7	6
4	9	8

The rule that connects the term number and the number of matchsticks is multiply by two and add one.

Term $\boxed{\times2}$ ⇨ $\boxed{+1}$ ⇨ number of matchsticks

For any term, *n*, this means that you multiply *n* by 2 and add 1 to find the number of matchsticks.

You can write that more simply as a formula. The *n*th term is $2n + 1$.

Example

Carl is setting chairs at rectangular tables in a banquet hall.

Find the *n*th term for the number of chairs.

Number of tables	Number of chairs	4 times table
1	6	4
2	10	8
3	14	12
4	18	16

The term-to-term rule is +4

The number of tables is two more than the 4 times table

The position-to-term rule is multiply by 4 then add 2

number of tables $\boxed{\times4}$ ⇨ $\boxed{+2}$ ⇨ number of chairs

The *n*th term is $4n + 2$

⬤ Use the term-to-term rule to find the position-to-term rule.

⬤ Use the position-to-term rule to find the *n*th term.

Exercise 13c

1 Write the *n*th term for these rules.

a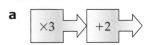

b

c ×2 −5

d ×4 +3

e ×3

f ×10 −4

2 Find the *n*th term for each sequence.

 a 3, 5, 7, 9, 11, ...
 b 5, 8, 11, 14, 17, ...
 c -3, -1, 1, 3, 5, ...
 d 3, 7, 11, 15, 19, ...
 e 2, 7, 12, 17, 22, ...
 f 11, 21, 31, 41, 51, ...
 g 9, 16, 23, 30, 37, ...
 h 6, 12, 18, 24, 30, 36, ...
 i 40, 36, 32, 28, 24, ...

Problem solving

3 A row of houses in a street are numbered using odd numbers as shown.
Find the *n*th term for this sequence.

4 A gardener lays slabs using the pattern shown.
 a Find the *n*th term for the number of white slabs.
 b Find how many white slabs the gardener will need for this pattern if he has 15 green slabs.
 c Find how many white slabs the gardener will need for this pattern if he has 90 green slabs.

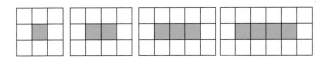

5 Felix finds the total of the numbers in the 'T' shape shown in the hundred square grid. The total is 40.

Mya finds the total of the numbers in the next 'T' shape. The total is 45.

1	2	3	4	5	6	7	8	9	10
11	12	13	14	15	16	17	18	19	20
21	22	23	24	25	26	27	28	29	30
31	32	33	34	35	36	37	38	39	40
41	42	43	44	45	46	47	48	49	50
51	52	53	54	55	56	57	58	59	60
61	62	63	64	65	66	67	68	69	70
71	72	73	74	75	76	77	78	79	80
81	82	83	84	85	86	87	88	89	90
91	92	93	94	95	96	97	98	99	100

1	2	3	4	5	6	7	8	9	10
11	12	13	14	15	16	17	18	19	20
21	22	23	24	25	26	27	28	29	30
31	32	33	34	35	36	37	38	39	40
41	42	43	44	45	46	47	48	49	50
51	52	53	54	55	56	57	58	59	60
61	62	63	64	65	66	67	68	69	70
71	72	73	74	75	76	77	78	79	80
81	82	83	84	85	86	87	88	89	90
91	92	93	94	95	96	97	98	99	100

Find the *n*th term for the total of the 'T' shape if Felix and Mya carry on with this sequence.

Look at the sequence 3, 9, 15, 21, **27**, **33**, ...

$$T(5) = 27 \quad \text{and} \quad T(6) = 33$$

T(5) just means the 5th term.

You can write $T(6) = T(5) + 6$

For any term in this sequence, you can write the **recursive formula**

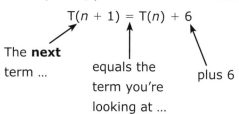

$$T(n + 1) = T(n) + 6$$

The **next** term ...

equals the term you're looking at ...

plus 6

A recursive formula is really just a term-to-term rule!

You can use a recursive formula to generate terms of a sequence.

Write the first five terms of each of these sequences.
a $T(n + 1) = T(n) + 2$ $T(1) = 3$
b $T(n + 1) = T(n) - 5$ $T(1) = 20$

a $T(1) = 3,$ $\quad\quad T(2) = 3 + 2 = 5,$ $\quad\quad T(3) = 5 + 2 = 7, ...$
3, 5, 7, 9, 11

b $T(1) = 20,$ $\quad\quad T(2) = 20 - 5 = 15,$ $\quad\quad T(3) = 15 - 5 = 10, ...$
20, 15, 10, 5, 0

Recursive sequences occur in real life.

A pond contains frogs and lily pads. Each month for a year,
the number of frogs is given by $\quad\quad T(n + 1) = T(n) + 20$
and the number of lily pads is given by $\quad T(n + 1) = T(n) + 10$
At the start of the year there are 4 frogs and 30 lily pads.

a Write the sequence of
   i the number of frogs for the first six months
   ii the number of lily pads for the first six months
b How many whole months have passed before there are more frogs than lily pads?

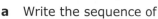

a **i** $T(2) = 4 + 20 = 24,$ $T(3) = 24 + 20 = 44, ...$
   4, 24, 44, 64, 84, 104
   ii $T(2) = 30 + 10 = 40,$ $T(3) = 40 + 10 = 50, ...$
   30, 40, 50, 60, 70, 80
b 4 months

Exercise 13d

1   For each sequence, write down the value
    of the term specified.

    Example: 3, 5, 7, **9**, 11, … $T(4) = 9$

    a   2, 5, 8, 11, 14, … $T(2) =$

    b   4, 7, 10, 13, 16, … $T(3) =$

    c   1, 7, 13, 19, 25, … $T(5) =$

    d   3, 8, 13, 18, 23, … $T(7) =$

    e   -15, -13, -11, -9, -7, … $T(8) =$

    f   6, 2, -2, -6, -10, … $T(9) =$

2   Write the first five terms of each of
    these sequences.

    a $T(n + 1) = T(n) + 1$, $T(1) = 2$

    b $T(n + 1) = T(n) + 2$, $T(1) = 0$

2   c $T(n + 1) = T(n) + 4$, $T(1) = 1$

    d $T(n + 1) = T(n) - 1$, $T(1) = -1$

    e $T(n + 1) = T(n) - 2$, $T(1) = 1$

    f $T(n + 1) = T(n) - 3$, $T(1) = -5$

3   Describe each of these sequences using
    a recursive formula.

    a   2, 4, 6, 8, 10, …

    b   3, 7, 11, 15, 19, …

    c   -2, 4, 10, 16, 22, …

    d   4, 1, -2, -5, -8, …

    e   -5, -9, -13, -17, -21, …

    f   0.5, 2.5, 4.5, 6.5, 8.5, …

Problem solving

4   Describe each of these sequences using
    a recursive formula. Careful – they
    have gaps!

    a   5, 8, ..., 14, ..., 20, …

    b   ....., 15, 17, ..., 21, 23, …

    c   ....., ..., 21, 27, 33, 39

    d   13, 27, ..., ..., 69, 83, …

    e   4, ..., 16, ..., 28, ...

    f   38, 31, ..., ..., 10, ...

5   Zachary starts up a savings account with
    £300. His bank gives him £5 interest
    each month. At the end of each month
    he records the amount in pounds sterling
    in his account:

    305, 310, 315, …

    a   Write a rule for this sequence using
        a recursive formula.

    b   Zadie starts up a bank account with
        £350. Her bank gives her £3 interest
        each month. Write out the amounts
        in Zadie's account for the first five
        months.

5   c   Who has the most money after
        two years: Zachary or Zadie?

    d   After how many months does Zachary
        have more money than Zadie?

6   Phoebe is a budding
    musician. She
    posts a song on the
    Internet and very
    soon it has gone
    viral! In the first

    week after its release, the number of hits
    was only 10, but then the weekly number
    of hits increased by the recursive formula
    $T(n + 1) = 2 \times T(n)$.

    a   Find the number of hits after

        i   3 weeks   ii   10 weeks

    b   Phoebe is aiming for 20 000 hits on
        her song. How many weeks will it take
        for this to happen?

7   Look back at the example on the opposite
    page. How many months will it take
    before each lily pad can have two frogs
    sitting on it?

MyMaths.co.uk

Check out

You should now be able to ...

Test it ➡
Questions

✓	Identify and use term-to-term rules.	6	1
✓	Generate sequences using term-to-term rules.	6	2
✓	Find and use position-to-term rules.	6	3 – 5
✓	Find and use the *n*th term.	6	6, 7

Language	Meaning	Example
nth term	A formula for the position-to-term rule of a sequence.	The *n*th term for the sequence 3, 8, 13, 18, 23, ... is 5*n* – 2
Rule	How you get from one term to the next in a sequence.	The rule for the sequence 3, 8, 13, 18, 23, ... is 'add 5'.
Sequence	A pattern of numbers or diagrams.	 3, 8, 13, 18, 23, ...
Term	A number in the sequence, identified by its position.	For the sequence 3, 8, 13, 18, 23, ..., the first term is 3, the second term is 8, etc.
Flow Chart	A flow chart is a diagram that describes a sequence of operations.	×2 ⇨ +1 ⇨ Means 'multiply by two' then 'add six'

1 For each sequence, find the term-to-term rule and write the next two terms of the sequence.

a   9   16   23   30

b   35   32   29   26

c   1   3   9   27

2 Write the first five terms of the sequences with these rules.

a   *Start with 6 and add 2*

b   *Start with 90 and subtract 8*

c   *Start with 5 and double*

d   *Start with 3, double and subtract 1*

3 This sequence of diagrams is formed by adding squares.

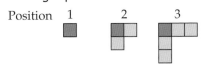

a   Draw the diagram for position 4.

b   How many squares are added to the previous pattern to make the next pattern?

c   State the rule that connects the pattern number and the number of tiles needed.

d   Find how many squares are in the 15th term of the sequence.

4 Find the position-to-term-rule for each of these sequences.

a   7   9   11   13   15

b   4   9   14   19   24

5 Find the 12th term of the sequences with these position-to-term rules.

a   multiply the position by 4 then subtract 9

b $2n + 11$

c $8n - 20$

d $4n - 4$

6 Write the nth term for these rules.

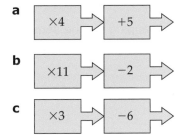

7 Find the nth term rule for each of these sequences.

a   14   24   34   44   54

b   5   13   21   29   37

c   7   8   9   10   11

d   150   250   350   450   550

What next?

13a

1 **a** Write the number sequence for this bead pattern.

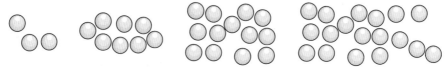

b What is the term-to-term rule for the sequence?

2 For each of these sequences

   i write the term-to-term rule

   ii add three more terms.

   a 4, 11, 18, 25, ...   **b** 12, 17, 22, 27, ...

   c 56, 48, 40, 32, ...   **d** 2, 4, 8, 16, ...

   e 480, 240, 120, 60, ...   **f** -2, 4, 10, 16, ...

13b

3 Here is a mapping for the sequence 5, 9, 13, 17, ...

Position		Term value
1	→	5 ⎞
2	→	9 ⎠ +4
3	→	13
4	→	17

a State the rule that connects the position number and the value of the term.

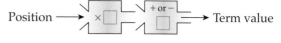

b Use your rule to calculate the value of these terms.

   i ninth term   **ii** fifteenth term   **iii** fiftieth term   **vi** hundredth term

13c

4 This is the function for a mapping.

a Copy and complete this mapping of the function.

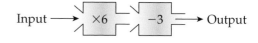

Input		Output
1	→	3
2	→	☐
3	→	☐
4	→	☐
5	→	☐

b What is the value of the nth term?

5 Jane boils water in her science lesson.

At the beginning of her experiment the temperature is 20 °C.

She checks the temperature of the water every minute.

The temperature rises by 3 °C every minute.

a Copy and complete this mapping for the first six minutes.

Time (minutes)		Temperature (°C)
1	➡	23
2	➡	☐
3	➡	☐
4	➡	☐
5	➡	☐
6	➡	☐

b Find the *n*th term.

6 For each of these sequences

  i find the *n*th term

  ii and write down the thirtieth term.

  a 5, 7, 9, 11, 13, ...   **b** 4, 11, 18, 25, 32, ...

  c 4, 9, 14, 19, 24, ...   **d** 1, 5, 9, 13, 17, ...

  e 7, 17, 27, 37, 47, ...   **f** 8, 11, 14, 17, 20, ...

7 Write the first five terms of each of these sequences.

  a $T(n + 1) = T(n) + 3$, $T(1) = 4$

  b $T(n + 1) = T(n) + 5$, $T(1) = -1$

  c $T(n + 1) = T(n) - 2$, $T(1) = 25$

  d $T(n + 1) = T(n) - 0.5$, $T(1) = 9.5$

8 Describe each of these sequences using a recursive formula.

  a 3, 6, 9, 12, 15 ...   **b** 22, 19, 16, 13, 10 ...

  c 3.5, 5, 6.5, 8, 9.5 ...   **d** 13, 8, 3, -2, -7 ...

  e -10, -6, -2, 2, 6, ...   **f** $\frac{1}{4}$, $\frac{3}{4}$, $1\frac{1}{4}$, $1\frac{3}{4}$, $2\frac{1}{4}$ ...

9 Viv won a fortune on the lottery but her motto is 'spend, spend, spend'. At the start of January she has three million pounds but each month she spends £75 000.

  a If T(*n*) represents the money Viv has at the start of the *n*th month

    i write a recursive formula for T(*n* + 1)

    ii write an *n*th term formula for T(*n*).

  b How much money does Viv have after **i** one year   **ii** two years?

  c When will Viv have spent all her money?

14 3D shapes

Introduction

Small animals such as meerkats eat only a few grams of food a day. However, it would take only about a week for a meerkat to eat the equivalent of its own body mass in food. A human on the other hand, eats about 1 kg of food a day but would take almost two months to eat the equivalent of his/her own body mass in food. Meerkats have a greater surface area in proportion to their volume than humans, meaning they lose relatively more heat and thus they need to eat relatively more.

What's the point?

The size and shape of different animals determines their metabolism. Understanding surface area and volume helps us to understand the animal kingdom.

Objectives

By the end of this chapter, you will have learned how to …

- Describe properties of solid shapes.
- Construct and use nets of solid shapes.
- Use plans and elevations.
- Find the volume of a cuboid.
- Find volumes of shapes made from cuboids.
- Find the surface area of a cuboid.

Check in

1 What is the area of each shape?
Give your answer in cm². **a** 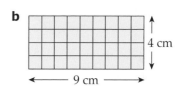 **b**

5 cm

4 cm

7 cm

9 cm

2 Find the area of each shape.

a 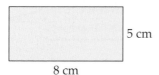 **b** 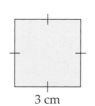 **c**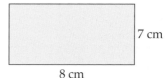

5 cm

8 cm

3 cm

7 cm

8 cm

3 Calculate.
  a $2 \times 7 \times 4$ **b** $6 \times 6 \times 2.5$ **c** $4 \times 5 + 6 \times 3$ **b** $1.5 \times 7 + 4 \times 9$

Starter problem

Here is an animal made from cubes.
Calculate the volume and surface area of the animal.

Build an enlargement of the animal which is twice as long,
twice as wide and twice as tall.
Calculate the volume and surface area of your new animal.
Investigate.

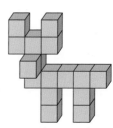

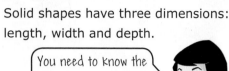

Solid shapes have three dimensions: length, width and depth.

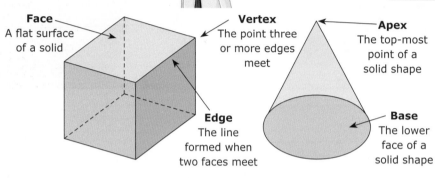

> You need to know the names for the parts of a solid.

> You use dashed lines to show the 'hidden edges' of a solid shape.

Face
A flat surface of a solid

Vertex
The point three or more edges meet

Apex
The top-most point of a solid shape

Edge
The line formed when two faces meet

Base
The lower face of a solid shape

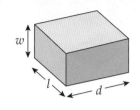

● The common names of 3D shapes which you need to know are:
cube, cuboid, pyramid, cone, sphere, triangular prism and cylinder.

> You also need to know how to recognise common 3D shapes.

Cube   **Cuboid**   **Square-based pyramid**   **Triangular-based pyramid**

Cone   **Sphere**   **Triangular prism**   **Cylinder**

Example

This is a cuboid.
Write the number of

a   edges
b   faces
c   vertices.

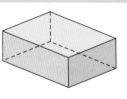

a   12 edges
b   6 faces
c   8 vertices

Exercise 14a

1 **a** How many edges has this shape?
  b How many faces has this shape?
  c How many vertices has this shape?
  d Identify one edge that is parallel to AE.
  e The shape is a cube. What shape is each face?

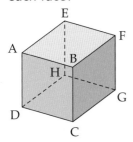

2 **a** How many edges has this shape?
  b How many faces has this shape?
  c How many vertices has this shape?
  d Which edge is parallel to BC?
  e How many edges are parallel to CF?

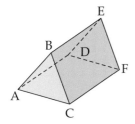

3 **a** How many edges has this shape?
  b How many faces has this shape?
  c How many vertices has this shape?

3 **d** What shape is the base of this shape?
  e How many triangles meet at the apex of this shape?

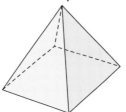

4 **a** Which three-dimensional shape has no edges, vertices, faces or base?
  b Which three-dimensional shape has four triangular faces and one square base?
  c Which three-dimensional shape has a circular base and an apex?
  d Which three-dimensional shape is made from only four triangular faces?
  e Which three-dimensional shape has six square faces?

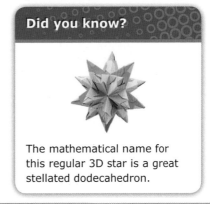

Did you know?

The mathematical name for this regular 3D star is a great stellated dodecahedron.

Problem solving

5 Kia cuts these shapes from card.
  What different solids can she make by sticking shapes together?

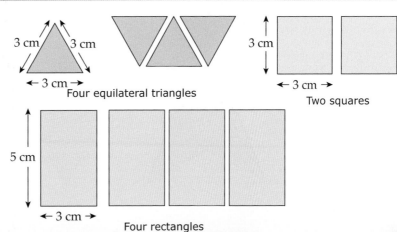

Four equilateral triangles

Two squares

Four rectangles

Collect some different shaped and sized boxes.

Cut them open and lay them flat to see what their nets look like.

A **net** is a **two-dimensional 'plan'** for making a **three-dimensional solid** shape.

When you fold this net it forms a cuboid.

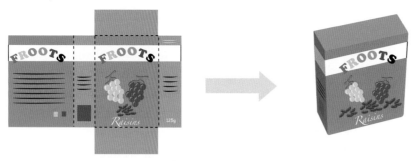

Example

Which of these will fold into a cube?

A broken line shows where the shape is to be folded.

a   b   c 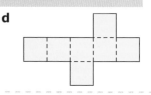   d

Shape **c** will fold into a cube.

Here are some common three-dimensional shapes and their nets.

Cube   Square-based pyramid   Triangular prism   Cylinder

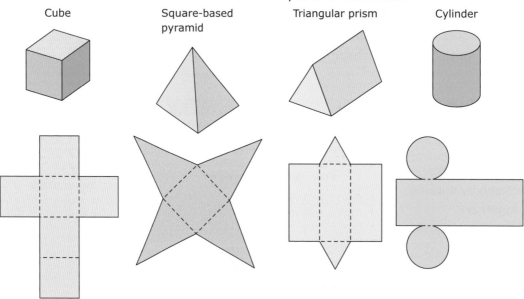

Exercise 14b

1 Name the three-dimensional shape that you can make by folding each of these nets.

a
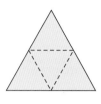

b
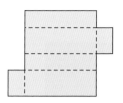

c
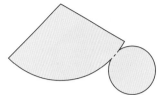

d
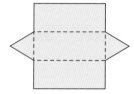

e
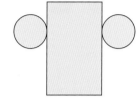

f
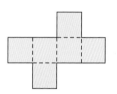

2 Draw the net of each of these shapes accurately on squared paper.

a
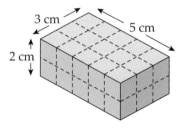
3 cm, 5 cm, 2 cm

b
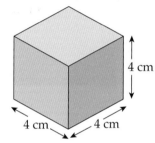
4 cm, 4 cm, 4 cm

c
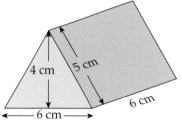
4 cm, 5 cm, 6 cm, 6 cm

Problem solving

3 Copy this shape onto centimetre-squared paper.
Cut it out and fold along the dashed lines. Glue it together.

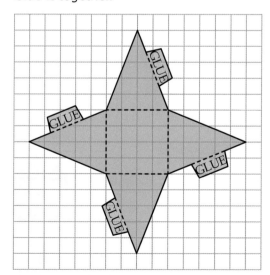

4 Use centimetre-squared paper to make a net for this shape.

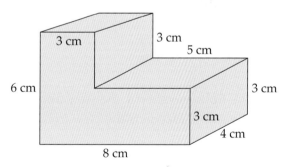
3 cm, 3 cm, 5 cm, 6 cm, 3 cm, 3 cm, 4 cm, 8 cm

14c Plans and elevations

A **plan** gives you a bird's-eye view of an object or scene.
This is the view seen from above the object.

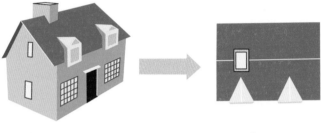

The object   The plan

Plans are drawn
to scale.

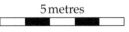
5 metres

> ◉ The plan is the view from directly above the object.

Elevations show an object from different viewpoints.

Plan
The view seen
from above

The object

Side elevation
The view from the side

Front elevation
The view from the front

> ◉ The front elevation is the view from the front of the object.
> ◉ The side elevation is the view from the side of the object.

Use thicker lines
to show changes
in 'depth'.

Example

Draw the plan, front elevation and side elevation
for this L-shape.

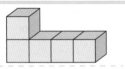

Plan   Front   Side
                    elevation   elevation

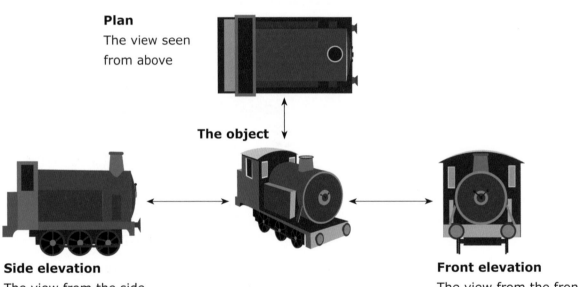

Exercise 14c

1 Match each of these three-dimensional shapes with its plan.

a
Cylinder

b
Cube

c
Triangular prism

d
Cuboid

e
Hexagonal prism

f
Square-based pyramid

i

ii

iii

iv

v

vi

2 These shapes are made from cubes. On squared paper, draw the plan, the front elevation and the side elevation of each shape.

a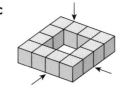

b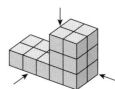

c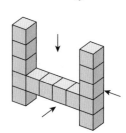

d

The plan is the view seen from above.

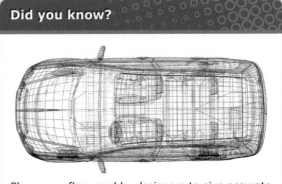
Problem solving

3 On squared paper, draw the plan, the front elevation and the side elevation of this shape.

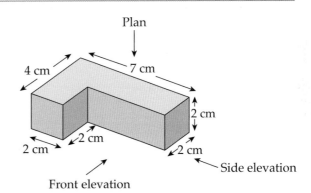

Plan

4 cm

7 cm

2 cm

2 cm

2 cm

2 cm

Front elevation

Side elevation

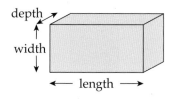

depth
width
length

- A 3D shape is 'solid' and has three dimensions: **length, width** and **depth**.

- 3D shapes have **volume**.
  ▶ Volume is the amount of space a shape occupies.
  ▶ Volume is measured in **cubic** units.

Cubic centimetres (**cm³**) and cubic metres (m³) are two common units of volume.

You use cubic millimetres (mm³) to measure tiny volumes.

You use cubic kilometres (km³) to measure very big volumes.

You write cubic units using the index ³.

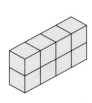 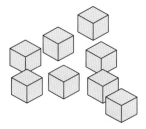

You find a shape's volume by counting exactly how many standard 1 × 1 × 1 cubes will fit inside it.

This cuboid is made from eight centimetre cubes.

The volume of the cuboid is eight cubic centimetres.

You can write this as 8 cm³.

- You find the volume of a cuboid by multiplying the length by the width by the depth.
  Volume = $l \times w \times d$

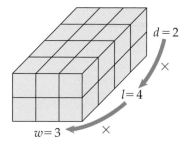

$d = 2$
$l = 4$
$w = 3$

Volume = $l \times w \times d$
$= 4\,\text{cm} \times 3\,\text{cm} \times 2\,\text{cm}$
$= 24\,\text{cm}^3$

The volume of the cuboid is 24 cubic centimetres.

Example

Find the volume of the cuboid.

Volume = $l \times w \times d$
$= 8\,\text{cm} \times 5\,\text{cm} \times 3\,\text{cm}$
$= 120\,\text{cm}^3$

The volume of the cuboid is 120 cubic centimetres.

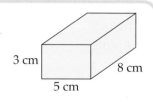

3 cm
8 cm
5 cm

Exercise 14d

1 Tahir puts centimetre cubes together.

a What is the volume of this layer?

b He adds a second layer. What is the total volume?

c He adds a third layer. What is the new total volume?

2 Find the volume of each of these cuboids using the formula
Volume = $l \times w \times d$.

a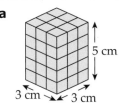
5 cm
3 cm   3 cm

b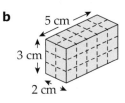
5 cm
3 cm
2 cm

c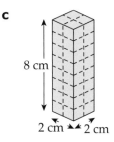
8 cm
2 cm   2 cm

d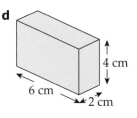
4 cm
6 cm   2 cm

e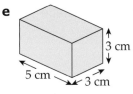
3 cm
5 cm   3 cm

f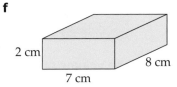
2 cm
7 cm   8 cm

Problem solving

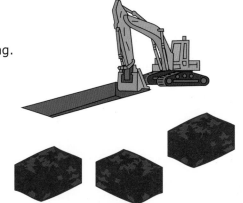

3 A trench is dug.
It is 2 metres wide, 3 metres deep and 10 metres long.
How many cubic metres of concrete will be needed to fill it?

4 Stone blocks measure 5 cm wide, 4 cm deep and 6 cm long.
Ten blocks are packed together.
What is the total volume of the blocks?

5 Find the volume of each of these.
Take care to use the correct units.

   a A tile is 10 cm long, 10 cm wide and 1 cm deep.

   b A crate arrives at the factory. It measures 3 m by 2 m by 5 m.

   c A packet of biscuits measures 2 cm by 6 cm by 5 cm.

   d Rita's mobile phone measures 11 cm by 5 cm by 2 cm.

   e A stone cube has sides of length 3 m.

To find the **volume** of a cube or cuboid we use this **formula**.

Volume = length × width × depth

or $V = l \times w \times d$

Volume has cubic units such as cubic centimetres (**cm³**).

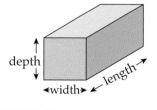

Example

Find the volume of this shape.

Volume = length × width × depth

= 4 cm × 3 cm × 2 cm

= 24 cm³

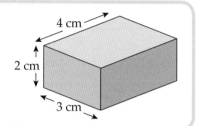

This shape is more complicated.

To find the volume of this shape you can split it into cubes and cuboids.

The volume of cuboid A is

4 cm × 2 cm × 2 cm = 16 cm³.

The volume of cuboid B is

2 cm × 2 cm × 2 cm = 8 cm³.

The total volume of the shape is

16 cm³ + 8 cm³ = 24 cm³.

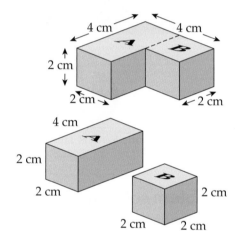

Example

Find the volume of this shape.

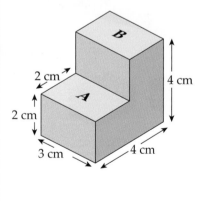

Split the shape into simpler cuboids.

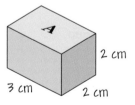

Volume of A = 3 × 2 × 2

= 12 cm³

The total volume is

12 cm³ + 24 cm³ = 36 cm³.

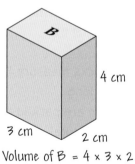

Volume of B = 4 × 3 × 2

= 24 cm³

Exercise 14e

1 Each of these shapes are made from centimetre cubes.
What is the volume of each shape?
Give your answers in cm³.

a

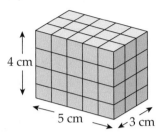

4 cm

5 cm   3 cm

b

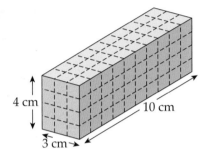

4 cm

10 cm

3 cm

c

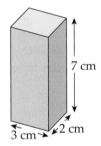

7 cm

3 cm   2 cm

d

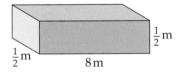

½ m

½ m   8 m

2 These shapes are made from centimetre cubes. A layer of cubes is added to make each new shape.
What is the volume of each shape?

a

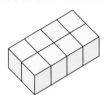

b

c

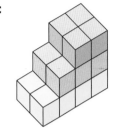

d

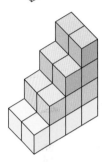

3 Calculate the volume of each of these shapes made from cuboids.

a

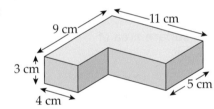

9 cm   11 cm

3 cm

4 cm   5 cm

b

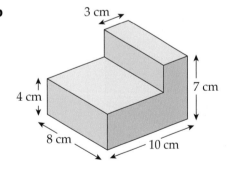

3 cm

7 cm

4 cm

8 cm   10 cm

Problem solving

4 a Find the volume of this shape.
b Sketch a shape made from cubes and cuboids that has a volume of 100 cm³. Label the shape with its dimensions.

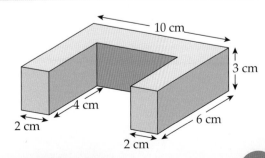

10 cm

3 cm

4 cm

2 cm   6 cm

2 cm

A cuboid has three dimensions:
  length, width and depth.

A three-dimensional shape has volume.

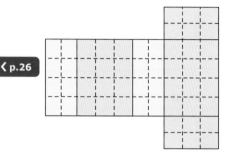

The **net** of the cuboid has two dimensions:
  length and width.

The net shows all six **faces** of the cuboid.

The net shows the **surface area** of the cuboid.

< p.26

> Opposite faces of cubes and cuboids have the same area.

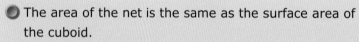

⬤ The area of the net is the same as the surface area of the cuboid.

  ▶ To find the area of the net you add the areas of all the faces.

The surface area of this cuboid is 12 + 12 + 8 + 8 + 6 + 6 = 52 cm².

Example

Find the surface area of this cuboid.

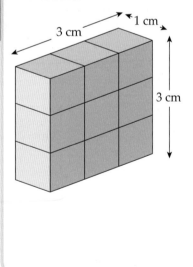

3 cm

1 cm

3 cm

This is the net of the cuboid.
It shows all six faces.

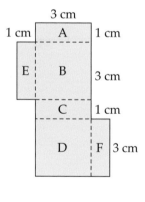

3 cm

1 cm   A   1 cm

E   B   3 cm

C   1 cm

D   F   3 cm

Calculate the area of each face.
Then add all the areas together.

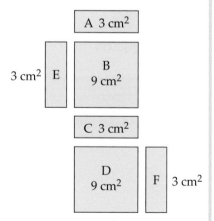

A 3 cm²

3 cm² E   B
             9 cm²

C 3 cm²

D
9 cm²   F   3 cm²

The surface area of the cuboid is
3 + 9 + 3 + 9 + 3 + 3 = 30 cm².

Exercise 14f

1 These nets are drawn on centimetre-squared paper. Find the area of each net. Give your answers in square centimetres (cm²).

a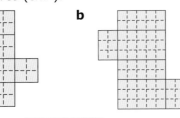

b

c

2 Calculate the surface area of each of these cuboids.

a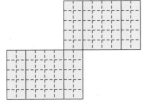

b

c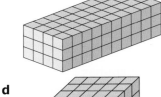

d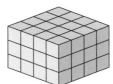

3 Calculate the surface area of each of these cuboids.

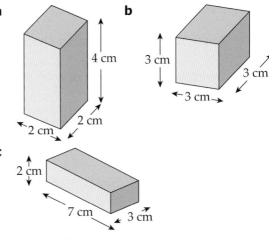

a 4 cm, 2 cm, 2 cm

b 3 cm, 3 cm, 3 cm

c 2 cm, 7 cm, 3 cm

d 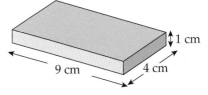 1 cm, 9 cm, 4 cm

e A cuboid whose length is 20 cm, width is half its length, and height is half its width.

Did you know?

The surface area of animals is a very important factor for controlling their body temperature. For example, elephants use their large ears to help keep themselves cool.

Problem solving

4 a Calculate the surface area of this cuboid. Give your answer in square centimetres (cm²).

b The cuboid is now cut in half. Can you think of a quick way to calculate the combined surface area of the two cuboids?

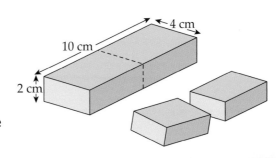

4 cm, 10 cm, 2 cm

Check out

You should now be able to ...

Test it ➡

Questions

✓	Describe properties of solid shapes.	6	1, 2
✓	Construct and use nets of solid shapes.	6	3
✓	Use plans and elevations.	6	4
✓	Find the volume of a cuboid.	6	5
✓	Find volumes of shapes made from cuboids.	6	6
✓	Find the surface area of a cuboid.	6	7

Language	Meaning	Example
Apex	The highest point of the shape.	apex / base
Base	The lowest face of the shape.	
Face	A flat surface of a solid.	Vertex / Edge / face
Edge	The line where two faces meet.	
Vertex	A point where three or more edges meet.	
Prism	A solid shape with the same cross-section throughout its length.	A triangular prism has the same cross-section throughout its length.
Net	A 2D shape which can be folded to make a 3D solid.	Folds to make a cube
Surface area	The total area of all the faces of a 3D solid.	The area of a net equals the surface area of the solid.

1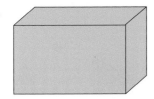

   a What is the mathematical name
for this solid?

   b How many faces does it have?

   c How many vertices does it have?

   d How many edges does it have?

2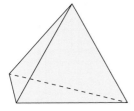

   a What is the mathematical
name for this solid?

   b How many faces does it have?

   c How many vertices does it have?

   d How many edges does it have?

3 Name the 3D solids that you can make by
folding each of these nets.

   a 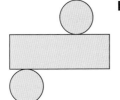   **b**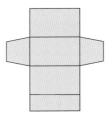

4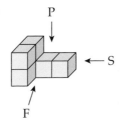

On squared paper draw

   a the front elevation (F)

   b the side elevation (S)

   c the plan view (P) of this solid.

5 Calculate the volume of
the cuboid. Give the units
of your answer.

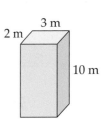

6 This shape is made from three cuboids.
Calculate its volume.

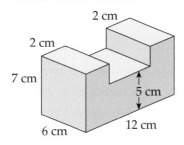

7 Calculate the surface
area of this cuboid.
Give the units of
your answer.

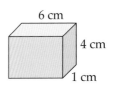

What next?

Score		
	0 – 3	Your knowledge of this topic is still developing. To improve look at Formative test: 3A-14; MyMaths: 1078, 1098, 1106, 1107 and 1137
	4 – 6	You are gaining a secure knowledge of this topic. To improve look at InvisiPen: 321, 322, 323, 324 and 325
	7	You have mastered this topic. Well done, you are ready to progress!

14a

1 Name these 3D shapes.

a   b   c   d   e

  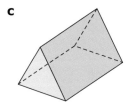

14b

2 Draw a net for this hexagonal pyramid.

6 cm

4 cm

3 What is the volume of the cuboid made from this net?

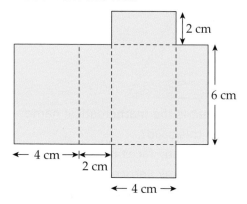

2 cm

6 cm

← 4 cm →

2 cm

← 4 cm →

14c

4 This shape is made from two cuboids.
  a Draw an accurate plan view of the object.
  b Draw the front elevation.
  c Draw the side elevation.

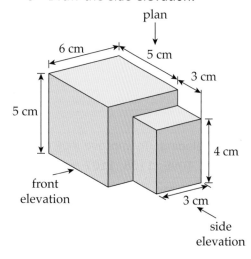

plan

6 cm   5 cm

3 cm

5 cm

4 cm

front elevation

3 cm

side elevation

5 A shape is made from cubes. Sketch the shape given its plan, front elevation and side elevation.

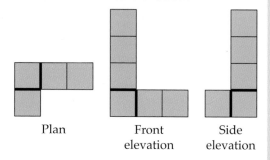

Plan   Front elevation   Side elevation

6 Use the formula $V = l \times w \times d$ to calculate the volumes of these cuboids.
(Give your answers in cm³.)

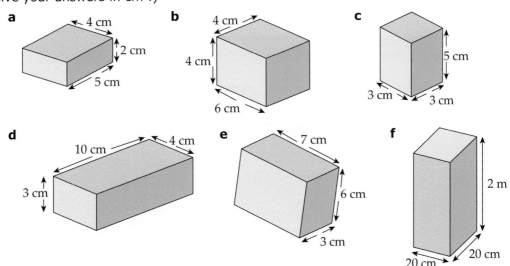

a 4 cm, 2 cm, 5 cm

b 4 cm, 4 cm, 6 cm

c 5 cm, 3 cm, 3 cm

d 10 cm, 4 cm, 3 cm

e 7 cm, 6 cm, 3 cm

f 2 m, 20 cm, 20 cm

7 Find the total volume of the shape in question **4**.

8 a Draw an accurate net of this cuboid.
  b What is the volume of the cuboid?
  c What is its surface area?

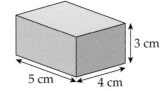

3 cm, 5 cm, 4 cm

9 Here is a net and the cuboid that it makes.
  a Which is the opposite face to C?
  b Which is the opposite face to B?
  c Which is the opposite face to F?
  d What is the surface area of the cuboid?
  e What is its volume?

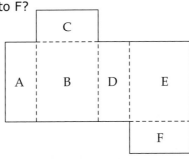

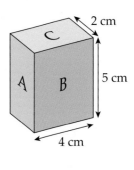

2 cm, 5 cm, 4 cm

The golden rectangle has fascinated scholars for over 2000 years. It's a special kind of rectangle, which is often found in art and architecture.

Task 1

Rectangles come in all shapes and sizes, or different **proportions**. If one shape is an enlargement of another shape then the two shapes are called **similar**. Here are six different rectangles.

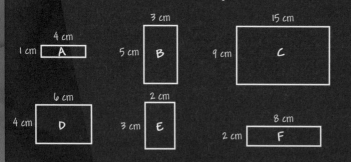

a Write down which three pairs of rectangles are similar.
b For each rectangle, divide the longer side by the shorter side and write down the result.
i What do you notice?
ii What can you say about similar rectangles and the **ratio** of their sides?

Task 2

Here is a square with a narrower rectangle next to it. Together they form a larger rectangle.

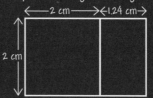

a Look at the larger rectangle.
Divide the longer side by the shorter side and write down the result, to 1 d.p.
b Now look at the smaller rectangle and do the same. What do you notice? Describe your findings using the word 'similar' if possible.

$$A:B = B:C$$
or
$$\frac{A}{B} = \frac{B}{C}$$

Task 3

Here is a **golden rectangle**.
The smaller rectangle is similar to the larger rectangle.
You can write this as a formula:

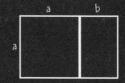

$$\frac{a+b}{a} = \frac{a}{b}$$ The value of $\frac{a}{b}$ is called the **golden ratio**.

a For each rectangle use the formula, decide if it is golden or not. Use a calculator to help you, rounding your answers to 1 d.p. If there is a slight difference in your calculator answers, suggest why this might be the case.

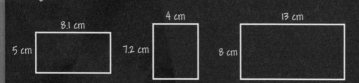

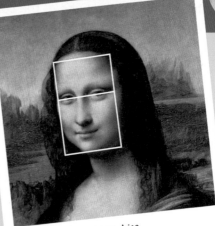

Leonardo da Vinci, Mona Lisa
The face fits within a golden rectangle.
A smaller golden rectangle splits the face at the eye line.

Task 4

Look at the portrait of Mona Lisa, which is shown on this page.
By measuring lengths, describe why her face is framed by a golden rectangle.

How to CONSTRUCT A GOLDEN RECTANGLE

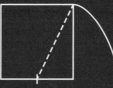

Draw a square.
Mark the mid point
of the base.

Set a pair of compasses to
the distance between the
mid point and the top
corner and draw an arc.

Extend the base of
the square to the arc
and complete the
rectangle.

Did you Know

One possible place where the
golden ratio occurs is in the
ratio of your height to the
top of your
head, to the
height to your
navel.

Task 6

In the **Fibonacci series,** each term is generated by adding the
previous two terms.

    0, 1, 1, 2, 3, 5, 8, 13, . . .
        0+1=1   3+5=8

a Find the ratio of any two adjacent numbers from the series,
dividing the larger one by the smaller one.

b Try this for several pairs of adjacent numbers, working towards
the larger numbers.

What do you notice as you use larger and larger numbers?

The Fibonacci series can be shown as a set of squares.

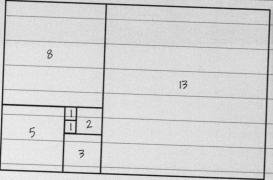

c Draw your own set of
squares in this way.

For each new size of rectangle
that you produce, find the ratio
of its length to its width.

d What do you notice about
the ratios?

What does this tell you
about the rectangle?

e You can draw arcs in each square
to produce a **Fibonacci spiral**.

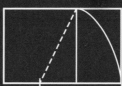

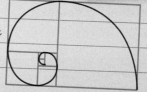

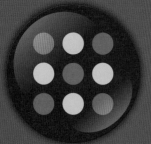

15 Ratio and proportion

Introduction

All of us need to eat! Eating provides the fuel that makes our bodies work but too much fuel can have serious consequences for our health. One way of burning off extra kilocalories is by walking. The faster you walk and the further you walk, the more kilocalories you will burn off. You can say that the number of kilocalories burned is proportional to the amount of exercise – or to put it another way: double the pain, double the gain!

What's the point?

Understanding proportion means that you can work out the effects of doubling and halving quantities.

Objectives

By the end of this chapter, you will have learned how to ...

- ● Simplify equivalent ratios.
- ● Divide an amount in a given ratio.
- ● Use multipliers to solve ratio and proportion problems.
- ● Express an amount as a percentage of another amount.
- ● Compare simple proportions by converting to percentages.
- ● Solve problems involving direct proportion.
- ● Make financial decisions.

Check in

1 Work out the answers to these in your head.

   a 3×6 **b** 8×9 **c** 7×4 **d** 5×12

   e 6×7 **f** 11×6 **g** 9×5 **h** 4×9

2 Work out the answers to these in your head.

   a $55 \div 5$ **b** $48 \div 6$ **c** $64 \div 8$ **d** $27 \div 3$

   e $40 \div 8$ **f** $108 \div 9$ **g** $54 \div 6$ **h** $63 \div 7$

3 Find three equivalent fractions to each of these fractions.

   a $\dfrac{1}{2}$ **b** $\dfrac{2}{3}$ **c** $\dfrac{2}{5}$ **d** $\dfrac{3}{4}$

   e $\dfrac{3}{20}$ **f** $\dfrac{7}{10}$ **g** $\dfrac{1}{7}$ **h** $\dfrac{2}{8}$

4 Simplify each of these fractions.

   a $\dfrac{4}{8}$ **b** $\dfrac{5}{10}$ **c** $\dfrac{20}{50}$ **d** $\dfrac{30}{100}$

   e $\dfrac{25}{100}$ **f** $\dfrac{85}{100}$ **g** $\dfrac{16}{20}$ **h** $\dfrac{15}{35}$

Starter problem

When you walk 3 miles you burn off 243 kilocalories.

How far do you have to walk to burn off the extra calories in a chocolate bar?

How far would you have to walk if you had to burn off the calories you eat at lunch today?

Investigate.

The **ratio** of colours in this bead pattern is

blue : yellow

1 : 3

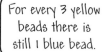

For every 3 yellow beads there is 1 blue bead.

The ratio in this pattern is

blue : yellow

3 : 9

In both patterns, the number of yellow beads is three times the number of blue beads.

$$3 \times 1 = 3$$
$$\text{and } 3 \times 3 = 9$$

For every 3 yellow beads there is still 1 blue bead.

$$\div 3 \left(\begin{matrix} 3 & : & 9 \\ 1 & : & 3 \end{matrix} \right) \div 3$$

The ratios 3 : 9 and 1 : 3 are **equivalent** ratios.
They are connected by a factor of three.

⬤ When you divide the numbers in a ratio by a factor, you **simplify** the ratio.

Example

a   Write the ratio of black to white tiles.

b   Rearrange the beads in this pattern so that you can write the ratio of blue to pink beads in the simplest way.

c   What factor connects the ratios 3 : 12 and 1 : 4?

---

a   The ratio of black : white tiles is

1 : 4

b   The ratio of blue : pink beads is

1 : 2

c   The factor is 3.

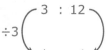

Example

Simplify the ratio 35 : 63

The common factor of 35 and 63 is 7.

$$\div 7 \left(\begin{matrix} 35 & : & 63 \\ 5 & : & 9 \end{matrix} \right) \div 7$$

35 : 63 simplifies to 5 : 9

‹ p.12

5

Exercise 15a

1 Write the ratio of blue to pink beads in each of these patterns.

a
b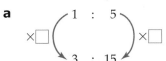

c
d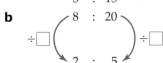

2 Copy and complete this statement for each of these patterns.

For every one grey bead there are ☐ yellow beads.

a
b

c

d

3 What is the factor that connects the ratios in each of these pairs of ratios?

a
×☐ $\begin{matrix} 1 & : & 5 \\ 3 & : & 15 \end{matrix}$ ×☐

b
÷☐ $\begin{matrix} 8 & : & 20 \\ 2 & : & 5 \end{matrix}$ ÷☐

c
÷☐ $\begin{matrix} 12 & : & 28 \\ 3 & : & 7 \end{matrix}$ ÷☐

4 Use the factors to simplify each of these ratios.

a
÷5 $\begin{matrix} 20 & : & 5 \\ 4 & : & \boxed{} \end{matrix}$ ÷5

b
÷3 $\begin{matrix} 6 & : & 15 \\ 2 & : & \boxed{} \end{matrix}$ ÷3

c
÷2 $\begin{matrix} 8 & : & 6 \\ \boxed{} & : & 3 \end{matrix}$ ÷2

5 Simplify each ratio fully.

a 5:20   b 12:6   c 10:30
d 15:45   e 9:6   f 12:8
g 16:12   h 20:25   i 15:20
j 60:10   k 12:36   l 20:60

Did you know?

Some recipes use very simple ratios – a traditional recipe for shortcrust pastry uses a ratio of two parts flour to one part fat.

Problem solving

6 The ratio of the length : width of this photograph is 2:1.
Which of these are the same photo made larger?

a
20
40

b
20
30

c
15
30

Karis and Donna wash car windscreens on Saturdays.
One Saturday they earned £15.

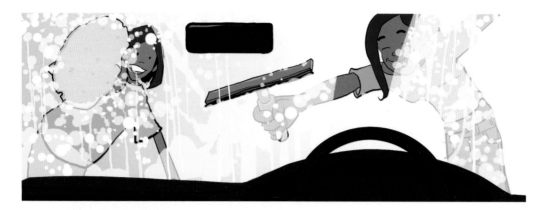

Donna washed 3 windscreens and Karis washed 2.
They divide the money in the ratio 3 : 2.

For every £3 that Donna receives, Karis receives £2.

Method 1

Donna : Karis

£3 : £2 → £5

£6 : £4 → £10

£9 : £6 → £15

Go up in £5s because the ratio 3 : 2 adds to 5.

Donna receives £9 and Karis receives £6.

Method 2

3 : 2 → 5 parts

Divide the money by 5 to find 'one part'.

£15 ÷ 5 = £3, so one part is £3.

Now multiply the ratio by £3.

×£3 ⟮ 3 : 2 ⟯ ×£3

£9 : £6

To divide an amount into a given ratio
▶ Find one part by dividing the amount by the total of the ratio.
▶ Multiply the ratio by your answer.

Example

Divide 20 sweets in the ratio 2 : 3.

Method 1

The ratio is 2 : 3.

2 : 3 → 5

4 : 6 → 10

6 : 9 → 15

8 : 12 → 20

Method 2

2 : 3 → 5 parts

20 ÷ 5 = 4

×4 ⟮ 2 : 3 ⟯ ×4

8 : 12

There are 5 parts of 4 sweets.

Multiply the ratio by 4.

20 sweets divided in the ratio 2 : 3 is 8 sweets and 12 sweets.

Exercise 15b

1 By drawing, share 15 sweets in these ratios.

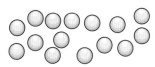

a 1:2 ◯ : ◯◯

b 4:1 ◯◯◯◯ : ◯

c 2:3 ◯◯ : ◯◯◯

2 Use jottings to divide these amounts in the given ratios.

a Divide £16 in the ratio 1:3

> Remember 1:3 → 4 parts

b Divide 18 kg in the ratio 5:1

c Divide 25 sweets in the ratio 3:2

d Divide 24 apples in the ratio 3:5

e Divide €28 in the ratio 4:3

Problem solving

3 Joubin and Alex deliver leaflets at the weekend.
They are paid £32 and divide their wages in the ratio 1:3.
How much will each receive?

4 Ashida wins £60 in an art competition.
She shares the money with her brother in the ratio 3:2.
Ashida keeps the larger amount.
How much will each receive?

5 Can Jamilla share out 25 counters in this ratio?
Explain your answer.

1 : 3

6 Steve mixes red and green paint to make 28 litres of brown paint.
He uses the ratio   Red : Green
                     3 : 4

How many litres of each colour does Steve use?

7 Sarah and Martin are collecting names for a school meal petition.
Sarah collects four names for every one name that Martin collects.

a Write this as a ratio.   Sarah : Martin =

b How many names does each one collect if they collect 30 names altogether?

8 Tom and Eli share £24.
Tom gets £9. In what ratio did they share the money?

9 Thomas makes 350 g of pastry.
He mixes fat and flour in the ratio 2:5.
How much of each ingredient does he use?

Ali picks fruit in his summer holidays.

I get paid £6 per hour. The ratio of time : wage is 1 : 6

Ali has worked for 5 hours today, so the multiplier is 5.

● **Proportional** relationships always keep to the same **ratio**.

Ali earns £30 when he works for 5 hours.

Example

a Copy this diagram.
Use the multiplier to complete it.

$\times 4 \left(\begin{array}{c} 2 : 5 \\ + \\ 8 : \square \end{array} \right) \times 4$

b Copy this diagram. Find the multiplier and complete the diagram.

$\times \square \left(\begin{array}{c} 3 : 5 \\ + \\ 18 : \square \end{array} \right) \times \square$

c Philippa earns £22 for 4 hours' work. How much will she earn for 20 hours' work?

a $5 \times 4 = 20$

$\times 4 \left(\begin{array}{c} 2 : 5 \\ + \\ 8 : 20 \end{array} \right) \times 4$

b The multiplier is 6 because $18 \div 3 = 6$.
$5 \times 6 = 30$

$\times 6 \left(\begin{array}{c} 3 : 5 \\ + \\ 18 : 30 \end{array} \right) \times 6$

c The multiplier is 5 because $20 \div 4 = 5$.
$22 \times 5 = 110$

hours wage

$\times 5 \left(\begin{array}{c} 4 : 22 \\ + \\ 20 : 110 \end{array} \right) \times 5$

Philippa will earn £110 for 20 hours' work.

Exercise 15c

1 Copy these diagrams.
Use the multipliers to complete them.

a
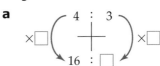
×3 (3 : 7) ×3
9 : ☐

b
×6 (4 : 11) ×6
24 : ☐

c
×3 (7 : 9) ×3
21 : ☐

d
×7 (5 : 9) ×7
35 : ☐

2 Copy these diagrams.
Find the multipliers and complete the diagrams.

a
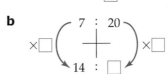
×☐ (4 : 3) ×☐
16 : ☐

b
×☐ (7 : 20) ×☐
14 : ☐

c
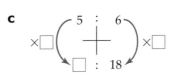
×☐ (5 : 6) ×☐
☐ : 18

d
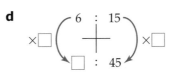
×☐ (6 : 15) ×☐
☐ : 45

Problem solving

3 Kia swims 50 m in 1 minute.
Use this diagram to calculate how many metres she
will swim in 8 minutes.

time   distance
×☐ (1 : 50) ×☐
8 : ☐

4 Soldiers are trained to carry a backpack with a mass of 41 kg.
Copy and complete the diagram to work out the mass that 12 soldiers can carry.

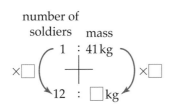

number of
soldiers   mass
×☐ (1 : 41 kg) ×☐
12 : ☐ kg

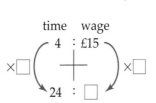

5 You will need a calculator for this challenge.
Keith works for 4 hours and is paid £15.

a Copy and complete the diagram to calculate
how much he will be paid for 24 hours' work.

b How much is Keith paid for working for
  i 2 hours
  ii 1 hour?

time   wage
×☐ (4 : £15) ×☐
24 : ☐

Here are Jemima's exam results.

Subject	Score	out of	%
Maths	90	100	90
English	85	100	85
Science	67	100	67
D&T	95	100	95
History	20	50	40

Jemima's maths score is $\frac{90}{100}$ which is 90%.

Her English score is $\frac{85}{100}$ which is 85%.

Jemima's history score is $\frac{20}{50}$.

For history the **denominator** is not 100 so her percentage cannot be 20%.

To write Jemima's score as a percentage you need to find the **multiplier** that changes the denominator from 50 to 100.

$$\frac{20}{50} \xrightarrow{\times 2} \frac{\square}{100}$$

The multiplier is 2 because $100 \div 50 = 2$.

$$\frac{20}{50} \xrightarrow{\times 2} \frac{40}{100}$$

$50 \times 2 = 100$ and $20 \times 2 = 40$.

Now you can **express** Jemima's history score as a percentage because $\frac{40}{100}$ can be written as 40%.

> ⬤ To convert a fraction into a percentage find the equivalent fraction with a denominator of 100.

Example

a Express $\frac{27}{100}$ as a percentage.

b Jo scored 67 out of 100 in her Spanish test. Write her score as a percentage.

c Fred scored 21 out of 25 for his D&T project. What was his score as a percentage?

a $\frac{27}{100} = 27\%$

b Jo's score is $\frac{67}{100}$ which is 67%.

c Fred's score is $\frac{21}{25}$.

$$\frac{21}{25} \overset{\times 4}{\underset{\times 4}{=}} \frac{\square}{100}$$

The multiplier connecting 25 and 100 is 4.

$25 \times 4 = 100$

$21 \times 4 = 84$

So Fred scored 84% in his assessment.

6

Exercise 15d

1 Write these fractions as percentages.

a $\dfrac{77}{100}$ **b** $\dfrac{33}{100}$ **c** $\dfrac{25}{100}$

d $\dfrac{30}{100}$ **e** $\dfrac{60}{100}$ **f** $\dfrac{15}{100}$

g $\dfrac{10}{100}$ **h** $\dfrac{9}{100}$ **i** $\dfrac{5}{100}$

j $\dfrac{1}{100}$ **k** $\dfrac{54}{100}$ **l** $\dfrac{63}{100}$

2 a A tortoise starts at 0 m.
Estimate the percentage of the distance travelled by the tortoise at each stop.

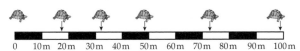

0   10 m 20 m 30 m 40 m 50 m 60 m 70 m 80 m 90 m 100 m

b Write your percentage estimates as fractions.

3 Colin scored 89 out of a possible 100 points in his BMX trial. Write his score as

a a fraction **b** a percentage.

4 For each of these pairs of **equivalent fractions**

i find the multiplier

ii copy and complete the pair.

a $\dfrac{1}{10} = \dfrac{\square}{100}$ **b** $\dfrac{2}{5} = \dfrac{\square}{100}$

c $\dfrac{3}{20} = \dfrac{\square}{100}$ **d** $\dfrac{1}{4} = \dfrac{\square}{100}$

e $\dfrac{12}{25} = \dfrac{\square}{100}$ **f** $\dfrac{9}{20} = \dfrac{\square}{100}$

g $\dfrac{23}{50} = \dfrac{\square}{100}$ **h** $\dfrac{3}{4} = \dfrac{\square}{100}$

5 In 2007 it was estimated that 47 out of every 50 young people in the UK aged 14 years owned a mobile phone.

a What fraction of 14-year-olds owned a mobile phone?

b Convert the fraction to an equivalent fraction with a denominator of 100.

c What percentage of 14-year-olds
i owned a mobile phone
ii did not own a mobile phone?

Problem solving

6 Kieran is working out in which subject he achieved the best scores.
His marks for each subject are out of different totals.

a Write Kieran's scores as fractions of the total possible scores.

b Write each fraction as an equivalent with a denominator of 100.

c Write Kieran's scores as percentages.

d Put his percentage scores in order from lowest to highest.

Subject	Score	out of	Fraction $\left(\dfrac{1}{100}\right)$	%
Maths	35	50		
English	14	20		
Science	23	25		
PE	3	5		
Citizenship	9	10		

● You can compare **proportions** by converting them to percentages.

English 34 ÷ 60 = 0.566.. = 56.7%

Maths $\frac{30}{50} = \frac{60}{100} = 60\%$

Change both of your results to percentages.
English 34 ÷ 60 = 0.566.. = 56.7%
Maths $\frac{30}{50} = \frac{60}{100}$ = 60%

I got 34 out of 60 in my English exam and 30 out of 50 in my Maths exam. Which subject did I do best in?

Tanya did better in her maths exam.

● When two quantities are in **direct proportion**, if one of them increases, the other one increases by the same proportion.

When two quantities are directly proportional:
– if you double one quantity, you double the other
– if you halve one quantity, you halve the other.

● You can use the **unitary method** to solve direct proportion problems.
  ▶ In this method you find the value of one unit of a quantity.

Example

The cost of 30 text messages is 36p.
What is the cost of 50 text messages?

Using a unitary method

	30 texts	36p	
÷30 (1 text | 1.2p) ÷30
×50 (50 texts | 60p) ×50

Find the cost of 1 text message by dividing by 30.

Multiply the number of text messages by the cost of 1 text message.

50 text messages cost 60p.

Exercise 15e

Problem solving

1 These are files being downloaded from the Internet.
For each file write

a

b

c

    i the fraction downloaded in its simplest form

    ii the percentage downloaded.

2 **a** Karen took two tests.
In French she scored 47 out of 60.
In German she scored 64 out of 80.
In which test did she do better?

    b Brian has scored 13 goals in 25 games for his club.
Dean has scored 18 goals in 32 games for the same club.

Who is the better goal scorer?
Explain your answer.

    c Rachel put £150 into a savings account.
After one year the interest was £9.
Debbie put £190 into a savings account.
After one year the interest was £13.
Who had the better rate of interest?

3 Chloe and Zoe both put money into two savings accounts both paying the same interest. Chloe put in £200 and after a year had £240. If Zoe put £150 into her account how much money will she have after a year?

4 Solve each of these problems using direct proportion.

    a 12 pizzas cost £36. How much will 7 pizzas cost?

    b 5 kg of apples cost £7.50. How much will 8 kg of apples cost?

    c A recipe for six people uses 720 ml of stock.
How much stock is needed for the same recipe for five people?

    d An advert says that 400 g of cheese costs £5.40.

      i What is the cost of 1 kg of cheese?

      ii What is the cost of 100 g of cheese?

5 **a** Copy this conversion table for converting between miles and kilometres.
Use direct proportion to complete it.

Miles	Kilometres (km)
1	
5	8
10	
	30
30	
	100

    b Draw a conversion graph for miles and kilometres.

6 Look back at question 3. The girls have a brother Eric who also put money into a savings account. He says his money grew by £50 after a year. How much money did he put into the account at the start of the year?

Nicole is a student taking a photography course at university.

Nicole wants to buy a brand new camera, priced at £474.
She already has £300 **saved**. She can save £30 per month.
After how many months would Nicole have saved up enough
money for the camera?

474 – 300 = 174

174 ÷ 30 = 5.8   Use a calculator

It will take Nicole 6 months.   Round up

Nicole needs to **budget** carefully as she has limited money to live on.

Nicole has £900 to live on each month. She plans her monthly **outgoings** on a spreadsheet.

Outgoing	Amount budgeted £
Accommodation	400
Food shopping	180
Household bills	50
Transport	50
Mobile phone	20
Clothes/other	30
Entertainment	80

a How much money does Nicole have left over each month?

b What proportion of Nicole's monthly expenses goes on

  i accommodation

  ii food shopping?

In each case, give your answer as a fraction in its lowest terms.

Budget Plan

The left-over amount is often referred to as **contingency**, which can be used for unforeseen expenses.

a   total amount = £810

     900 – 810 = 90

     Nicole has £90 left over

b **i** $\frac{400}{900} = \frac{4}{9}$

    ii $\frac{180}{900} = \frac{1}{5}$

When Nicole goes to the supermarket, she makes choices based on **value for money**.

£1.20

BRAND A
PASTA
500g

Buy 1
get 1 free

90p

BRAND B
PASTA
500g

Buy 1
get 1 half price

Nicole is choosing between two similar brands of pasta,
A and B. Which brand gives better value for money?

Brand A   1.20 + 0   = £1.20 for 1kg

Brand B   90p + 45p   = £1.35 for 1kg

So brand A is better value for money.

The **cheapest** option is brand B, just buying one bag of pasta. The cheapest is not always the best value. Which would you choose?

Exercise 15f

1 Work out how long it would take to be able to afford each of these items, starting from nothing and at the rate of saving given.

   a 32 GB tablet, price £320, can save £50 per month.

   b 18 inch laptop, price £299, can save £40 per month.

   c Classic designer boots, price £160, can save £45 per month.

   d 100 watt guitar amp, price £429.95, can save £28 per week.

2 Laura has created a budget for her monthly expenses.

Expense type	Amount budgeted £
Accommodation	500
Food shopping	200
Household bills	50
Transport	60
Other essential expenses	90
Amount left over	

Did you know?

Many companies allow you to buy now and pay later. You need to be very careful, as you can end up paying a lot more than the retail price!

   a Laura takes home £1200 **salary** each month. How much does she have left over each month for herself?

   b Work out the proportion of Laura's salary for each of the six categories in the spreadsheet. In each case, give your answer as a fraction in its lowest terms.

   c Laura's friend Marie says '£1200 per month means you take home £400 per week.' Describe why this is only an **estimate**, and explain whether Laura's weekly pay will be more or less than this.

Problem solving

3 Oscar is deciding which of these two brands of coffee to buy, *Mountain Brand* or *Club Coffee*. He thinks: 'Mountain Brand's got an offer on, but it's a lot smaller.'
Which one would you advise Oscar to buy? Give your reasoning.

Buy 1 get 1 free

£3.99 for 300 g   £2.40 for 100 g

4 Maisie likes houmous! Two competing brands are normally fairly identical, but they now both have offers. Which should Maisie choose, and why?

Brand X
Normally £1.50 for 200 g, now 50% off!

Brand Y
Bigger size, still only £1.50 for 300 g!

5 Look again at Nicole's budget spreadsheet on the opposite page. Due to **price inflation**, the amount she pays for accommodation has gone up by 10%. She still only has £900 to spend each month. Advise Nicole on where she can make a saving to ensure that she still has £90 left over as contingency.

Check out

You should now be able to ...

✓ Simplify equivalent ratios.	**5**	1 – 3
✓ Divide an amount in a given ratio.	6	4, 5
✓ Use multipliers to solve ratio and proportion problems.	6	6
✓ Express an amount as a percentage of another amount.	6	7
✓ Compare simple proportions by converting to percentages.	6	8
✓ Solve problems involving direct proportion.	6	9
✓ Make financial decisions.	6	10

Language	Meaning	Example
Ratio	Ratio compares the size of one part with the size of another part.	2 : 3 means for every two red beads there are three green beads.
Equivalent	Two things are equivalent if they have the same value.	$\frac{3}{5}$ and $\frac{12}{20}$ are equivalent fractions. 2 : 7 and 10 : 35 are equivalent ratios.
Proportional	Proportional relationships always keep to the same ratio.	Donna gets paid £9 per hour. The ratio of time worked to the amount earned is always 1 : 9, regardless of how many hours are worked.
Simplify	Means to write as simply as possible by dividing the numbers in a ratio by the highest common factor.	42 : 54 simplifies to 7 : 9. The highest common factor of 42 and 54 is 6, so divide them both by 6.
Unitary method	A method in which you find the value of one unit of a quantity to solve direct proportion problems.	The cost of 12 packets of crisps is £2.04. The cost of 1 packet = £2.04 ÷ 12 = £0.17 = 17p. You can now use the cost of one packet to find the cost of any number of packets of crisps.

1 Write the ratio of squares to triangles.

2 Write each of these ratios in its simplest form.
   a 12 : 15
   b 40 : 60
   c 24 : 32
   d 28 : 42

3 A farm has 54 cows and 27 sheep. What is the ratio of cows to sheep?

4 Larry and Gary share apples in the ratio 5 : 6.
   If Larry gets 35 apples, how many does Gary get?

5 Divide
   a £60 in the ratio 1 : 3
   b 40 kg in the ratio 3 : 5
   c 120 days in the ratio 1 : 5
   d 250 students in the ratio 7 : 3.

6 A recipe for one person requires 80 g of pasta. How much will be needed for six people?

7 Convert these fractions into percentages.
   a $\frac{37}{100}$ b $\frac{3}{10}$

   c $\frac{7}{20}$ d $\frac{3}{4}$

   e $\frac{6}{15}$ f $\frac{1}{2}$

   g $\frac{15}{75}$ h $\frac{10}{10}$

8 Medication A cured 65 out of 100 patients and medication B cured 75 out of 150. Which is the most effective medicine?

9 The cost of 60 eggs is £14.40.
   a What is the cost of 15 eggs?
   b What is the cost of 75 eggs?

10 Laura saves £30 per month.
   a How long will it take before she can afford a scooter that costs £499?
   b While she is saving the price rises by 10%. How much longer will Laura need to keep saving?

What next?

Score		
	0 – 4	Your knowledge of this topic is still developing. To improve look at Formative test: 3A-15; MyMaths: 1036, 1037, 1038, 1039 and 1052
	5 – 8	You are gaining a secure knowledge of this topic. To improve look at InvisiPen: 162, 191, 192, 193 and 194
	9 – 10	You have mastered this topic. Well done, you are ready to progress!

15 MyPractice

15a

1 Write the ratio of green to yellow beads in each of these patterns.

a

b

c

d

2 Use the factors to simplify each of these ratios.

a $\div 3 \left(\begin{array}{cc}12 & : & 9 \\ 4 & : & \square\end{array}\right) \div 3$

b $\div 4 \left(\begin{array}{cc}16 & : & 4 \\ 4 & : & \square\end{array}\right) \div 4$

c $\div 3 \left(\begin{array}{cc}27 & : & 6 \\ \square & : & 2\end{array}\right) \div 3$

d $\div 3 \left(\begin{array}{cc}15 & : & 24 \\ 5 & : & \square\end{array}\right) \div 3$

15b

3 Use jottings to divide these amounts in the given ratios.

a Divide £18 in the ratio $1:2$.

> Remember $1:2 \rightarrow 3$ parts

b Divide 20 g in the ratio $4:1$.

> Remember $4:1 \rightarrow 5$ parts

c Divide 25 sweets in the ratio $3:2$.

> Remember $3:2 \rightarrow 5$ parts

d Divide 30 m in the ratio $2:3$.

> Remember $2:3 \rightarrow 5$ parts

e Divide \$35 in the ratio $2:5$.

> Remember $2:5 \rightarrow 7$ parts

f Divide 28 litres in the ratio $9:5$.

> Remember $9:5 \rightarrow 14$ parts

15c

4 Copy and complete these diagrams.

a $\times 3 \left(\begin{array}{cc}6 & : & 7 \\ 18 & : & \square\end{array}\right) \times 3$

b $\times \square \left(\begin{array}{cc}4 & : & 9 \\ \square & : & 63\end{array}\right) \times \square$

c $\times \square \left(\begin{array}{cc}3 & : & 8 \\ 12 & : & \square\end{array}\right) \times \square$

d $\times \square \left(\begin{array}{cc}5 & : & 12 \\ \square & : & 72\end{array}\right) \times \square$

5 Change each of these fractions to an equivalent fraction.

a $\dfrac{4}{5} = \dfrac{\square}{100}$

b $\dfrac{3}{10} = \dfrac{\square}{100}$

c $\dfrac{7}{10} = \dfrac{\square}{100}$

d $\dfrac{23}{50} = \dfrac{\square}{100}$

e $\dfrac{19}{25} = \dfrac{\square}{100}$

f $\dfrac{7}{20} = \dfrac{\square}{100}$

g $\dfrac{4}{25} = \dfrac{\square}{100}$

h $\dfrac{13}{20} = \dfrac{\square}{100}$

i $\dfrac{17}{20} = \dfrac{\square}{100}$

6 Change each fraction in question **5** to a percentage.

7 Change each of these fractions to percentages.

a $\dfrac{3}{4}$

b $\dfrac{3}{5}$

c $\dfrac{9}{10}$

d $\dfrac{41}{50}$

e $\dfrac{13}{25}$

f $\dfrac{11}{20}$

g $\dfrac{24}{25}$

h $\dfrac{19}{20}$

i $\dfrac{11}{25}$

j $\dfrac{8}{40}$

k $\dfrac{8}{50}$

l $\dfrac{8}{25}$

8 **a** Betty took two tests.

In history she scored 24 out of 40.

In geography she scored 42 out of 60.

In which test did she do better?

b Rufus put £200 into a savings account.

After one year the interest was £8.

Christabel put £160 into a savings account.

After one year the interest was £7.

Who had the better rate of interest?

9 Solve each of these problems using direct proportion.

a 10 pizzas cost £25. How much will 15 pizzas cost?

b 3 kg of pears cost £6. How much will 14 kg of pears cost?

c A recipe for four people uses 200 g flour.

How much flour is needed for the same recipe for seven people?

10 Geoff's earns £325 per week. His rent is £530 per month.

His monthly travel pass costs £75. He spends £60 a week on food. Other expenses are £85 per month.

a How much money does Geoff have left over each month?

b What proportion of Geoff's expenses is spent on travel?

c Geoff's food costs rise by 10% how much money does he now have left over a month?

11 Ed has to decide between two brands of rice.

Brand A: £4.75 for 1 kg

Brand C: £3.00 for 450 g + buy one bag get second bag half price

Which brand should Ed buy? Give your reasons.

MyMaths.co.uk

16 Probability

Introduction

Buying a new car or TV is a major purchase for a family. It is important that when you spend a lot of money on an item it is reliable, works well and does not break down. However no product is 100% perfect. Most consumer items have experiments carried out on them to find out their probability of breaking or becoming defective under different conditions.

What's the point?

Reliability theory is important to ensure the quality of manufactured goods but it is also vitally important in ensuring the safety levels of cars, planes and trains.

Objectives

By the end of this chapter, you will have learned how to ...
- Understand and use the probability scale from 0 to 1.
- Find the probabilities for mutually exclusive events.
- Find probabilities based on equally likely outcomes.
- Use a sample-space diagram to show the possible outcomes of two events.
- Find and interpret probabilities based on experimental data.
- Use Venn diagrams to find probabilities.

Check in

| impossible | unlikely | even chance (50/50) | likely | certain |

A fair dice is rolled. Use these words to describe these outcomes.

a An odd number   **b** The number 5   **c** Any number from 1 to 6

d The number 8   **e** Any number less than 6

2   0   —————————————————   1

A fair dice is rolled. Copy the probability scale, and put the letter of these possible outcomes onto the scale.

a A zero   **b** An even number   **c** Any number from 1 to 6

d The number 6   **e** Any number greater than 1

3   A fair dice is rolled. Use a fraction to describe these outcomes.

a An odd **or** even number   **b** A number greater than 3

c The number 1, 2, 3, 4 or 5   **d** A number less than 1   **e** The number 1

Starter problem

If you roll a dice what is the probability of a 5?

If you roll two dice what is the probability of a 5?

Does the probability of getting a 5 change if you roll more dice?

Investigate.

🔘 You can describe probability in words or fractions on a **probability scale**.

Certain

City are winning 15–0 with 2 seconds left; they are **certain** to win!

The probability of picking a card with a triangle is 'two chances out of three' or $\frac{2}{3}$.

It is **likely** to rain again.

1 ─ Certain

$\frac{2}{3}$

Even

There is an **'even chance'** of a coin landing with 'heads' showing.

The probability of a coin landing with 'heads' showing is 'one chance in two' or $\frac{1}{2}$.

$\frac{1}{2}$ ─ Even

It is **unlikely** he will win the Lottery.

It is **impossible** to walk on the Sun.

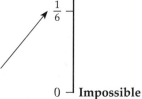

The probability of rolling a 6 with a **fair** dice is 'one chance in six' or $\frac{1}{6}$.

$\frac{1}{6}$

Impossible

0 ─ Impossible

🔘 If the chance of an event happening is impossible, it has the probability 0.

🔘 If the chance of an event happening is certain, it has the probability 1.

Example

Raj has to get a green card to win the game.
a   What is the probability of getting a green card?
b   What is the probability of choosing a red card?

There are five cards; three are green and two are red.
a   The probability of choosing a green card is '3 out of 5' = $\frac{3}{5}$.
b   The probability of choosing a red card is '2 out of 5' = $\frac{2}{5}$.

Exercise 16a

1 Decide which word best describes the probability of each event.

Impossible
Likely
Certain
Unlikely
Even chance

a You will eat something in the next 24 hours.

b By flapping your arms you will fly around the classroom.

c You will find a £20 note on the way home from school.

d You will roll a dice and score 6.

e You will have a cup of tea today.

f The next person to walk into your classroom will be female.

2 Use a fraction to describe the probability of these events.

a The spinner stopping on red.

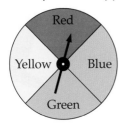

b Picking a red ball from the bag.

2 c Picking the card with 3 on it.

d The spinner stopping on blue.

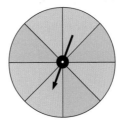

e Picking a green cube at random.

f Picking a yellow ball from the bag.

3 Copy this probability scale.
Show the probabilities from question **2** on your scale. The first one is done for you.

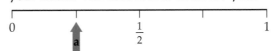

0   a $\frac{1}{2}$ 1

Problem solving

4 Here are ten cards numbered from 1 to 10. You take a card at random. What is the probability of getting

a a number greater than 6

b an even number

c the number 7

d a number less than 7

e the number 3 or the number 8

f a number that is a multiple of 3?

16b Mutually exclusive events

> Two **events** are **mutually exclusive** if it is *impossible* for them to happen together.

When you spin the arrow it can land on A or B or C.
These three outcomes are mutually exclusive.

The **probability** it lands on A, P(A), is $\frac{1}{3}$.

The probability it lands on B, P(B), is $\frac{1}{3}$.

The probability it lands on C, P(C), is $\frac{1}{3}$.

$\frac{1}{3} + \frac{1}{3} + \frac{1}{3} = 1$ The total of the probabilities is 1.

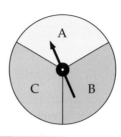

P(A) is short for 'the probability of the arrow landing on A'.

To win, I need to roll a 6. The probability of this is $\frac{1}{6}$

The probability of you losing then is $\frac{5}{6}$ because the events win and lose are mutually exclusive!

> If you know the probability of an event occuring is P, then the probability that it will not occur is $1-P$.

‹ p.56

Example

Riaz picks a coloured ball at **random** from this group.
List all the probabilities and show that their total is 1.
Explain why the total is 1.

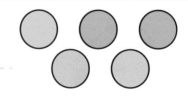

The probability of choosing a green ball, P(A), is $\frac{2}{5}$.

The probability of choosing a blue ball, P(B), is $\frac{1}{5}$.

The probability of choosing a red ball, P(C), is $\frac{2}{5}$.

$\qquad$ P(A) + P(B) + P(C) $= \frac{2}{5} + \frac{1}{5} + \frac{2}{5} = 1$

The three outcomes are mutually exclusive so the total of their probabilities must be 1.

> Outcomes are **exhaustive** if between them they include all the possible outcomes of an event.

Exercise 16b

1 For each of the spinners
   i what is the probability of a favourable outcome?
   ii what is the probability of an unfavourable outcome?

Remember the total of the probabilities for all the outcomes is 1.

a
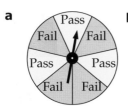

b
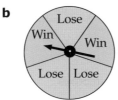

1 **c**
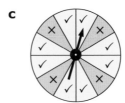

d

2 The following are the probabilities that an event happens. What are the probabilities that the event does not happen?

   a $\frac{3}{7}$ **b** $\frac{4}{9}$ **c** $\frac{2}{3}$ **d** $\frac{1}{8}$

Problem solving

3 Roy makes ten sandwiches.
   He makes two chicken, five beef and three cheese sandwiches.
   He offers the sandwiches to Mandy. Mandy loves chicken and beef but she hates cheese.
   Suddenly there is a power cut. Mandy takes a sandwich in the dark.
   a What is the probability that Mandy will get a chicken sandwich?
   b What is the probability that Mandy will get a beef sandwich?
   c What is the probability that she will get a chicken or a beef sandwich?
   d What is the probability of Mandy getting a cheese sandwich?

4 Ryan is playing snakes and ladders. He has landed on 10. On his next throw of the dice he wants to avoid the snakes on squares 12 and 14. Favourable outcome A: Ryan can throw 6 to avoid the snakes. Favourable outcome B: Ryan can throw an odd number, 1, 3 or 5 to avoid the snakes.

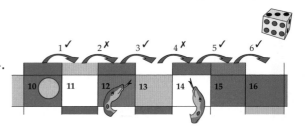

   a What is P(A)
   b What is P(B)
   c What is the probability of Ryan throwing 6 or an odd number?
   d What is the probability of Ryan landing on a snake?

5 An experiment has two outcomes A and B. If P(A) = $\frac{2}{3}$ and P(B) = $\frac{4}{9}$ can you say whether events A and B are
   a mutually exclusive   **b** exhaustive?

16c Theoretical probability

Outcomes are **equally likely** if each outcome has the same chance of happening.

The probability of the arrow landing on any particular colour is different for each of these spinners.

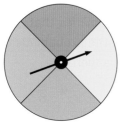   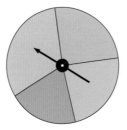

There is a greater probability of the arrow landing on blue than on the other colours.

With this spinner each **outcome** is **equally likely**.

With this spinner the outcomes are not equally likely.

If all the outcomes are equally likely then the **theoretical probability** of an event is given by the **formula**:

$$\text{Probability of an event} = \frac{\text{number of } \textbf{favourable} \text{ outcomes}}{\text{total number of outcomes}}$$

Favourable outcomes are the results you are looking for.

Five balls are placed in a bag.
What is the probability of picking a blue ball?

$$P(B) = \frac{\text{number of blue balls}}{\text{total number of balls}}$$

$$= \frac{2}{5}$$

The probability of picking a blue ball is $\frac{2}{5}$.

P(B) is short for probability of picking a blue ball.

Example

Nina rolls a fair dice.
What is the probability she will roll an even number?

There are six equally likely outcomes: 1, 2, 3, 4, 5 or 6
There are three favourable outcomes: 2, 4 or 6

$$P(E) = \frac{\text{number of favourable outcomes}}{\text{total number of outcomes}} = \frac{3}{6}$$

$$P(\text{even number}) = \frac{3}{6} = \frac{1}{2}.$$

Statistics and probability Probability

Exercise 16c

1 Which of these spinners will have an equally likely chance of landing on each different colour?

a 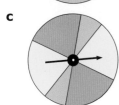 **b**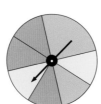

c  **d**

2 Charles closes his eyes and picks a ball from each of these jars.
Use the formula

$$P(E) = \frac{\text{number of favourable outcomes}}{\text{total number of outcomes}}$$

to find the theoretical probability of picking a pink ball from each of the jars.

a   **b**

2 **c**  **d**

e  **f**

3 A card is picked at random from this set. Use the formula to calculate the probability of picking

a a circle **b** a triangle.

4 A card is picked at random from this set. Use the formula to calculate the probability of picking

a a square **b** a cross.

Problem solving

5 Use the formula to calculate these probabilities.
Give your answers as fractions.

a You roll a dice.
What is the probability of rolling an odd number?

> Call it P(odd number) for short.

b A jar contains six green marbles and nine blue marbles.
A marble is picked at random.
What is the probability it will be green?

> Call it P(green) for short.

c You roll a dice. What is the probability of rolling a number greater than 4?

> Call it P(5 or 6) for short.

d A bag of small plastic toys contains five dogs, two monkeys, four cats and three bears.
What is the probability of picking a dog or a cat?

You can list all the possible outcomes of two events in simple cases.

The Year 9 Girls' Hockey squad are choosing colours for their sports kit.

They can choose from

Blue skirt   Orange skirt

The events are choosing a shirt and choosing a skirt.

Blue shirt   Red shirt

⬤ Using a table makes it easier to list the outcomes in a systematic way.

They draw the different possible combinations and put them in a table.

Skirts		Shirts	
		Blue	Red
	Blue	Blue Blue	Red Blue
	Orange	Blue Orange	Red Orange

The table shows that there are four different combinations to choose from.

⬤ A table used to list all the outcomes of two events in a systematic way is called a **sample-space diagram**.

They add another colour of skirt to the table.

Skirts		Shirts	
		Blue	Red
	Blue	Blue Blue	Red Blue
	Orange	Blue Orange	Red Orange
	White	Blue White	Red White

The table shows that there are now six different kit combinations.

Exercise 16d

1 **a** Copy and complete the table to list all the combinations of flipping 2 coins. The table has been started for you.

1st option

2nd option	Heads	Tails
Heads		Tails Heads
Tails		

b How many combinations are there altogether?

2 Here are all Mr Ross's shirts and ties.

a Copy and complete the table to show all the different combinations he could choose.

Shirts

Tie	Striped	Yellow	Blue	White
Red		Yellow		
Blue Striped				White Blue Stripe

b How many different combinations are there altogether?

3 Most Year 9 students will be able to choose their GCSE options before their summer holidays.

Here are two option groups that Henry Compton School offers.

Option A	Option B
French	ICT
Art	Food Tech
History	Geography
	Latin
	Photography

		Option B	
		ICT	
Option A	French		

The Year 9 options table has been started for you.

a How many columns will you need for Option B?

b How many rows will you need for Option A?

c Copy and complete the table for both option groups.

d How many different combinations can Henry Compton students choose from?

Problem solving

4 Oscar rolls two dice and finds the total scores. Draw a table to show all the possible outcomes. Part of the table has been started for you.

Blue dice

Red dice	+	1	2	3

Jake and Maisy are playing the card game Snap.

Jake has these cards in his hand.   Maisy has these cards in her hand.

Mother   Father   Daughter   Son   Mother   Father   Daughter   Son

What is the probability that they will both put down the same card?

● Use a **sample-space diagram** to find all the possible outcomes in a **systematic** way.

There are 16 possible outcomes and
4 **favourable** outcomes.

The favourable outcome is 'they both put
down the same card'.

$$P(\text{same card}) = \frac{4}{16} = \frac{1}{4}$$

		Maisy's cards			
		M	F	D	S
Jake's cards	M	(MM)	MF	MD	MS
	F	FM	(FF)	FD	FS
	D	DM	DF	(DD)	DS
	S	SM	SF	SD	(SS)

So the probability that Jake and Maisy put down the same card is $\frac{1}{4}$.

● You can use a sample-space diagram to find the probability for two events.

Reece has a dice and a coin.
He tosses the coin and rolls the dice.
The coin can show either heads or tails.
The dice can show 1, 2, 3, 4, 5 or 6.

a How many possible outcomes are there?

b What is the probability of getting a tail and a 3?

Draw a sample-space diagram.
Use H for heads and T for tails.

a There are twelve possible outcomes.

b P (tail and 3) = $\frac{1}{12}$.

		Outcome of dice roll					
		1	2	3	4	5	6
Outcome of coin toss	Heads	H1	H2	H3	H4	H5	H6
	Tails	T1	T2	T3	T4	T5	T6

Exercise 16e

1 Robert has four shirts and two ties.

a Copy and complete the table to show all the combinations he could choose.

Shirts

	Blue	Green	Pink	Yellow
Dotty				
Striped				Yellow + Striped

Ties

b How many different combinations of shirt and tie are there?

2 In the game show *Spin 'n' Win*, contestants answer a question.

If they answer correctly they spin Wheel 1 to earn points.

Then they spin Wheel 2 to multiply their score.

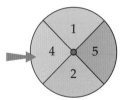 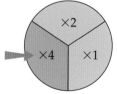

They can win either 1, 2, 4 or 5 points.

They can multiply their points by 1, 2 or 4.

2 a Copy and complete the sample-space diagram with the final scores.

Wheel 1

Wheel 2		1	2	4	5
	×1	1			5
	×2			8	
	×4				

b How many possible outcomes are there?

c What is the highest number of points that can be won?

d What is the probability of winning 2 points?

e What is the probability of winning 4 points?

3 The outcomes recorded in this table show the different ways that these spinners can land.

a How many outcomes will there be altogether in the table? You can copy and complete the table to help you.

First spinner

Second spinner		Yellow	Blue	Green	Red
	Blue	Yellow Blue		Green Blue	
	Red		Blue Red		Red Red
	Green			Green Green	

b What is the probability of either of the two spinners landing on a red?

Problem solving

4 Pete rolls two dice and adds their scores. The table shows some of the outcomes.

a How many outcomes are there altogether?

b Explain how you could calculate your answer to **a**.

c Which score is the most frequent?

d What is the probability of scoring 7?

e Is it possible to score 13?

f Which two scores both have a probability of $\frac{1}{12}$?

First dice

Second dice	+	1	2	3	4	5	6
	1	2		4	5		7
	2		4				
	3						9
	4		6				
	5			8		10	
	6			10			

Jake and his friends build a ball maze for the school fair.

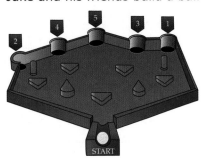

Players roll a golf ball into the maze.
There are five possible scores: 1, 2, 3, 4 or 5.

There is a 1 in 5 probability $\left(\frac{1}{5}\right)$ of each score.

No, that's not true. The outcomes are not equally likely.

If you do not know whether or not the outcomes are equally likely you can estimate the different probabilities by doing an **experiment**.

> ● The formula for **experimental probability** is
>
> $$\text{Experimental probability} = \frac{\text{number of successful trials}}{\text{total number of trials}}$$
>
> ▶ Increasing the number of trials in an experiment makes the experimental probability more reliable.

Jake carries out ten trials.

Score	1	2	3	4	5
Frequency	1	0	3	3	3

An experiment is a series of trials. Each time Jake rolls a ball into the maze is a trial.

These results do not give enough information.
So Jake does 100 trials.

Score	1	2	3	4	5
Frequency	5	2	25	18	50

From these results he works out the experimental probabilities.

$$\text{Experimental probability of scoring 1} = \frac{\text{number of times score is 1}}{\text{total number of trials}}$$

$$= \frac{5}{100} = 0.05$$

There is a high probability of scoring 5 and a low probability of scoring 2.

$$\text{Experimental probability of scoring 2} = \frac{\text{number of times score is 2}}{\text{total number of trials}}$$

$$= \frac{2}{100} = 0.02$$

In the same way he calculates the other experimental probabilities respectively.

$$P(3) = 0.25 \qquad P(4) = 0.18$$
$$P(5) = 0.5$$

5

Exercise 16f

1 Jake and his friends build another attraction for the school fair.
A marble is dropped into the 'Zig-Zag' and it comes out at tray A, B, C, D, E or F.

Jake and his friends think that the marble will be equally likely to come out at each of the trays so that the probability of each outcome is $\frac{1}{6}$.
They carry out an experiment. They do 100 trials and here are their results.

Tray	A	B	C	D	E	F
Frequency	10	25	12	15	27	11

a Are the frequencies what Jake and his friends expected?
b What are the experimental probabilities of the marble coming out at each tray? Give your answers as fractions.

1 c If you had to guess which tray the marble would come out at, which tray would you choose?
d Look closely at the 'Zig-Zag'. Can you explain why the outcomes are not equally likely?

2 Clive is bored and is throwing rolled-up balls of paper at the recycling bin.
He decides to find the probability of a ball landing in the bin. He carries out an experiment.
He has 20 throws. Five balls land in the bin.

▲ Each throw is a trial.

a Use the formula for experimental probability to find the probability of Clive getting his next throw into the bin.
b Clive takes 100 throws at the bin. Estimate how many times he will get a ball in the bin.

Problem solving

3 Clive is right-handed.
He decides to repeat the experiment using his left hand.
The **conditions** have to remain the same.
Clive cannot move his chair closer or use a bigger bin.
Clive does 50 trials.
Here is the record of the experiment.

a What is the probability that Clive's next throw will go in?
b Does Clive have a greater probability of hitting the bin using his left or his right hand?

✓ = hit								X = miss	
X	X	X	X	✓	X	X	✓	X	✓
✓	X	X	X	X	X	✓	X	X	X
X	✓	X	X	X	X	X	X	✓	X
X	X	X	X	X	✓	X	X	X	X
X	X	X	✓	X	X	X	✓	X	X

⬤ The **universal set** is the set containing all the **elements**.

▶ It has the symbol Ω.

Example

Ω = {2, 3, 6, 7, 11, 15}, P = {prime numbers} and E = {even numbers}.

a List the elements in set P. **b** List the elements in set E.

c Which element is in P and E? **d** Which element is not in set P or set E?

---

a $P = \{2, 3, 7, 11\}$ **b** $E = \{2, 6\}$ **c** 2 **d** 15

‹ p.12 ⬤ Venn diagrams use circles to sort objects into sets.

A ∩ B means 'the **intersection** of A and B'.

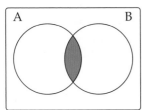

A ∪ B means 'the **union** of A and B'

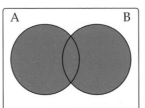

A′ means 'the **complement** of A'.

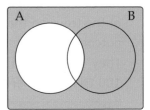

⬤ You can use Venn diagrams to work out probabilities.

$$P(A) = \frac{\text{number of elements in set A}}{\text{number of elements in } \Omega}$$

P(A) means the probability of A.

Example

Tara asked 14 students at her school about their family.

She sorts them into S = {has a sister} and B = {has a brother}.

She showed her results on a Venn diagram.

Tara picks a student at random. Find: **a** P(B′) **b** P(S ∩ B)

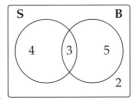

---

a

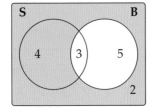

There are 4 + 2 = 6 students in B′.
There are 14 students total.

$$P(B') = \frac{6}{14} = \frac{3}{7}$$

b

There are 3 students in the intersection.

$$P(S \cap B) = \frac{3}{14}$$

Exercise 16g

1 For the sets

  a Ω = {whole numbers from 1–12},
    A = {multiples of 3} and
    B = {even numbers}.

  b Ω = {1, 2, 3, 5, 8, 13, 21, 34, 55},
    A = {whole numbers less than 20} and
    B = {factors of 24}.

  c Ω = {whole numbers from 1–16},
    A = {odd numbers} and
    B = {prime numbers}.

  list the elements in

  i   A

  ii the complement of A

  iii B

  iv the complement of B

  v the union of A and B

  vi the intersection of A and B

2 Alexa manages a gym.
She surveys 30 members to find out
which exercise classes they take.
She sorts her results into the sets
A = {aerobics} and K = {kickboxing}.

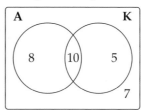

Alexa picks one member at random.
Find the probability of these events.
Give your answer as a fraction in its
simplest form.

  a P(A)   **b** P(K)   **c** P(A′)

  d P(K′)   **e** P(A ∩ K)   **f** P(A ∪ K)

Problem solving

3 **a** Cori sorts 19 objects into the sets A and B.
    She knows that

$$P(A \cap B) = \frac{4}{19}, \quad P(A) = \frac{10}{19}, \quad P(B) = \frac{11}{19}$$

    Complete the Venn diagram for Cori's objects.

  b Cori sorts another group of objects into the sets X and Y.
    She knows that

$$P(X \cap Y) = \frac{1}{9}, \quad P(X) = \frac{5}{9}, \quad P(Y) = \frac{1}{3}$$

    Jaime draws a Venn diagram for Cori's objects.
    Explain why Jaime might be wrong and draw another possibility.

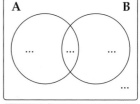

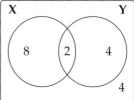

4 Rini sorts a group of objects into the sets A and B.
She draws a Venn diagram to show her results.

  a Explain why Rini must have started with 25 objects.

  b Use $x = 2$ to find

    i P(A)   **ii** P(B′)   **iii** P(A ∪ B)   **iv** P(A ∩ B)

  c If $P(A \cap B) = \frac{1}{5}$, find the value of x.

5 Ω = {whole numbers from 1–10}, A ∩ B = {3, 7} and A ∪ B = {1, 3, 4, 6, 7, 10}.
Investigate the possibilities for the sets A and B.

Check out

You should now be able to ...

Test it ➡

Questions

✓ Understand and use the probability scale from 0 to 1.	5	1
✓ Find probabilities for mutually exclusive events.	5	2
✓ Find probabilities based on equally likely outcomes.	5	3, 5
✓ Use a sample-space diagram to show the possible outcomes of two events.	6	4, 5
✓ Find and interpret probabilities based on experimental data.	5	6, 7
✓ Use Venn diagrams to find probability.	6	8

Language   Meaning   Example

Language	Meaning	Example
Outcome	The result of an activity.	For a regular dice the outcomes are 1, 2, 3, 4, 5, and 6.
Event	A group of one or more possible outcomes.	The event 'odd number' consists of the outcomes 1, 3 or 5.
Trial	A single occurrence of an activity whose outcome is random.	Tossing a coin once is a trial. Tossing a coin 100 times is an experiment.
Experiment	A collection of repeated trials.	
Mutually exclusive	Events that cannot both happen at the same time.	Rolling an even number and an odd number on a regular dice.
Experimental probability	The number of favourable outcomes divided by the total number of outcomes in an experiment.	If a coin is tossed 50 times and comes up heads 23 times, then the experimental probability of heads is $\frac{23}{50}$.
Theoretical probability	Assuming all outcomes are equally likely, the number of favourable outcomes divided by the total number of outcomes.	For a regular dice, the theoretical probability of obtaining a factor of 6 (that is a 1, 2, 3 or 6) is $\frac{4}{6} = \frac{2}{3}$.

1 A bag contains 2 white and 7 red counters. What is the probability that a randomly chosen counter will be
   a red
   b green?

2 The probability that Jeremy wins his game of chess is 0.6. What is the probability he doesn't win?

3 Mandy has a pack of 76 cards. Twenty of the cards have pictures on them. Find the probability of Mandy selecting a picture card at random. Give your answer as a fraction in its lowest terms.

4 Ashleigh can choose white, brown or seeded bread for her sandwiches. As a filling she could have cheese, ham or egg.
   a Draw a sample-space diagram to show all the possible outcomes.
   b How many different combinations can she choose from?

5 A game involves flipping a coin and rolling a dice.
   a Copy and complete the sample space diagram to show all the possible outcomes.

		Dice					
		1	2	3	4	5	6
Coin	H	H1					
	T						

5 **b** How many possible outcomes are there?
   c What is the probability of getting a head and a 5?
   d What is the probability of getting an odd number and a tail?

6 The test results of 15 students are as follows:

12	10	13	10	16
18	15	13	9	7
10	12	14	15	17

A mark of 12 or more was needed to pass.
Estimate the probability that a student chosen at random would have passed the test.

7 Zak plays a game 40 times and wins 16 times.
   a Estimate the probability he will win the next time he plays.
   b If Zak plays the game 30 more times, how many times would you expect him to win?

8 Construct a Venn diagram from this information.
   Ω = {whole numbers 1–40}
   $P(A) = \frac{1}{2}$, $P(A \cap B) = \frac{1}{8}$, $P(A \cup B)' = \frac{1}{4}$

What next?

Score	0 – 3		Your knowledge of this topic is still developing. To improve look at Formative test: 3A-16; MyMaths: 1199, 1209, 1210, 1211, 1262 and 1263
	4 – 6		You are gaining a secure knowledge of this topic. To improve look at InvisiPen: 451, 452, 453, 454, 461 and 462
	7 – 8		You have mastered this topic. Well done, you are ready to progress!

16a

1 Twelve cards numbered from 1 to 12 are shuffled and placed face down.

| 1 | 2 | 3 | 4 | 5 | 6 | 7 | 8 | 9 | 10 | 11 | 12 |

As a fraction, what is the probability of picking a card which is

a a number greater than 8   **b** an odd number

c a multiple of 5   **d** an orange card

e a prime number   **f** a green card

g a multiple of 3?

2 This is a **fair** spinner.

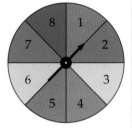

a What is the probability of the arrow pointing to 5?

b What is the probability of the arrow pointing to a pink sector?

c What is the probability of the arrow pointing to a number less than 4 **or** a green sector?

16b

3 When choosing a ball at random from the bag there are three possible outcomes.

First outcome ➡ P(red) – the probability of choosing a red ball.

Second outcome ➡ P(green) – the probability of choosing a green ball.

Third outcome ➡ P(blue) – the probability of choosing a blue ball.

a As a fraction, what is the probability of choosing red?   P(red) = ☐

b As a fraction, what is the probability of choosing green?   P(green) = ☐

c As a fraction, what is the probability of choosing blue?   P(blue) = ☐

d Add the outcomes: P(red) + P(green) + P(blue) = ☐ What is the total?

16c

4 Ellen throws 12 darts at a target.

a Give an estimate of the probability that her next throw will hit red.

b Give an estimate of the probability that her next throw will hit blue.

c Give an estimate of the probability that her next throw will miss the target.

d Give an estimate of the probability that Ellen's next throw will hit red or blue.

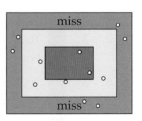

5 a Copy and complete the table to list all of the possible combinations of flipping a coin and rolling a dice.

b How many combinations are there altogether?

		Dice		
		1	2	3
Coin	H			
	T			

6 Stefan buys a bag of mixed flower bulbs. There are

8 snowdrop bulbs   6 daffodil bulbs

10 crocus bulbs   12 iris bulbs.

If Stefan takes a bulb at random from the bag, what is the probability that it will be

a a daffodil bulb   **b** an iris bulb?

Stefan takes two bulbs at random and plants them in a flowerpot.

c Draw a sample-space diagram to show the possible combinations of flowers that might grow.

7 Sandra has sowed tomato seeds in trays. Each tray holds 12 seeds.

Sandra records how many seeds have grown and how many have failed in the first 10 trays.

Tray	1	2	3	4	5	6	7	8	9	10	Totals
Seeds grown	8	10	12	10	8	11	10	9	12	10	= 100
Seeds failed	4	2	0	2	4	1	2	3	0	2	= 20

a Give an estimate of the probability that the eleventh tray will have 12 seeds growing successfully.

b Give an estimate of the probability that the eleventh tray will have less than 12 seeds growing successfully.

c What is the **mean** average number of seeds grown successfully in each tray?

8 Two hundred students were sorted into the sets

B = {has a brother} and S = {has a sister}.

The results are shown in the Venn diagram.

A teacher picks one student at random.

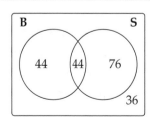

Find the probability of these events.

Give your answer as a fraction in its simplest form.

a P(B)   **b** P(S)   **c** P(B')

d P(S')   **e** P(B ∩ S)   **f** P(B ∪ S)

MyMaths.co.uk

Case study 6: Crime scene investigation

Forensic experts have used mathematical techniques to solve crimes for a long time. Probability, formulae and graphs are three of the topics that they need to be familiar with.

The Weekly Bugle

Following a jewellery shop raid in Park Street, Tooting, on Saturday afternoon, in which shots were fired but nothing was stolen, a getaway car was found abandoned at the junction with Fisher Row. The Ford Fiesta had narrowly missed a cyclist after skidding 53 metres. The driver and passenger of the car were seen running from the scene. A male in his 20s suspected of being the passenger was apprehended by police officers later that day. Police investigating the incident are keen to trace the driver of the car.

POLICE LINE DO NOT CROSS   PO

Task 1

Detectives searching for clues at the jewellery shop notice that a safe has been tampered with, though not successfully unlocked. The safe has a combination lock consisting of five windows that can be any one of five colours: **Green, Red, Blue, Purple or Yellow.**

Only one combination will open the safe. How many possible combinations are there?

Task 2

Detectives at the jewellery shop notice a bullet hole in a wall, at a height of 4 m from the floor. They calculate that the equation of the path of the bullet is

$$y = 1.5 + \frac{x}{8}$$

where y is the height of the bullet above the floor in metres and x is the horizontal distance of the bullet from the gun in metres. It is believed that the person firing the shot was somewhere between 10 and 20 metres away from the wall when they fired the shot. Set up an equation and solve it to find a more accurate estimate.

Task 3

A DNA analysis of the abandoned car shows that two samples of DNA match the detained suspect's DNA. It is estimated that there is a one in a billion chance that a single sample of DNA will provide an exact match to another sample of DNA.

a Write the number 1 billion in standard form.
b For two independent samples of DNA you can multiply their probabilities. Calculate the probability that the two samples match. Give your answer in standard form.
c Comment on whether or not the analysis provides evidence to support the theory that the suspect was in the car at the time of the crime.

CONFIDENTIAL

Task 4

The length of the tyre marks left by a skidding car depends on its speed when it started skidding.

These are typical values for a tarmac road surface and dry weather conditions.

Initial speed	length of tyre marks
10 mph	1.5 metres
15 mph	3.3 metres
20 mph	5.9 metres
25 mph	9.3 metres
30 mph	13.3 metres
35 mph	18.1 metres
40 mph	23.7 metres
45 mph	30 metres

a   What happens to the length of the tyre marks as the speed doubles ?

b   What happens as the speed trebles ?

c   Use the data to draw a graph of the length of the tyre marks against speed.

d   Join the points with a smooth line.

e   Extend your graph to get an approximate speed for the car in the news article.

Task 5

The relationship between speed and the length of the skid is given by the equation

$$speed = \sqrt{90 \times length \times friction}$$

where friction is the drag factor of the road.

a   Using your answer from task 4, how far would the car have skidded if it had been on a concrete road surface with a drag factor of 0.9 ?

b   How far would it have skidded if it had been on snow with a drag factor of 0.3 ?

- The tarmac road has a drag factor of 0.75

c   Was the resident right in thinking that the car was doing at least 80 mph?

d   How quickly would it have been travelling if it skidded for 53 metres on a concrete road ?

309

These questions will test you on your knowledge of the topics in chapters 13 to 16.
They give you practice in the types of questions that you may see in your GCSE exams.
There are 90 marks in total.

1 Write the first five terms of these sequences.
   a *Start with 25 subtract 3*   (2 marks)
   b *Start with 4, double and subtract 3.*   (3 marks)
   c The nth terms is $2n - 7$ (2 marks)

2 For each of these sequences
   i find the term-to-term rule   (3 marks)
   ii write the next two terms in each sequence.   (3 marks)
      a 9, 14, 19, 24, …   **b** 25, 16, 7, -2, …   **c** 2, 10, 26, 58, …

3 For each of these sequences
   i   find the term-to-term rule   (3 marks)
   ii use this to find the position-to-term rule   (3 marks)
   iii write each position-to-term rule as an equation in terms of n
           where n is the nth term   (3 marks)
   iv use this nth term formula to find the 20th term of each sequence. (3 marks)
      a 3, 10, 17, 24, …   **b** 12, 8, 4, 0, …   **c** 21, 28, 35, 42, …

4 Describe these shapes in terms of the number of
   i edges   (2 marks)   **ii** faces   (2 marks)   **iii** vertices.   (2 marks)

   a 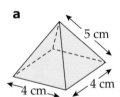   **b**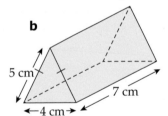

5 For the two shapes in question **4**
   a name the particular shapes shown   (2 marks)
   b on centimetre squared grid paper draw the nets of these two shapes. (4 marks)

6 Here is a six-cube shape.
   On squared paper draw
   a the plan view (P)   (2 marks)
   b front elevation (F)   (2 marks)
   c side elevation (S).   (2 marks)

   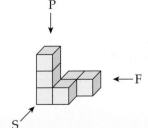

7 An earth trench is being dug to take concrete as a foundation for brickwork. The trench is 25 cm wide, 40 cm deep and 4 m long. What volume of concrete is needed to fill the trench? (3 marks)

8 For the two cuboids shown
   i calculate the surface area (8 marks)   **ii** calculate the volume. (6 marks)

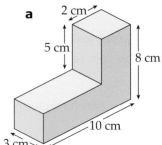
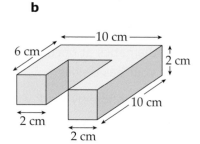

9 a In a school there are 396 students with a ratio of boys to girls of 10:8. How many boys and girls are there in the school? (3 marks)
  b £1350 was left between two children in the ratio of 7:2. How much does each child receive? (3 marks)

10 a The hourly rate for a part-time job is £6.50 per hour. Lara works a shift of seven hours. How much does she receive? (2 marks)
  b Lara spends £4.55 on travel. What is this as a percentage of Lara's wages? (1 mark)

11 Solve these problems by direct proportion.
  a In a recent set of exams Sophie scored 43/60 in Maths and 29/40 in Biology. In which exam did she do better? Show your working to support your answer. (3 marks)
  b Adam scored 14 goals in 11 games and Tom scored 16 goals in 13 games. Who is the better goal scorer? (3 marks)

12 There are 12 marbles in a bag: 5 red marbles, 4 blue marbles and 3 green marbles. A marble is chosen at random from the bag.
  a Find the probability that the marble is
    i green   **ii** blue   **iii** either red, or blue or green. (3 marks)
  b Are the events red and green mutually exclusive? Explain your answer. (1 mark)

13 A four sided dice is thrown at the same time as a coin is tossed.
  a Draw a sample space diagram to show all the possible outcomes. (3 marks)
  b What is the probability of getting a tail and a 3. (1 mark)

14 a Draw a Venn diagram to show these sets A = {2, 3, 5, 6, 8} B {3, 5, 7, 10} and Ω = {1–10} (4 marks)
  b Calculate   **i** P(A n B)   **ii** P(A ∪ B)   **iii** P(A') (3 marks)

You are about to meet six students who have volunteered to go to Kangera in East Africa to work with a charity helping to rebuild a school. There is a lot of work to be done and your mathematical skills will be put to good use helping them.

Solving real life problems often requires you to think for yourself and to use several pieces of mathematics at once. If you are going to be successful you will need to practice your basic skills.

- **Fluency** – Can you confidently work with numbers, graphs and formulae?

- **Reasoning** – Can you use algebra to describe a situation?

- **Problem solving** – Can you cope if a problem doesn't look familiar?

Fluency

Being good at mathematics doesn't just mean being able to do sums and solve equations.

It can also mean how you think about things. Can you look at a 2D drawing and see the 3D shape?

Scale drawings, based on careful measurement and 3D reasoning, are used in architecture and engineering to plan projects. Many of the same ideas are used to produce the graphics in computer games.

Reasoning

It is often said that we are living in the information age. Newspapers, television, the internet... they are all bombarding us with statistics and they are not always right.

To make sense of all this information you need to understand the mathematics and be able to reflect on what the statements might mean.

Perhaps you will be asked to produce a report yourself explaining some statistics.

Problem solving

Scientists use mathematics to describe the world around us. By understanding how forces change on a scale model, engineers can investigate the drag on a real car.

They can then use real and mathematical models to ensure that cars are more fuel efficient.

The AfriLinks project links schools in Europe with schools in Africa.

Six British students travel to Kangera in East Africa.

Greg   Ella   Imran   Maxine   Josh   Wah Wah

The local school has been destroyed in a mudslide. The students will help build a new school.

Before they depart, the students find out about the Kangera region.

1   The population is 9953.
    Round this number to the nearest 1000.

2   The pie chart shows the population by age group.

    a   Which age group is the largest?

    b   Which is the smallest age group?

    c   Rounding each age group to the nearest 100, how many people are aged

        i   between 0 and 20   **ii**   21 to 40

        iii   41 to 60   **iv**   over 60?

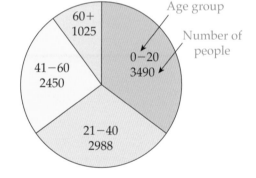

3   The graph shows average monthly temperature and rainfall over a 30 year period in the Kangera region.

    a   On average, which is the warmest month?

    b   What is the range of temperatures?

    c   On average, how many millimetres of rain fall in May?

    d   On average, which is the driest month?

    e   On average, which is the coolest month?

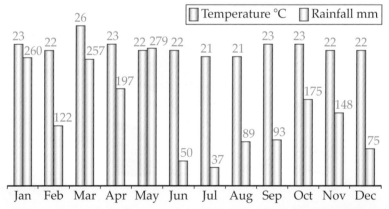

6

4 The table shows rainfall measurements for the first five months of this year.

Month	Jan	Feb	Mar	Apr	May
Rainfall (mm)	180	242	368	492	481

a What do you notice when you compare these figures with the average rainfall?

b Explain why you think the school building was destroyed.

5 Most pupils walk to school in Kangera.
The map shows some of the pupils' journeys.

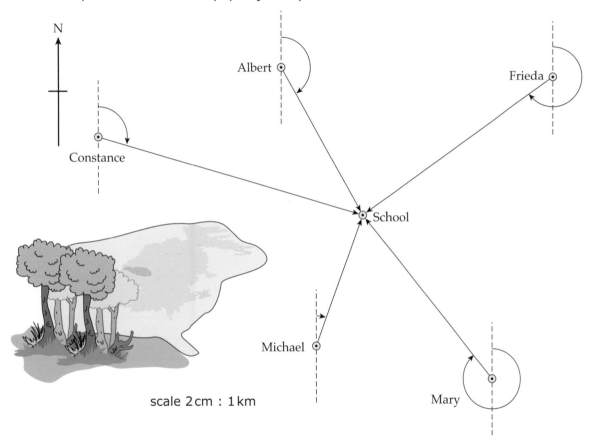

scale 2 cm : 1 km

Copy and complete the table.
Use a ruler to measure the distance travelled to school.
Use a protractor to measure the direction that each student takes when walking to school.
Give each answer as a three-figure bearing.

Name	Distance (km)	Bearing in °
Albert		
Constance		
Michael		
Mary		
Frieda		

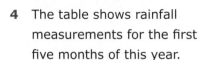

The project to build the schoolhouse starts here!
This is a 3D drawing of the team's idea for the schoolhouse.

To build the school house they need a plan.
Here is a rough draft. It is not drawn to scale.

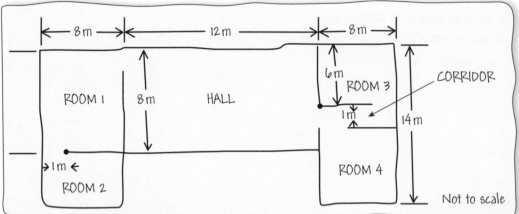

1 Redraw the plan neatly using a scale of 1 cm : 200 cm.
   Use a ruler and protractor for accurate measurements.

2 **a** Calculate the area of each room.
         Put your answers into a table like this.

   b What is the total area of the school floor?

3 The team decide to cover the floor with wooden boards.
   The boards cost $14 per m².

   a To the nearest hundred dollars, how much will
         the floor cost?

   b The flooring budget was $3500.
         How much is the overspend?

Room	Area (m²)
1	
2	
3	
4	
Hall	
Corridor	
Total	

4 Imran has to buy breeze-blocks to build the walls of
   the schoolhouse.
   Each block measures 20 cm × 50 cm × 10 cm.

   a What is the volume of one breeze-block?

         The blocks are delivered on pallets.

   b Look at the drawing.
         What shape do the blocks make on the pallet?

   c How many breeze-blocks will there be on a full pallet?

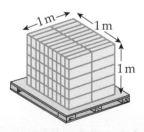

The blocks are held together by a cement mortar.

The mortar is made by mixing sand, cement and water.

Stronger mortar uses more cement, weaker mixtures use more sand.

The label shows the ratio of three mixes.

Mix	Sand	Cement
Strong	3	1
Medium	9	2
Weak	6	1

5 a What strength of mix are each of these?

   i 6 parts sand and 2 parts cement

   ii 9 parts sand and 1.5 parts cement

   iii 6 parts cement and 27 parts sand.

b Maxine uses 27 parts sand to make a medium mix. How much cement will she need to use?

c A strong mix is needed for the path. Maxine mixes a total of 800 kg. How much sand and how much cement did she mix?

6 This drawing shows one of the gable walls of the school.

a What is the total area of the wall? Use the correct units.

Josh has to paint both gable walls white. The label on the paint tin says that the paint will cover 10 m² per litre.

b How many litres will Josh need to paint two coats each for both gable walls?

7 Paint is sold in 2.5 litre tins that cost 18 dollars each.

What will the paint cost?

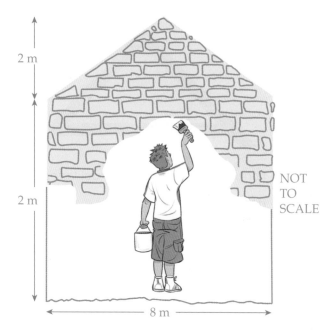

2 m

2 m

NOT TO SCALE

8 m

8 Josh only gets half of the first coat of paint on one gable and before he is called away. It is decided to employ someone else to finish the job. The local painter charges 8 dollars an hour and says he can do 12 m² every hour

a How long will it take to finish the whole job?

b How much will it cost?

MyMaths.co.uk

The roof of the schoolhouse is made from 'A' frames, and covered with sheets of corrugated steel.

The 'A' frames must all be **exactly** the same shape and size.

1   Use a ruler and protractor to find out which frame is not congruent.

A    **B**

C    **D**

The corrugated roof sheets are delivered by lorry.

2   The delivery firm charges $3 for every kilometre travelled and a call-out fee of $15.

   a   Calculate the cost of delivery if the school site is 25 km from the builders' shop.

   b   Use these symbols to write the formula for the cost of delivery.

   C = total cost   d = distance travelled

> Remember to add on the call-out fee of $15.

   c   For a distance of 10 km, the cost will be $45. Use this example to check if your formula is correct.

   d   Once your formula works for part **c**, use it to calculate the charges for these deliveries.
   i 20 km   **ii** 50 km   **iii** 12 km   **iv** 10.5 km

Greg and Wah Wah design different patterns for the path.
This is their first design.

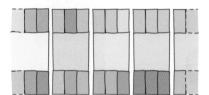

3 a What is the ratio of red to yellow tiles?

b Complete this rule to connect the number of yellow and red tiles.

yellow ⟶ □ ⟶ red

c Wah Wah thinks that the pattern is too simple.
Here is her new idea.
What is the ratio of yellow to red tiles now?
She says that the ratio of yellow to red is 2 : 40.
Greg says that the ratio is 1 : 20.

Explain how they are both correct.

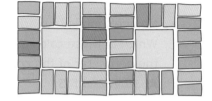

4 Greg wants to try out his own ideas using blocks and slabs.

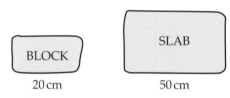

This is his repeating pattern.

a How many green slabs must they lay before the blocks and slabs end up finishing level with each other?

b If the path is 9 m long, how many times will the pattern repeat itself?

c How many
   i blocks will they need to buy
   ii slabs will they need to buy?

d If a block costs $2 and a slab costs $3, how much will the whole path cost?

Imran, Ella, and Maxine are going to mark out a basketball court.

1 Ella makes the basket rings.
She cuts metal strips and
shapes them into circles.

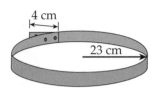

The radius of the ring has
to be 23 cm.
She leaves a 4 cm
overlap to fix the ring.

a How long will she need to cut the strips of metal?

b If she makes both rings using a 3 m strip of metal,
roughly how much metal will be wasted?

> Use π = 3.14 and round
> your answers to the
> nearest cm.

2 a Maxine's job is to mark out the court with tape.
Which of these calculations could she use to work out
the perimeter of the court?
 A 15.75 × 25.5
 B 2 × 25.5 + 15.75
 C 2(25.5 + 15.75)

b Use the correct calculation to find out
how much tape she would need to go
all around the court.

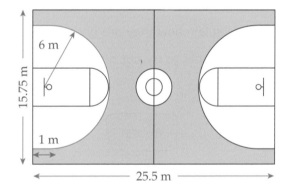

c The 'D' shapes have a radius of 6 m.
The straight lines at the end are 1 m long.
What is the length of the red line?

Imran marks out one of the centre
circles using a rope fixed to a peg in
the ground.

3 The circumference of the circle
has to be about 6.5 m.
Estimate to the nearest cm
how long Imran will need
to make the rope.

> Circumference
> = 2 × π × radius

To celebrate the opening of the basketball court the students will play a match against the workers.

They start training for the big match!

4 The students practise shooting. Here is a record of each student's success.

Name	Score	Miss
i Greg	8	12
ii Maxine	15	15
iii Imran	15	10
iv Ella	9	18
v Josh	4	12
vi Wah Wah	12	3

    a Estimate the probability that each of the students will score with their next shot.

    b Explain who is the best shot taker.

    c How many baskets were scored altogether?

5 The students play a number of one-on-one games.
Here is how many games they played and the number of points they scored.

scored 36
played 6

scored 45
played 9

scored 49
played 7

Maxine
scored 56
played 8

Josh
scored 44
played 8

Wah Wah
scored 120
played 15

    a What is the mean score for each student?

    b Using both sets of data, who is the strongest player in the group?

    c Over ten full games, which players have maintained their mean score?

Player	Greg	Ella	Imran	Maxine	Josh	Wah Wah
Score	60	53	70	68	55	88

MyMaths.co.uk

17e The school garden

Imran, Ella and Josh are planning a 'Junior Garden'
for the younger students.

The Junior Garden is a rectangle, 8 m by 5 m, in which
there will be four growing areas.

8 m

5 m   The Junior Garden

Chilli	Tomato		
6 m²	9 m²	Sweet potato	Maize
		10 m²	15 m²

1 Work with a partner to fit these four growing areas onto
the 8 m by 5 m plot. Use squared paper to help.

2 The students find some old gardening items in a shed.

Some useful conversions
1 inch ≈ 2.5 cm
1 ounce ≈ 30 g
1 pint ≈ 0.6 litres
1 lb (pound) ≈ 0.45 kg

A ruler that
measures inches.

A watering can
that measures
pints and gallons.

A weighing scale that
measures pounds
and ounces.

All their instructions are in metric measures; they will have to
convert units into imperial to complete the task!

a How many pounds of compost will be measured?

b How many pounds of sharp sand will be measured?

c How many ounces of fertiliser will be measured?

d Imran says that he needs 3.5 pints of water.
Show that his answer is not right.

e Ella dug the trench 6 inches deep.
Will it be the right depth?

f How many inches long is the trench?

Mix 5 kg of
compost with
2 kg of sharp
sand.

Mix 100 g of
fertiliser with
3.5 litres of
water.

Dig a trench
15 cm deep
and 60 cm
long.

3 The 'size' of a flowerpot is the distance across the top – the diameter.
Josh measures these with a 12-inch ruler.

a   **b**   **c** 12 inches   **d**   **e**

9 inches

6 inches

4 inches

3 inches

What are the sizes in centimetres?

4 Ella weighs the following items.

a 5 pounds of bananas   **b** 4 ounces of chillies   **c** 8.5 pounds of maize   **d** 12 ounces of coffee beans

Convert these amounts to the metric equivalent.

3D view

5 The field behind the school has to be set out in a special way.
The head teacher gives these instructions:

• $\frac{1}{4}$ of the field must be fenced-off for goats.
• In the rest of the field, I want four congruent sections for four different crops.
• The sections should tessellate – there must be no spaces between the edges of the sections.

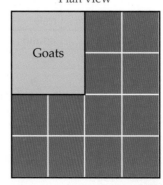

Congruent means the same shape and size.

a With your partner, experiment to find the single shape that the children need to use for the four congruent sections.

b If the area of the whole field is 1600 m², what is the area of the goat paddock?

c What will be the area of each of the four other sections?

Plan view

Goats

MyMaths.co.uk

Check in 1

1. **a** ÷   **b** ×   **c** +
   d ÷   **e** ×   **f** −
2. **a** 9   **b** 25   **c** 49
   d 100   **e** 64
3. **a** 27   **b** 72   **c** 56
   d 42
4. **a** 8   **b** 9   **c** 8
   d 7

MyReview 1

1. **a** 7.8   **b** 3.25   **c** 0.9
   d 0.06   **e** 70   **f** 1.7
   g 350   **h** 0.092
2. **a** 6097   **b** 6100   **c** 6100
   d 6000
3. **a** 13   **b** 22   **c** 96
   d 50   **e** 33   **f** 1
4. 1, 2, 8
5. 8, 16, 24
6. **a** Yes $5 + 6 + 4 = 15$, a multiple of 3
   b No $610 ÷ 2 = 305$, not even
   c Yes   not divisible by 2, 3, 5 or 7 ($11^2 > 103$)
   d Yes   ends in a 5
7. **a** $2 × 3 × 7$ **b** $5 × 5 × 7$
8. 3, 7
9. **a** 9   **b** 12
10. **a** 88   **b** 140
11. **a** 3.0 3.2 3.5 4
    b 0.01 0.1 0.12 0.21
    c 8.99 9.08 9.8 9.91
    d 0.09 0.78 0.8 0.81

Check in 2

1.

Metric	Imperial
gram	pint
millimetre	ounce
kilometre	foot
litre	inch
centimetre	mile
kilogram	pound
millimetre	yard

2. **a** 1 mile   **b** 1 kilogram
   c 1 metre   **d** 1 inch   **e** 1 litre
3. **a** 20 cm²   **b** 18 cm²   **c** 25 cm²

MyReview 2

1. **a** 250   **b** 250   **c** 12 000
   d 4300

2. **a** 24   **b** 80
3. **a** 10 kg (≈ 22 lbs)   **b** 7 miles (≈ 10.5 km)
4. **a** 66 cm²
5. **a** 54 mm²   **b** 60 cm²
6. **a** 60 cm²   **b** 6000 cm² or 0.6 m²
7. 31 cm
8. 74.4 cm

Check in 3

1. **a** 21   **b** 4   **c** 5
   d 1   **e** -1   **f** -3
2. **a** 18   **b** 28   **c** 45
   d 84   **e** 48   **f** 63
   g 21   **h** 32
3. **a** -12   **b** -10   **c** -45
   d 24   **e** -48   **f** 18
   g -25   **h** 28
4. **a** 26 cm   **b** 18 cm   **c** 28 cm

MyReview 3

1. **a** $4b$ **b** $4n + 12m$
   c $g - 12h$ **d** $11j - 10i + 5$
2. **a** $24a$ **b** $12cd$ **c** $3h$
   d 2   **e** $42x$ **f** 3
   g $30pq$ **h** 8
3. **a** $12a + 12b$ **b** $12v - 16$ **c** $6x + 2$
   d $10s - 20t$ **e** $21 - 12s$
   f $4p + 8q - 12r$ **g** $18 + 3t$ **h** $4m + 2n$
4. **a** 99 cm²   **b** 3 cm
5. **a** $t + p$ **b** $t - 1$ **c** $2p$
6. **a** $P = 2n + 24$ **b** $P = 3s + 9$
   c $P = 10v + 5$ **d** $P = 14a + 10d$

Check in 4

1. Missing labels from left to right are
   10%, 20%, 30%, 50%, 60%, 70%, 90%
2. **a** £5   **b** 8 kg   **c** 12 cm
   d 25 mm
3. **a** $\frac{3}{8}$ **b** $\frac{3}{4}$ **c** $\frac{1}{3}$
   d $\frac{5}{9}$ **e** $\frac{1}{2}$ **f** 1

MyReview 4

1. **a** $\frac{2}{7}$ **b** 1
2. **a** $\frac{3}{6} = \frac{1}{2}$ **b** $\frac{4}{20} = \frac{1}{5}$ **c** $\frac{11}{12}$
3. **a** £6   **b** 3 students
4. **a** 16 g   **b** 15 cm
5. **a** 3   **b** 15
6. **a** 150   **b** 5

7	**a**	0.3	**b**	0.4	**c**	0.25
8	**a**	0.17	**b**	0.44		
9	**a**	7	**b**	72		
10	**a**	210	**b**	15		

11 £95
12 £16.20
13 40 %

14	**a**	£321	**b**	£187.11		
15	**a**	£769.60	**b**	£800.38	**c**	£1095.38

Check in 5
1	**a**	43mm	**b**	76mm		
	c	8mm	**d**	51mm		
2	**a**	27°	**b**	108°	**c**	313°
	d	98°				
3	**a**	50°	**b**	29°		

MyReview 5
1 $a = 76°$ Angles on a straight line add to 180°
$b = 104°$ Vertically opposite angles are equal /
Angles on a straight line: $a + b = 180°$
$c = 76°$ Angles on a straight line add to 180° /
Vertically opposite angles: $c = a$ /
Angles around a point add to 360°
$d = 125°$ Alternate angles are equal
$e = 125°$ Corresponding angles are equal /
Vertically opposite angles
$f = 55°$ Angles on a straight line

2	$a = 48°$		$b = 69°$		$c = 50°$
	$d = 99°$		$e = 95°$		$f = 70°$
3	$a = 33°$		$b = 80°$		$c = 100°$
4	**a** Trapezium		**b** Rectangle		
5	**a** 7cm		**b** 55°		**c** 125°

Check in 6
1 WELCOME
2	**a**	2	**b**	3	**c**	-1
	d	-3	**e**	-4	**f**	-5
3	**a**	3	**b**	-2	**c**	-2
	d	4				

MyReview 6
1	A	$x = 3$	B	$y = -1$
	C	$x = -4$	D	$y = 5$

2 **a**

x	0	1	2	3	4
2x	0	2	4	6	8
+1	+1	+1	+1	+1	+1
y	1	3	5	7	9

2 **b**

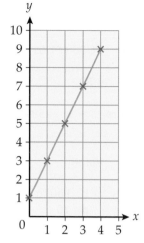

3 **a** The points move three squares up for
every one square across
b $y = 3x$
4	**a**	30 km/h	**b**	20 km
	c	He stops for 5 minutes		
5	**a**	£200		
	b	Between 12 noon and 1 pm		
	c	Between 3 pm and 4 pm		

Check in 7
1	**a**	10	**b**	8	**c**	13
	d	6	**e**	8	**f**	5
	g	13	**h**	13		
2	**a**	10	**b**	4	**c**	12
	d	10	**e**	5	**f**	12
	g	20	**h**	3		
3	**a**	20	**b**	70	**c**	20
	d	20	**e**	10	**f**	100
	g	30	**h**	40		
4	**a**	£2	**b**	£1	**c**	£4
	d	£4	**e**	£5	**f**	£6
	g	£10	**h**	£8		

MyReview 7
1	**a**	215	**b**	27		
2	**a**	56	**b**	54	**c**	6
	d	140	**e**	50	**f**	0.75
	g	6.4	**h**	350		
3	**a**	192	**b**	245		
4	**a**	249	**b**	273	**c**	77.1
	d	73.7				
5	**a**	1620	**b**	4264	**c**	8645
	d	17 791				
6	**a**	132.3	**b**	146.3		

7 a 17 **b** 21 **c** 15 r 2
 d 20 r 7 **e** 25 **f** 26
8 35.88 m²
9 a £1 (84 p) **b** £1.50 (£1.51)
 c 2 (1.798)
10 a 3.85 **b** 4.80
11 42 weeks, 2 days
12 a 95 days, 20 hours **b** 259 200

Check in 8
1 a 7 **b** Norah **c** 4
 d 20
2 a Steak and kidney **b** Potato
 c 30 **d** 10

MyReview 8

1

Gender (M/F)	Own bags (Y/N)

2 Frequencies: 3, 3, 2, 3, 1, 1, 2, 1

Amount spent (£)	Tally	Freq
0 – 9.99	|||	3
10 – 19.99	|||	3
20 – 29.99	||	2
30 – 39.99	|||	3
40 – 49.99			1
50 – 59.99			1
60 – 69.99	||	2
70 – 79.99			1

3 Did you bring your own bag?

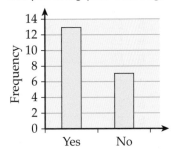

4 School dinner choices

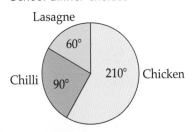

5 a 1 **b** 30 ÷ 12 = 2.5
 c (2 + 2) ÷ 2 = 2 **d** 6 − 1 = 5
6 a Café sales

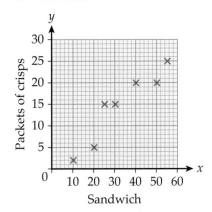

b Positive correlation

7

0	4
10	8
20	3 8
30	1 2 2 4 6 8
40	0 2 3 3 3 7

Key   20 | 3 means 23

Check in 9
1 a Yes, 2 **b** No **c** No **d** Yes, 1
2 Only **c** same size
3 a 90° **b** 180° **c** 270° **d** 360°
4 Enlarged by a scale factor 2

MyReview 9
1 a One horizontal line of symmetry
 b Order 1
2 a

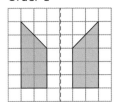

b

3 A rhombus with vertices at (7, 0), (6, 3), (7, 6) and (8, 1)

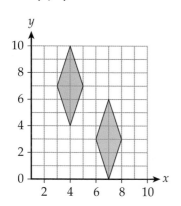

4

5 **a**

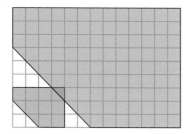

b $\frac{1}{3}$

6

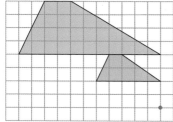

7 A 10 cm by 3 cm rectangle.

Check in 10

1	**a**	22	**b**	3	**c**	3
	d	8	**e**	-1	**f**	4
2	**a**	$x + 5$	**b**	$3y$		
	c	$t - 6$	**d**	$\frac{a}{10}$		

3 $4 \times 3 - 5 = 7$
4 No, left hand side is 28 but right hand side is 30

MyReview 10

1	**a**	$35 = 35$	**b**	$41 \neq 40$	**c**	$42 \neq 41$
2	**a**	$5 < 8$	**b**	$14 > 12$	**c**	$55 < 56$
3	**a**	13	**b**	45	**c**	10
	d	15	**e**	45	**f**	9
	g	16				
4	**a**	7	**b**	11	**c**	1
	d	12				
5	**a**	$5p + 4 = 39$	**b**	7		
6	**a**	2	**b**	6	**c**	2
	d	2	**e**	6	**f**	3
7	**a**	$16x = 32$	**b**	2 cm		
	c	$5x = 10$ cm, $3x = 6$ cm				

Check in 11

1	**a**	30	**b**	32	**c**	27
	d	42	**e**	72	**f**	21
	g	108	**h**	28		
2	**a**	6	**b**	7	**c**	5
	d	7	**e**	7	**f**	4
	g	4	**h**	7		
3	**a**	600	**b**	54	**c**	320
	d	6700	**e**	89.7	**f**	372
	g	2734	**h**	7400		
4	**a**	3.6	**b**	12.4	**c**	3.45
	d	7.21	**e**	0.94	**f**	0.87
	g	4.829	**h**	0.029		

MyReview 11

1	**a**	9	**b**	1	**c**	100
	d	6	**e**	9	**f**	8
2	1, 4, 9, 16					
3	7 cm					
4	$4 \times 12 = 48$ cm					
5	**a**	64	**b**	625	**c**	729
6	**a**	2^8	**b**	6^3	**c**	7^6
	d	5				
7	**a**	d^3	**b**	e^5	**c**	f^7
8	**a**	3^7	**b**	7^{12}	**c**	11^5
9	**a**	r^{11}	**b**	s^{13}	**c**	t^{14}
	d	y^2z^3				
10	**a**	560	**b**	200 000	**c**	9 400 000
11	**a**	4×10^3	**b**	7.6×10^4	**c**	8.3×10^7

Check in 12

1 Check lines are accurate to within 1 mm.

	a	2.9 – 3.1 cm	**b**	4.1 – 4.4 cm
	c	7.3 – 7.5 cm	**d**	5.5 – 5.7 cm
	e	17 – 19 mm	**f**	28 – 30 mm

2 **a** **i** 4 cm, 5 cm, 7 cm
    ii 40 mm, 50 mm, 70 mm
    iii Scalene
  b **i** All 4.3 cm   **ii** All 43 mm
    iii Equilateral

MyReview 12

1 Check angles are accurate to within 1°.
  a 54 – 56°   **b** 144 – 146°
  c 169 – 171°   **d** 224 – 226°
2 Check third angle and missing sides are as given.
  a 50°, 5 cm, 5.1 cm   **b** 55°, 7.3 cm, 4.2 cm
3 Check accuracy of drawing.
4 Check line is 3 cm from end, at 90° to vertical line.
5 Check line is at 33° to both original lines.
6 Check third side and missing angles are as given.
  a 5.9 cm, 53°, 75°   **b** 7.8 cm, 37°, 38°
7 Check the three sides and three angles are as given.
  90°, 53°, 37°
8 **a** 055°   **b** 200°

Check in 13

1 **a** 33   **b** 16   **c** 56
  d 25   **e** 43   **f** 29
2 Output in order is: 1, 4, 7, 10, 13, 16
3 **a** 3, 6, 9, 12, 15   **b** 7, 14, 21, 28, 35
  c 5, 10, 15, 20, 25   **d** 4, 8, 12, 16, 20
  e 11, 22, 33, 44, 55   **f** 9, 18, 27, 36, 45

MyReview 13

1 **a** *Start with 9,*   *add 7*   37, 44
  b *Start with 35,*   *subtract 3*   23, 20
  c *Start with 1,*   *triple*   81, 243
2 **a** 6, 8, 10, 12, 14   **b** 90, 82, 74, 66, 58
  c 5, 10, 20, 40, 80   **d** 3, 5, 9, 17, 33
3 **a**   **b** 2
  c *Multiply the position by 2 and subtract 1 or 2n – 1*
  d 29
4 **a** *Multiply the position by 2 and add 5*
    (2n + 5)
  b Multiply the position by 5 and subtract 1
    (5n – 1)
5 **a** 39   **b** 35   **c** 76
  d 44
6 **a** $4n + 5$ **b** $11n - 2$

7 **a** $10n + 4$ **b** $8n - 3$ **c** $n + 6$
  d $100n + 50$

Check in 14

1 **a** 35 cm²   **b** 36 cm²
2 **a** 40 cm²   **b** 9 cm²   **c** 56 cm²
3 **a** 56   **b** 90   **c** 38
  d 46.5

MyReview 14

1 **a** Cuboid   **b** 6   **c** 8
  d 12
2 **a** Triangular-based pyramid
  b 4   **c** 4   **d** 6
3 **a** Cylinder   **b** Trapezium prism
4 **a**   **b**   **c**
5 60 m²
6 408 cm³
7 68 cm²

Check in 15

1 **a** 18   **b** 72   **c** 28
  d 60   **e** 42   **f** 66
  g 45   **h** 36
2 **a** 11   **b** 8   **c** 8
  d 9   **e** 5   **f** 12
  g 9   **h** 9
3 Possible equivalent fractions include
  a $\frac{1}{2} = \frac{2}{4} = \frac{3}{6} = \frac{10}{20} = \frac{50}{100}$
  b $\frac{2}{3} = \frac{4}{6} = \frac{6}{9} = \frac{8}{12} = \frac{20}{30}$
  c $\frac{2}{5} = \frac{4}{10} = \frac{6}{15} = \frac{8}{20} = \frac{40}{100}$
  d $\frac{3}{4} = \frac{6}{8} = \frac{9}{12} = \frac{15}{20} = \frac{75}{100}$
  e $\frac{3}{20} = \frac{6}{40} = \frac{9}{60} = \frac{12}{80} = \frac{15}{100}$
  f $\frac{7}{10} = \frac{14}{20} = \frac{21}{30} = \frac{35}{50} = \frac{70}{100}$
  g $\frac{1}{7} = \frac{2}{14} = \frac{3}{21} = \frac{4}{28} = \frac{10}{70}$
  h $\frac{2}{8} = \frac{1}{4} = \frac{3}{12} = \frac{6}{24} = \frac{25}{100}$
4 **a** $\frac{1}{2}$ **b** $\frac{1}{2}$ **c** $\frac{2}{5}$
  d $\frac{3}{10}$ **e** $\frac{1}{4}$ **f** $\frac{17}{20}$
  g $\frac{4}{5}$ **h** $\frac{3}{7}$

MyReview 15

1 3 : 4
2 **a** 4 : 5   **b** 2 : 3   **c** 3 : 4
   d 2 : 3
3 2 : 1
4 42
5 **a** £15, £45   **b** 15 kg, 25 kg
   c 20 days, 100 days
   d 175 students, 75 students
6 480 g
7 **a** 37%   **b** 30%   **c** 35%
   d 75%   **e** 40%   **f** 50%
   g 20%   **h** 100%
8 A (0.65 > 0.5)
9 **a** £3.60   **b** £18
10 **a** 17 months   **b** 2 more months

Check in 16

1 **a** Even chance (50/50)   **b** Unlikely
   c Certain   **d** Impossible   **e** Likely
2

   a   d   b   e   c

3 **a** $\frac{6}{6} = 1$ **b** $\frac{3}{6} = \frac{1}{2}$ **c** $\frac{5}{6}$
   d $\frac{0}{6} = 0$ **e** $\frac{1}{6}$

MyReview 16

1 **a** $\frac{7}{9}$ **b** $\frac{0}{9} = 0$
2 $1 - 0.4 = 0.6$

3 $\frac{20}{76} = \frac{5}{19}$

4 **a**

		Bread		
		White	Brown	Seeded
Filling	Cheese	(C, W)	(C, B)	(C, S)
	Ham	(H, W)	(H, B)	(H, S)
	Egg	(E, W)	(E, B)	(E, S)

   b $3 \times 3 = 9$

5 **a**

		Dice					
		1	2	3	4	5	6
Coin	**H**	H1	H2	H3	H4	H5	H6
	T	T1	T2	T3	T4	T5	T6

   b $2 \times 6 = 12$ **c** $\frac{1}{12}$ **d** $\frac{3}{12} = \frac{1}{4}$

6 $\frac{10}{15} = \frac{2}{3} = 0.67 \, (2\,dp)$

7 **a** $\frac{16}{40} = \frac{2}{5} = 0.4$ **b** $0.4 \times 30 = 12$

8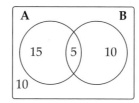